The Glasgow Rape Case

Ross Harper is a solicitor in Glasgow. He is a Temporary Sheriff in Scotland, a lecturer in advocacy at the University of Strathclyde and a former President of the Glasgow Bar Association. He is Chairman of the Scottish Tory Reform Group and Chairman of the Society of Scottish Conservative Lawyers.

Arnot McWhinnie has been chief crime reporter with the *Daily Record* since 1966, and since then has covered most of the major crime stories in Scotland, including one where his uncovering of fresh evidence has resulted in the release of a man from a ten-year prison sentence. For his investigative reporting on the Glasgow rape case, he received the 'Provincial Journalist of the Year' award in the spring of 1983.

The Glasgow Rape Case

Ross Harper & Arnot McWhinnie

Hutchinson

London Melbourne Sydney Auckland Johannesburg

Hutchinson & Co. (Publishers) Ltd

An imprint of the Hutchinson Publishing Group

17–21 Conway Street, London W1P 6JD

Hutchinson Group (Australia) Pty Ltd
30–32 Cremorne Street, Richmond South, Victoria 3121
PO Box 151, Broadway, New South Wales 2007

Hutchinson Group (NZ) Ltd
32–34 View Road, PO Box 40-086, Glenfield, Auckland 10

Hutchinson Group (SA) Pty Ltd
PO Box 337, Bergvlei 2012, South Africa

First published as a Hutchinson Paperback 1983
© Ross Harper and Arnot McWhinnie 1983

This book is sold subject to the condition that it shall not
by way of trade or otherwise be lent, resold, hired out or
otherwise circulated without the publisher's prior
consent in any form of binding or cover other than that
in which it is published and without a similar condition
including this condition being imposed on the subsequent
purchaser

Phototypeset in Linotron Century by Input Typesetting Ltd, London

Printed in Great Britain by The Anchor Press Ltd
and bound by Wm Brendon & Son Ltd,
both of Tiptree, Essex

British Library Cataloguing in Publication Data

Harper, Ross
    The Glasgow rape case.
    1. Rape–Scotland
    I. Title   II. McWhinnie, Arnot
    364.1′532′09411   HV6569.G7

ISBN 0 09 151731 1

Contents

Illustrations

Acknowledgements

Photographs Carol X courtesy of Strathclyde Police. Photograph of
Lord Ross courtesy of Stephen Parry Donald. All other photographs
reproduced by kind permission of the *Scottish Daily Record* and the
Glasgow Herald.

Preface

On 31 October 1980, I was assaulted and raped in the Barrow-field district of Glasgow. Three youths had sex with me without my consent. They were soon caught, but I was so frightened of giving evidence against them that I tried to kill myself.

When the Crown dropped the case I was horrified and felt, once again, like taking my own life. But I was told that through an old Scottish law I could bring a private prosecution. After a great deal of agony, and with a lot of help, I finally did so.

This is my story and the story of those who helped me. I have asked my lawyer to cooperate with the journalist who uncovered the scandal and to tell my story honestly – warts and all.

It is a horrific story but I hope it will help by giving courage and comfort to people in the same position as me.

Carol X

Part One

1 Nightmare Alley

There was little traffic. Urgently, he turned right into Bellfield Street, avoiding a skid by pressing the accelerator of his ambulance precisely at the moment of cornering. The driver turned left into Duke Street, the three-litre engine responding to his summons. As reflections of the pulsating blue light bounced off the dingy tenement windows of the East End, the late-night parties drew to their close.

Reaching speeds of forty and fifty miles per hour, the ambulance sped through the heart of Glasgow towards the entrance of the Glasgow Royal Infirmary which was now just a right turn away into High Street. The driver braked as he passed through the main gates and jammed to a halt in the precincts of the hospital.

The journey which had taken somewhere between four and five minutes would, in normal daytime traffic, have taken twenty minutes. As the ambulance pulled up outside the Casualty Department its back doors were immediately opened. Inside, covered by a blanket and being comforted by the driver's attendant, lay the cause of the emergency, the reason for the early-morning dash – a young woman horribly mutilated and covered in blood.

Gently stretchered out onto a trolley, she was wheeled into the emergency room. No time could be wasted. A team of neatly uniformed nurses walked beside her. They were used to injuries caused by violence, but they were horrified at what they saw.

It was exactly 1.27 a.m. on the morning of 1 November 1980.

Eddie O'Neill, the ambulance driver, breathed a sigh of relief
. . . she was still living. In thirteen years of ferrying the victims of muggings, assaults, knifings and road accidents to
Glasgow's hospitals, he had never seen a human being so
cruelly injured, yet still continuing to breathe.

Even the casualty surgeon, a young woman herself, was
appalled by the severity of the wounds. But doctors have work
to do and cannot let their judgement be coloured by emotion.
There was work to do here. The patient, a tiny, fragile girl in
her late twenties, had a face that was barely recognizable. It
was literally falling apart, sliced open by six gaping slash
wounds across her cheeks, nose, forehead and neck. There were
also vicious bone-deep wounds in both thighs and another less
serious one on her buttock. To those who saw the injured
woman that morning, it looked as if someone had played a
sadistic game of noughts and crosses on her face and legs with
something lethally sharp.

The medical team set to work, stripping off what few
blood-stained clothes covered the victim. When she had been
brought in, it was immediately observed that she was naked
from the waist down. The wounds were ingrained with clotted
blood and dirt. The young doctor realized that the woman
would have to undergo major surgery.

In the meantime, she did what she could to alleviate the
suffering. The young woman was in a state of shock. She was
pale, bloodless and trembling. Her blood pressure was falling.
A transfusion would be needed but, before it could be done, a
blood sample would have to be taken.

The doctor tried to find out who her patient was – and what
had happened to her. A nurse informed her the girl had said
something about being raped. She mumbled her name – Carol.
The nurses and doctor could hardly make out a word she was
saying, but gradually they were able to piece together a rough
idea of what had happened.

The details were entered in the Accident and Emergency
Department admission sheet. 'Name: Carol. Suffering from:
Multiple slashing-type wounds, assault. History: Assaulted
flick knife . . . raped? . . . uncertain of time . . . happened in
old tenement.'

The doctor, realizing that the police would be involved, and that she might be a medical witness at a criminal trial in the future, drew sketches of Carol's face and lower body showing the exact position of the injuries. These would help jog her memory at a later date. The battle to repair Carol's wounds began. It would be later in the morning, near lunchtime, before the job would be completed.

Carol was an East Ender who lived with her boyfriend, Billy, in the shadow of Celtic Park, the home of the famous football team. Their home, a top-floor tenement flat, was a stone's throw from one of Glasgow's most deprived and lawless areas. The 2000 people who live there, the bulk of them poor, honest and decent, nicknamed their district 'Nightmare Alley'. Its real name is Barrowfield. When the news filtered through Barrowfield members of one of the local gangs, the Torch, openly accused their rivals, the Spur, of having attacked the woman. A police officer was approached at a street corner by one of the Torch members. He said, 'We do a lot of bad things but we don't attack lassies – even in Barrowfield.'

2 Barrowfield

When the police came to the Royal Infirmary that night to investigate what had happened to Carol, they heard where she lived and nodded uneasily but knowingly. Injuries like that, they suspected, could only have been inflicted by someone drunk, psychopathic, or high on solvents, and there were a few mindless teenagers in Nightmare Alley who fell into that category.

Barrowfield had not always had such a reputation. A century before, as part of the East End, it had belonged to the power house of Glasgow, generating the wealth and energy which helped to make the city so great. The growth began earlier in the nineteenth century with the introduction of cotton manufacturing in the textile industry. Factories and mills sprung up all over the area. Later, heavy engineering arrived and there were forges and ironworks with famous names, such as Beardmore's at Parkhead and Arrol's at Dalmarnock. But with the economic changes of the twentieth century, the East End became decayed and derelict. The old tenements no longer met the needs of a rapidly changing society. Yet there were 150,000 people crammed into the area, three to every habitable room; most of them were out of work after many of the factories shut their gates for the last time.

As unemployment increased, East Enders moved out to look for work elsewhere. The effect was dramatic. By the 1960s the population was diminishing by thousands every year. By 1978 the East End population had plummeted from 150,000 to 45,000. The people who escaped were the skilled workers, the young and the healthy. Many of those who remained were unemployed, elderly or disabled.

At the same time as this exodus, the facilities which had grown up over the years to support a vigorous community also fell into decline. Shopkeepers went out of business, underused bus routes were cancelled, schools, cinemas and pubs closed down. The heart was being plucked out of the East End. As tenements emptied, they fell into dereliction.

By the middle 1970s poverty and unemployment were on a scale unmatched by any other inner-city area in Britain. Unemployment amongst East End men had risen to more than twenty per cent. Those who did work brought low wages home. The inner section of the East End round Barrowfield was the worst hit. A fifth of the area was vacant land surrounded by scrap-yards and derelict factories. Vandalism, which grew during the sixties, deterred further investment.

There were still people who remembered Barrowfield as a pleasant place in which to live, but it was slowly turning into a ghetto. Tenement homes began to crumble, rats were an everyday part of life, traditional corner-shops closed down, and residents continually struggled for survival against mud and dirt, rubble and bad drains, poor lighting and cracked pavements. They also had to fight against the feeling that they were second-class citizens.

Barrowfield is a violent place. In the 1960s, in common with many of the other areas of Glasgow, it spawned its own teenage gangs. They called themselves the Spur and the Torch. Their slogans began to appear on every gable-end and wall: 'OK – Kill' . . . 'Torch Rules' . . . 'Spur Ya Bass'. Anywhere the young thugs could use spray-paint to mark out their territories they did so. Yet there were only ten streets in the area which rapidly became known as an 'island of fear' and 'the most deprived housing scheme in Europe'.

Barrowfield is guarded by Gallowgate at its northern boundary, London Road at its southern, Fielden Street at its western, and a railway line and Celtic Football Club's Parkhead stadium at the eastern boundary. The Torch and the Spur split the territory in half, the Torch occupying the north of Barrowfield and the Spur the south. There was a no-man's-land in one of the streets, ironically called Law Street. But in between, if any gang dared to stray out of its own territory, violence would follow.

Fights between the two opposing factions happened frequently, day or night. In a decade of violence which reached a peak in the seventies, youngsters butchered each other with boning knives, cleavers, hatchets, daggers, swords, iron bars, garden railings and fences – anything they could get their hands on. Murders and attempted murders resulted in lurid trials at the High Court in Glasgow. One by one, young gangsters were detained, either during Her Majesty's Pleasure (if they were not old enough to go to prison), or were sentenced to life in Scotland's toughest jails. But they were always quickly replaced by other young thugs who were as ruthless and dangerous.

Most people living in Barrowfield were law-abiding. Inevitably, however, some were innocently caught up in the violence: a youth was stabbed to death by the Spur in mistake for his brother who was a member of the Torch; two housewives in the middle of a gang battle were injured by flying bricks; four young men from Gretna Green lost in the East End were battered and bruised by a gang when they stopped off in a nearby chip shop; a young mother using her last ounce of strength held her front door shut while, on the other side, thugs with swords tried to smash it down; a woman sitting in her bath was hit by a huge stone which crashed through her window; families regularly barricaded their windows with wardrobes.

In one night in the mid-seventies a young man died a cruel and slow death, stabbed through the skull. The next day a gang of hoodlums jumped up and down outside his home waving copies of newspaper reports on the killing and shouting, 'We are dancing on your grave.' Then they rampaged along Stamford Street, throwing bricks, stones, hatchets and bayonets through windows, smashing ninety of them.

Another infamous incident resulted in a small shopkeeper fleeing Glasgow to go into semi-retirement in the Highlands, almost an invalid. Thugs had finally put him out of business

when they threw a concrete sleeper through his window,
wrecking the interior and injuring him severely.

Amazingly, at the height of the violence, the two gangs
joined forces, but for only one reason: to form a bigger 'army'
to fight the police. As one officer who knew the area reported:
'It was them and us. They would dial 999 to report a phoney
accident and when we arrived to investigate we would be set
upon with sticks and bricks. I once found myself with a colleague surrounded by two hundred of them. We were lucky to
escape alive.'

A police car called to a mobbing and rioting – in Glasgow
the authorities described it as a 'group disorder' – was over-
turned. As a result of this, police officers were ordered never
to leave their vehicle unattended in Barrowfield. If CID officers have to visit the area, they make a prior arrangement
with the uniformed branch to watch their car while they conduct inquiries. In another incident a Land Rover was virtually
impaled by a long, four-inch by two-inch piece of wood thrown
like a javelin. It crashed through the windscreen, narrowly
missing the officers inside, continued through the wire-mesh
grill separating the front compartment from the rear, and
finally smashed through the back window. Firemen and ambu-
lancemen also received violence, occasionally being stoned by
mobs as they attended emergencies.

Vandalism became endemic. In 1972 a community centre
was erected at a cost of £100,000 in waste-ground in Barrowfield. It was deliberately destroyed by fire three weeks later.
The centre was rebuilt, destroyed by fire again, and finally
demolished by the local authority.

One by one, however, decent people from Barrowfield started
to stand up and be counted. In 1976, frustrated mothers, terrified to go out shopping or to let their youngsters play in the
street, demanded that Glasgow District Council Housing Department settled its plans to evict antisocial tenants. There
were eighty families on whom the local authorities had bulg-
ing files for antisocial activities, such as running a brothel,
building up substantial rent arrears, vandalizing their own
homes, giving shelter to absconders from approved schools,
dealing in stolen property and housing relatives who had van-

ished from their own council homes because of rent arrears. For the first nine months of 1976 the police made 400 arrests in Barrowfield and decent families held a series of meetings with local businessmen, councillors and Church leaders, to discuss how to rid the area of violence. Some women offered to start up 'petticoat vigilante' patrols, an idea which was quickly discouraged. Local organizations were set up for young mothers, pensioners, children and teenagers. But these activities were overshadowed by the violence.

The area's councillor, who helped spearhead the law-and-order campaign, found himself the target of thugs. He was twice badly beaten up near his home in Barrowfield. His windows were shattered by bricks and air-gun pellets. A dead cat was pushed through his kitchen window and burning paper through his letter-box. His wife was intimidated in the street by gangs. Slogans were daubed on his front door and he received so many threatening telephone calls that he had his phone disconnected.

Nevertheless, the people of Barrowfield were rising, loyal to themselves and their neighbours, all intensely interested in taking hold of their grim environment and shaking some life into it. As a result of pressure from the Tenants' Association the local authority decided to inject millions of pounds into Barrowfield. At the end of 1976 a £4 million contract was placed with a big building firm for the modernization of 600 houses. They were gutted and refurbished, flat roofs replaced with pitched ones, new bathrooms, kitchens and central heating installed. Environmental and landscaping work was included in the contract. Over the next few years Barrowfield certainly improved its appearance but the gang problem never really went away.

The Spur and the Torch can muster at least fifty regular members each. Many people who do not live in the area are under the misapprehension that the members are teenagers. The majority are young married men. The leader of the Spur, for instance, is not only married but has a young family. The younger thugs are responsible for most of the violence but, in a confrontation, the older ones flock out in droves. The area can be quiet for a month, then suddenly there is another month of trouble. This festering violence is never far away. And neither is the feeling amongst the local people that they are just not wanted.

The area became a no-go zone for delivery-van drivers. Theft from vehicles reached such alarming proportions that a number of companies decided, as a matter of policy, not to enter Barrowfield to deliver carpets, furniture, televisions, washing-machines or anything that was too bulky for the customer to take home himself. Before going to Barrowfield, delivery drivers report to the police station and arrangements are made for an officer to guard their vehicles while goods are being unloaded. One big television hire company pulled out of Barrowfield altogether, cancelling contracts even with householders who were fully paid up. They had lost too many sets, stolen from their repair men's vans.

Many folk are still desperately anxious to get out of Barrowfield. Some arrive, cannot take it, and apply for another council house a few weeks later. Others have managed to adjust, compensating for their surroundings by turning their homes into mini-palaces. They live, however, under the constant threat of theft, and so families seldom go on holiday together. One member has always to remain at home to guard against burglaries and vandalism.

No one could get rid of the gangs, not even the beat policemen who were put into the area to patrol three shifts a day. Two Community Liaison Officers were also drafted into Barrowfield and put to work with them, all briefed to listen to complaints from residents and help with their problems. Many of the locals, however, complained that the beat officers were not in the area long enough to make the police policy pay off. They would be just getting to know their jobs, when they were pulled out, transferred to another area and replaced by other young officers.

By 1980 £60 million had been spent on the East End of Glasgow in the Glasgow Eastern Area Renewal project (GEAR), half of a promised £120 million from central government. More than £6 million of that alone was spent on Barrowfield. But many people, with good reason, believe that, at the start of the eighties, Barrowfield was just as bad an environmental jungle as it was between the mid-sixties and the mid-seventies – despite all the money spent on it.

3 The Row

Halloween, 31 October 1980, a Friday, and Carol's man, Billy, had wakened at his usual time of 7 a.m. to slip quietly out of bed so that he would not disturb her. He was looking forward to the weekend.

His son, Billy junior, a fourteen-year-old, had been staying at Billy's for the past six days, having travelled to Glasgow for a holiday from his mother's new home in Coventry. Carol and Billy had promised him a farewell treat before he returned on Saturday morning. That night they were taking him to the cinema and afterwards, perhaps, they would have supper at a Chinese restaurant in the city centre.

Billy washed, shaved and snatched a cup of coffee. He made an extra cup for Carol and brought it into the bedroom. Opening her eyes, she stretched and gratefully took the cup from him. 'What would you like for your tea tonight?' she asked. Billy didn't ponder for long. 'Gammon steaks and maybe a trifle for afters.' As he left, heading for the Clydeside shipyard where he was a foreman painter, Billy placed some cash on the dressing-table. His son wanted to buy some clothes before returning to Coventry.

Carol fell asleep again, wakening a couple of hours later to the sound of young Billy making a cup of tea in the kitchen. She got dressed. Over breakfast she reminded him, 'We are going into Glasgow this morning to get your new denims. And don't forget you're going to the pictures tonight.'

Carol had been brought up in the Gallowgate, a famous Glasgow street which touches the city centre before cutting through the heart of the East End. Much hardship and heartbreak had been packed into her twenty-eight years of life. She had been reared in a typical dingy tenement, its stone-work pitted and crumbling, the legacy of years of erosion by industrial pollution. Her parents had faced a tough struggle for survival, scratching money together to feed and clothe them all. There was little space in the tiny flat; it had one room – complete with traditional bed recess – and a kitchen. An outside toilet was shared with the neighbours. There was no privacy for a little girl to have day-dreaming moments on her own, or for parents to sit down and talk without half-a-dozen pairs of inquisitive ears eavesdropping. Consequently, Carol sought refuge in a graveyard where, every day after school, she would play with her friends. Her father clawed a meagre living in a canning factory, processing anything from chicken to peas. He was a brickie to trade, as the Scots say. Eventually, he moved back to the building industry.

At primary school Carol was a bright and intelligent child, tiny, with long hair and elfin features. She was a promising pupil, always in the top three in her class. The school selected her for the Duke of Edinburgh Award course at an Outward Bound centre for girls in Wales. The trip to Wales was a memorable experience for her – freedom in the midst of wide, green, open countryside, gin-clear rivers and rolling hills: six weeks of canoeing, rock-climbing, hill-walking and camping. The Glasgow schoolgirl enjoyed every moment and inwardly developed a greater strength of purpose. She dreamed of being a nurse in a grand hospital or a secretary in a large office.

A year later Carol faced the harsh realities of life as she walked through the school gates of City Public for the last time. It was not the best school in Glasgow. Carol could have gone to Whitehill Secondary, a superior academy in every way. But her father could not afford to buy the uniform. Nevertheless, Carol had done exceptionally well at City Public. The art teacher had wanted her to continue her schooling, take her final exams and earn a place in Glasgow's College of Art. She regarded her as a promising artist – perhaps a future teacher like herself. Had she not won third prize in the prestigious

Glasgow schools' art competition? But like so many gifted
children in the deprived working-class areas of Britain's cities,
Carol was never to be given the chance she deserved. Her
family had to come first, and since she was the oldest child,
Carol's father insisted that she leave school at fifteen to get a
job. 'We all need the money,' he told her. 'Every little counts.'

Carol ended up in a ragtrade sweat-shop, sitting for eight
hours a day at one of dozens of clattering sewing-machines.
The noise was constant and even the banter of gossiping girls
and pop blaring over the loudspeakers couldn't quite drown it
out. Wages were meagre too, most of them going into the
family kitty to help pay for her keep. Teenage girls long to
buy make-up, a new blouse, perhaps a skirt, and Carol was no
exception. To afford the little extras, however, she was forced
to work weekends in a shellfish bar, carrying plates of freshly
boiled, steaming mussels to customers who sat at scrubbed
wooden tables. Such restaurants were, and still are, popular
in Glasgow's East End. The shell-fish come from the north-
west coast of Scotland and are rushed south to be eaten before,
or after, weekend sessions in the pubs. Sometimes the mussels
would be carried out, dripping with vinegar and wrapped in
newspaper, to be eaten in the street. The hundreds of discarded
empty shells, crackling underfoot, were testimony to the
Glaswegian taste. Carol later thought that the steamy atmosphere in the kitchen caused a kidney ailment which plagued
her ever afterwards.

The years passed by and the family moved farther east to
Parkhead, living in the shade of Celtic's famous football stadium. From Parkhead, they moved about the city, ending up in
the north at Easterhouse, a sprawling housing scheme which
attracted considerable notoriety because of teenage gangs.
Carol's father was very strict, always insisting she was home
by 9 p.m. Carol rebelled. At one point she ran away from
home, living in derelict buildings with another girl of sixteen
and a boy of seventeen. The police caught up with her and she
refused to go back to her family. Carol was sent to a girls'
assessment centre for thirty-eight days. When she returned
she developed a better relationship with her father. Still, East-

erhouse was a foreign country to her and she returned to the
East End as often as she could.

When she was eighteen Carol found her first real romance.
He was an East Ender from Parkhead. She had been out with
a few lads in the past, 'winching' as it is known in Glasgow.
And Carol knew what sex was all about. However, unlike so
many girls of her age, she had managed to retain her virginity.
For four months this particular boy took 'No' for an answer.
Every time he 'winched' Carol in an unlit back court or in his
home, where they would steal a few hours together while his
parents were out, he continually demanded sex and was continually refused. One night he suddenly exploded in rage. They
had been at a dance and the boy had taken too much to drink.
The young man, who had once been so tender towards her,
was determined to have sex whether she objected or not. He
pulled at her trousers and blouse. Carol screamed and struggled. But it was no use. She was taken by brute force, totally
against her will.

Carol staggered from the tenement towards the nearest
bus-stop at Parkhead Cross, where she collapsed. People just
walked by, glancing at her, only to continue on their way.
They thought she was just another young girl who had taken
too much to drink at a party. Carol, however, did not drink at
that time. One man who passed by and recognized her, knew
that. 'What's wrong with you, Carol?' he asked. Carol lied, 'I
don't feel well.' The man hailed a passing taxi and Carol was
taken to the Royal Infirmary; she was admitted and detained
for observation for a few days. The unhappy victim never told
anyone about the rape, not even her close friends, far less her
parents.

A fortnight later Carol missed her period! She hoped against
hope, fearful, ashamed and, above all, alone. She could not
bring herself to tell anybody. The second month passed and,
again, her period failed to arrive. An anxious visit to the doctor
followed and, a few days later, Carol was given the news. At
eighteen years of age, never having had sex voluntarily, she
was pregnant.

When the youth found out he asked Carol, through her
father, to marry him. Carol, however, had turned completely

against him. She could not bear to see him again and, to this day, she never has. But the incident left permanent scars.

Carol was forced to leave work to have her baby. She gave birth to a little boy and stayed with her parents. When the child was old enough to be looked after by her mother she went back to her job.

At twenty-one, Carol was to find some happiness. She fell in love with, and married, another East Ender, and bore his child, a boy. Carol had worked until she was only two weeks away from the confinement. But for the next three years she was a happy housewife and mother, until it became necessary to work again to make ends meet. The child was placed in a day nursery. Two years later, Carol became pregnant again. This time she gave birth to a girl. By then, however, the marriage was beginning to founder. Carol's husband had been in and out of trouble with the law, leaving her to fend for herself and her children while he served prison sentences. Eventually, when she could take no more, she left him. Divorce proceedings began and Carol returned to Easterhouse, staying again with her parents and her first child. The two other children were looked after by her mother-in-law. Work was hard to find and she remained unemployed.

Another three years passed and a new man entered Carol's life. Billy was a shipyard painter in Clydeside, yet another East Ender. Carol had known him only by sight. They met for the first time at a dance run by a Roman Catholic church club in Barrowfield. Neither were Catholics, but they had been invited by friends. Like Carol, Billy was going through the throes of a divorce. He had left his wife. They were introduced that night and were immediately attracted to each other.

When too much drink was taken an argument broke out between Billy's friend and another man. Carol was kicked in the ankle as she tried to separate them. Billy's friend received a slight injury and they took him to the Royal Infirmary for minor treatment. At 1 a.m., back at Billy's home in the shadow of Parkhead, he invited her in for a drink. 'Why don't you stay the night?' he asked. 'You can have the spare bedroom, and I'll sleep there.' He pointed to his own bedroom. Carol did stay the night, but in Billy's arms.

For the next two and a half years, until they married, Carol and Billy lived in the same flat he had once occupied with his now estranged wife. In Billy's words, 'If she was there she was there. If she wasn't it didn't matter.' Carol feared Billy might decide to go back to his wife before the divorce came through. She did not want to become too involved and suffer further pain and disappointment.

In October 1979, although neither of their divorces had come through, Carol and Billy knew enough of each other to settle down as man and wife. That year was the happiest year of Carol's life. Her man was working, unlike so many others in the East End, and there were no money problems. For twelve unbroken and happy months they lived together.

On Halloween, 31 October 1980, Carol's life changed irrevocably. That Friday morning, like a mother and son, Carol and Billy junior boarded a 64A green-and-yellow double-decker, and headed for the city centre to buy Billy's denims. In a shop called What Every Kid Wants, in Glasgow's famous Argyle Street, young Billy proudly bought his new pair of trousers and a belt. He also purchased a sleeveless woollen top, with white, pink and green hoops, which Carol thought a bit much for a boy. Anyway, she fancied it for herself and so bought the youngster a conventional shirt. Over the next two years this flimsy woollen top would be produced as evidence in courts in Glasgow and Edinburgh.

For the rest of the morning Carol and Billy junior window-shopped along Argyle Street, making for one of the big stores where Carol planned to buy Billy's tea. It was nearing lunch-time. 'Could you eat anything just now?' she asked young Billy. He was feeling hungry and they had a snack meal in the store's cafeteria. Afterwards, Carol decided to go home as quickly as possible. She wanted the youngster to try on his denims. If they didn't fit she would take them back to town in the afternoon. They jumped in a taxi and ten minutes later arrived home. Billy junior immediately tried on his new trousers. Apart from being long in the leg they were a perfect fit; Carol hemmed the legs, then pressed them.

She glanced at the living-room clock and suddenly remembered that she had promised to visit Babs, a neighbour who lived farther along the road. Babs had travelled with Carol on the 64A bus that morning. She was pregnant and anxious for some girl talk, especially from a woman like Carol who had three children of her own.

Carol put on her new top to show Babs and told Billy where she was going. It was shortly after 3 p.m. when she knocked on Babs's door. The talk all that afternoon was about babies, interrupted only by a short shopping trip for groceries. When they returned, Carol was offered a drink. Babs produced some Carlsberg Special Brew from a cupboard. The time just flew as they chatted and Carol forgot all about Billy coming home for his tea.

At 5 p.m. Ricky, the father of Babs's child, arrived home with a 'carry out' of wine. He had been drinking for most of the afternoon and pressed wine on Carol. Carol didn't really enjoy the taste of it, so she asked him to drown it with lemonade. As she was sipping her second glass Billy arrived home from work. It was 6.30 p.m. 'Where's Carol?' he asked his son. The boy immediately sensed that his father was angry. 'She's down the road at Babs's,' he told him. Billy didn't like Ricky and objected to Carol visiting Babs. He was also furious because his tea wasn't ready and they were going to be late for Billy junior's last treat.

Billy stormed out, intending to bring Carol back immediately. 'Right, come on,' he told her. Ricky, however, was not too happy about his impromptu party being interrupted. 'She's not going!' he shouted. 'You're not spoiling my party.' He disappeared from the living room and Billy heard the sound of a key turning in the front door. Ricky returned seconds later, brandishing an axe. Billy was sober but furious. He had foregone his customary drink on the way home so that he would have plenty of time to get ready for the big night out. 'I came in through that door,' he warned Ricky, 'and I'm going out of it -- and Carol is going with me.'

Carol, in the meantime, was trying to calm things down. 'I shouldn't have been drinking,' she apologized to Billy. She turned to Ricky and Babs, 'I'll have to go and make his tea.' After a few more heated words, Ricky relented and unlocked the door to let Carol and Billy out. But Billy's anger hadn't subsided. When they got home and Carol had made him a cup of tea, trying to explain, trying to calm him down, they were interrupted by a knock at the door. It was Babs. She was terrified of Ricky and wanted to keep out of his way.

Babs poured out her troubles. 'I'm going to my mother's for the night, but I haven't got any cash.' Billy escorted her to the main road in case Ricky was still about, dug into his hip-pocket and gave her a pound. 'Get a taxi,' he said. When he returned Carol had gone. 'Where's Carol?' he asked his son for the second time that evening. They looked round the flat. Carol had vanished.

Billy had never laid a finger on Carol before but, for a few anxious moments when she had seen the look of rage on his face, she had been scared. 'I'm going to get a battering,' she thought. So while Billy was talking to Babs she slipped out of the house and ran to the bus-stop, muttering, 'I'll go to my mother's for the night too.' Babs was at the bus-stop and, seconds later, a bus came and they both got on. By the time Billy was in the street looking for her, Carol was on her way into the city centre. The two women who had travelled on the same bus route together nine hours earlier, at the start of an ordinary day, were now fleeing their respective men, both to go home to mother. But their mothers were not to see them that night.

To reach her parents' home – at this time they lived in the south of the city – Carol had to change buses at Glasgow Cross. Babs stepped off the bus with her. They stood near a pub preparing to say farewell. The sound from inside could be heard quite clearly, the jukebox, clinking of glasses, laughter. Carol had never been in the Mecca Bar before, but Babs had. In fact, she reckoned some of her friends might be inside.

'Fancy one before we go?' Carol agreed. They walked through the door. Shakin' Stevens was rocking at full blast on the jukebox. Three girls stood next to it, constantly feeding in coins to keep the music going. They looked under-age. One of them bore love bites on her neck, brazenly exhibiting them. 'Hey, you three!' bellowed the barman, a middle-aged man with a bullet head. 'What age are *you*?' 'Nineteen.' 'Don't give

us that . . . *out.*' The three girls left but returned a few minutes
later, trying to hide themselves in a crowded corner. The barman spotted them again. 'I told you – *out.*'

A peroxide blonde, aged fifty plus, with black hair sprouting
at her roots, stood by the public telephone at the far end of the
bar dialling a call. Every table was occupied. Three old women,
dressed in scruffy coats with mottled legs and no nylons, chatted animatedly with each other. A few yards away, an elderly,
toothless and smiling man staggered up to a younger woman
in her forties who was standing with some women of her own
age. He asked her to dance. Shakin' Stevens's latest hit was
being played for the third time in succession. They jived in the
middle of the floor. Two women suddenly had the same idea.
'OK, cut that out!' roared the barman. 'No dancing in here.'
He rushed from behind the bar to break the party up. Roars
of disapproval from many of the customers followed within
seconds. The two barmaids dispensing drink at full tilt – pints,
sherries, whisky and wine – carried on unconcerned.

Babs waved at some women sitting at a table, who invited
Carol and her to join them. Between them Babs and Carol
didn't have much money, but they had enough for a few drinks.
Carol started with vodka and lemonade. They chatted and
laughed, feet tapping to the rhythm of the jukebox. Carol
finished another vodka and lemonade and then started on a
Carlsberg Special Brew. She sipped it, but it was too gassy
and, anyway, the amount she had taken in mid-afternoon and
early evening was beginning to have its effect. The nicotine-
stained walls of the pub began to swirl. Carol looked round for
Babs. She was nowhere to be seen. She thought of Billy, the
row, and of the happy evening they should have been spending
at the cinema with Billy junior on his last night. It was time,
she decided, to go home.

In the meantime, Billy was in the Clansman Bar in Springfield Road, not far from their flat. His son had decided he did
not want to go out without Carol and had gone to play with
his pals instead. Billy got steaming drunk.

As she left the Mecca, Carol discovered she had no money
in her bag. A girl called Rosie gave her 15p for her bus fare
home. She headed for London Road and waited for a bus going

to the East End. It was shortly after 10 p.m. None came and
Carol decided to walk. The road was long but straight. A bus
drove past her. As she headed home, anxious for the reconciliation with Billy, the cool night air began to sober her.

4 The Hunters

At 7.30 p.m. that night, scores of teenagers from Barrowfield and the surrounding areas were heading out to enjoy themselves at the start of another weekend. Many were going to a youth-club disco at a school hall in Queen Mary Street, near London Road. Run by a youth leader, the regular Friday nights were popular with local boys and girls, allowing them to let off a bit of steam instead of hanging around street corners.

Seventeen-year-old Joe Sweeney, one of the leaders of the Spur gang, and his brother Gordon, who was three years younger, had decided to go to the club. Joe bounded down the stairs of his tenement home at 185 Barrowfield Street to join up with a friend. The two boys swaggered into London Road, stopping at an off-licence to buy a bottle of cheap wine. Joe, like many lads of the same age, thought it was 'the big thing' to get drunk on a Friday night. Alcohol gave him the confidence to chat up girls. It made him feel like a man. Inside the club, Joe met Gordon and two other boys, fifteen-year-old John Thomson, who lived just a few doors down the road from him, and seventeen-year-old Stephen Cameron.

When the disco finished the boys walked out together, separating on the way home. Joe and John Thomson brazened their way into another off-licence to buy more wine. They took turns to swig from the bottle, sitting just inside the entrance to a tenement flat in Stamford Street. Afterwards, they walked aimlessly around the area. Stephen Cameron met his girlfriend, Charlotte, who hailed from another part of Glasgow altogether. She had arrived in Barrowfield to babysit for a friend. He strolled to the house with her and, when the children were put to sleep, Stephen and Charlotte sneaked into another bedroom to make love. Later he returned to the street and met Joe. 'Come on up to the house,' Joe suggested. 'I've got a few cans of Carlsberg.' Stephen jumped at the chance. He hadn't had a drink that night.

In the meantime, young Gordon and John Thomson roamed the area, lounging at street corners to see who was about. They were bored and had nothing to do to fill in the rest of the evening.

Carol, still feeling under the influence of drink but gradually sobering up, was making her way home. She was not staggering; nevertheless, her steps were made more difficult by a combination of vodka and her fashionable but impractical high-heeled sandals.

Carol didn't see the two boys standing in the shadows as she walked by. But they had spotted her, and also her uneasy movements. It was a sign of weakness. Gordon Sweeney and John Thomson looked at each other knowingly and began to follow the woman. Carol didn't hear their footsteps. She had just passed Celtic Park, heading for the corner of London Road, when the boys homed in.

Carol was later to tell the court her alleged version of how it happened . . . how one of the boys, rolling a cigarette between his fingers, blocked her way, asking for a light.

Later she remembered lying on her back, not on the street but somewhere else. She didn't know where she was. It was inky black. She heard four voices; when she tried to pick herself up she saw the glint of a blade and heard a menacing voice, 'You are going to get it, you cow!' Carol realized she was in danger of being killed. 'You don't need to use that,' she pleaded. For the second time she lapsed into unconsciousness. . . .

When Carol awoke again she was all alone, trapped in darkness. She found a door and just managed to push it open. She fell on her hands and knees to crawl over the ground. Not far away she saw street lights. As she neared them she recognized the familiar tenements of London Road. She was back at the same spot where it had all started. Struggling to her feet,

Carol began to run. The safety of her home was only a few hundred yards away. She fell several times. She felt something trickling down her legs, her own blood.

She managed to stagger barefoot to the flats. Only three flights of stairs to go and, at last, she would be at the door. Carol made it. She tried to knock but could not. Her fingers were all cut and the faint tapping was not loud enough to wake up Billy who was sleeping off the drink he had taken after their row.

In desperation Carol stumbled down the stairs again. Gathering up her last reserves of strength she ran across to London Road. Some passers-by merely looked at her, not stopping to offer any help.

Carol knew there was one person who would be able to help, Mrs Kate Dobbin, a middle-aged woman who was almost like a second mother. Kate's flat was on the ground floor. She was watching television when the door-bell rang.

Mrs Dobbin was met by a sight she was never to forget. Carol stood at the door, her face masked in blood and dirt and, for a few moments, almost unrecognizable. She reeled along the hall into the living room and collapsed, a pathetic bundle lying in front of the fireside. 'An ambulance, an ambulance,' she pleaded, unable to get her words out properly.

Mrs Dobbin's son, James, was in bed. His mother shook him. He awoke, blinked his eyes and, still half-asleep, walked to the living room to see what was wrong. James immediately came to his senses. He ran faster than he had ever run before, praying that the public phone-box several hundred yards away in Springfield Road would be working. James lifted the receiver and put it to his ear. He sighed with relief when he heard the familiar dialling tone and, with trembling fingers, dialled emergency services. As he sprinted back, the ambulance and the police alerted, Mrs Dobbin was trying to comfort Carol. The girl was in a state of terror, her hands shaking so violently she couldn't hold a cup of tea. 'What happened to you?' Mrs Dobbin asked. Carol's eyes stared straight ahead without flickering. She never answered.

At exactly 1.10 a.m. Constables John Alexander and Alan Wardie, on routine patrol, drew up to the Dobbins' home in response to a radio call to attend an assault. They saw blood on the ground and on the half-open door, and were immediately taken by James into the living room.

The officers had never seen such appalling injuries. The flesh on Carol's face and thighs was almost falling apart and blood still oozed from the gaping slash wounds. She was naked from the waist down and Mrs Dobbin put her coat over her shoulders. Both constables feared that Carol might die; one of them radioed his controller, asking him to urge the ambulance to waste no time.

When it did arrive, James Dobbin was allowed to go with Carol. He held her hand but she was in a trance. He was to sit in the Royal Infirmary's Casualty Department for five hours and, despite his long vigil, James was not allowed to see Carol again.

Between them Constables James Porte and Gordon Lindsay had only four years' service, but already they were battle-hardened in the violent streets of Glasgow's East End.

Soon after the attack on Carol the two officers spotted the Sweeney brothers, Thomson and Cameron. Porte and Lindsay knew them well. Over the past few months they had studied the young trouble-makers in the area and examined 'mug shots' pasted in the police gang-book which was kept in the Eastern Division's headquarters at Tobago Street. The gang-book details names, addresses and previous convictions of members of the various rival gangs who cause problems in the area.

As they walked into Barrowfield Street, only fifteen yards from its junction with Stamford Street, the Sweeneys, Thomson and Cameron spotted the two officers and prepared to make their getaway. Stephen Cameron bolted into the back close at 200 Barrowfield Street and, as the officers approached the three remaining boys, Joe Sweeney also took to his heels. Constable Lindsay, young and fit, chased him across Stamford Street into the close at number 61 and then into the back court. Twice, in his panic to get away, Sweeney slipped on some unknown object in the darkness. It allowed Constable Lindsay to gain a few yards on him. Even then he couldn't catch up. Sweeney went through the back close at 105 Barrow-field Street and bolted into his own home.

In the meantime, Constable Porte stopped young Sweeney and John Thomson. He immediately detected their nervousness. 'What have they been up to?' he thought. He contacted Lindsay over the personal radio and agreed to link up with him at the Sweeney home. Frog-marching the two youths in front, Porte soon joined Lindsay in the close. Together they frisked the youths. They were trembling. But why? The officers found nothing incriminating on them. No stolen property, no offensive weapons. They let them go free.

Porte and Lindsay decided to turn their attention to the Sweeney home and Joe Sweeney, who they believed was inside. First of all, they tried the door handle. It was locked. A split-second later they heard noises from within. 'Quick, quick, it's the police. Jump.' The constables started battering on the front door. Porte, realizing they were about to lose Sweeney, turned to run down the stairs. He planned to head for the back court to cover the rear windows.

But just as he had taken his first few steps down the well-worn close stairs, the front door suddenly opened and Sweeney's mother appeared. Porte returned and he and Lindsay quickly invited themselves in, explaining to Mrs Sweeney that they were looking for her son Joe. By that time Joe had climbed down the veranda to leap to the street below. Mrs Sweeney gave the two officers permission to search her home, her husband accompanying them as they looked round the rooms. Joe had vanished.

His brother, Gordon, and John Thomson arrived at the front door but, as soon as they saw the police, they turned back. Minutes later outside, Porte and Lindsay spotted the youths again. They followed them into the close at 212 Barrowfield, but they, like Sweeney, vanished into thin air.

As the abortive investigation into the mischief-making of the Sweeney brothers, Thomson and Cameron ended, Carol was only a few hundred yards away, trapped and terrified in the darkness of a scrap-yard cabin, blood still pumping from her appalling wounds. Unaware of what had happened, Constables Porte and Lindsay continued their beat patrol.

Hardly a Friday night passes without detectives visiting Glasgow Royal Infirmary to take statements from the victims of weekend violence. Four officers were in the hospital investigating another matter when Carol was wheeled in. Detective Constables Adam Drummond, Arthur Chatfield, Thomas Moulds and Leslie Darling were all from the Eastern Division. A nurse told the officers of Carol's hideous injuries. 'She is one of the worst victims of slashing we have ever seen. We think she might have been raped as well.'

Drummond and Chatfield asked if they could see the victim. Carol was in the Casualty Department operating theatre and they were allowed only a few minutes with her. They could not get much sense out of her. She mumbled something about having been raped in London Road.

Both teams headed out in their CID cars to search every property in the area in order to find the spot where Carol might have been attacked. But it proved useless.

In the meantime other officers were zeroing in on Billy who was to find himself the number one suspect, albeit a temporary one, for the razor attack on Carol. At 2.45 a.m. a squad of officers began to batter on his door. Billy junior got up to answer. As soon as he unlocked the door, six plain-clothes policemen charged into Billy's bedroom while he was putting on his trousers. An officer pushed him back onto the bed and told him, 'Take them off, you are not going anywhere, pal. Just stay there.' Another detective asked, 'Do you know Carol X?' 'Yes, she is my girlfriend,' Billy told them. 'Has anything happened to her?' 'She's fuckin' dead,' was the crude reply. Billy couldn't believe it and broke down. One of the officers whispered, 'She's OK, she's OK. She's just been injured.' Billy was asked to explain the blood at his front door. He couldn't. It took an hour to persuade the police that he was innocent and that he had not seen Carol since tea-time the previous evening. When the police left, young Billy confessed to his father that he had heard faint tapping at the door at 11.55 p.m. 'I tried to wake you,' he said. 'But you were so drunk I couldn't. I was scared to go to the door on my own.'

By the time the uniform early shift began to arrive at the Eastern Division headquarters at dawn on the Saturday morning, the detectives were no further forward with their inquiries. At 7 a.m. Drummond briefed the beat patrol officers who were about to start their day's work. 'A serious assault and rape has taken place somewhere in this division,' he told them. 'And we still don't know where it happened, the victim can't tell us. As soon as you go out, search your beat. You will know when you see blood – there will be a lot of it about.'

Constables James Russell and William Allan were the beat men for Barrowfield that day. Just as they were about to leave the office, Detective Constable Drummond gave them an extra piece of information. 'The victim managed to get to her home after the attack, so therefore it is possible the assault was carried out nearby.'

Russell and Allan began the search by walking round the perimeter of Barrowfield. At the entrance to Carol's flat they found spots of blood a yard apart and followed them up three flights of stairs. There was more blood at the door. The two officers then retraced the bloody trail back down to the street and when they reached London Road they noticed the drops getting bigger and closer together. From London Road they tracked them into Davaar Street, like two stalkers hunting a wounded stag. The trail ended outside Wilson's, a derelict scrap-yard. The large, double wire gates were open two feet. The constables walked inside.

Even in daylight Wilson's yard is a place of degradation and neglect, a jumble of outbuildings and old machinery, scrap metal, rusty chains, empty chemical drums, bricks, rubble and hardened bags of cement. The ground was covered in mud and red chippings, much of which had been contaminated by oil, petrol and chemicals. It was littered with jagged pieces of glass, nuts and bolts, and stones.

To the right as they walked in, the officers spotted a large green container sprayed in black and yellow paint with gang slogans. 'OK kill' was emblazoned across the container's entrance. The door was lying open and Constables Russell and Allan saw more blood, this time not just drips of blood, but pools, black and congealed. There was one pool just outside the container door, others inside. Even old harnesses which had been kept in the container were blood-spattered. It was undoubtedly the spot where the previous night's attack had taken place. Carol's denims, pants, tights and red high-heeled sandals were still lying there. So were other grim mementos: blood-stained locks of hair which had almost certainly been scalped from her head by a razor. The two beat men realized that there would be vital clues inside. They stood guard at the container's doors.

At 8 a.m. Detective Constables Drummond and Chatfield, on duty by this time for ten hours, arrived at the scene. They were relieved that the two uniformed officers had touched nothing; they informed the civilian Scenes of Crimes men who would photograph and fingerprint the grim find. They arrived ninety minutes later, one from Strathclyde Police headquarters in the centre of Glasgow, and the other from Motherwell police office. The two experts took coloured photographs of a sequence of views of Carol's home, showing the blood stains on the pavement outside and on her front door, and of the scrap-yard, the container and what they found inside.

One of them, using a brush and powder, began to look for fingerprints. On a disused gas fire outside the container door, he found a clear fingerprint and, with a strip of adhesive tape, almost like ordinary household sellotape, lifted it off the metal. To conform with police procedure, which often comes under the microscope in a court, he and Detective Constable Drummond signed a label to confirm that they had taken possession of the print. It would be sent to the Scottish Criminal Records Office, housed in Glasgow's Police headquarters, for experts to examine. Samples of the blood and hair found in the cabin were put in glass containers, along with controlled sweepings of earth from the cabin floor. Carol's clothes were also taken and put in polythene bags.

On Sunday morning a police photographer visited Carol's bedside to take official pictures of her injuries. His operational colleagues in the CID were chasing up various leads, none of them productive. On Monday the big breakthrough came. Detective Constables Drummond, Chatfield, Darling and Moulds had been hitting the streets of the East End in an effort to unmask whoever had assaulted Carol. The home of every young villain in the area capable of carrying out such an atrocity was visited. Barrowfield was humming with stories about the incident. At the end of the day the team of detectives got what they had set out to find. They call it 'information received', a polite expression for somebody 'grassing'. The information received was that Carol had been assaulted by the Sweeney brothers, John Thomson and Stephen Cameron.

That night the detectives made their plan for an early-morning raid on the homes of the suspects. They went to the Sweeney home first, at precisely 7.40 a.m. on Tuesday, 4 November. Detective Constables Drummond and Chatfield stood at the door while their colleagues, Darling and Moulds, covered the rear windows. This time Joe Sweeney and his brother had no chance of doing a disappearing act. The two brothers were led out of their home and put into separate CID cars which took them off to Tobago Street police station where they were placed in separate rooms. Twenty minutes later the four detectives were repeating the same routine, this time at Stephen Cameron's home at 61 Fraser Street. He too was taken to Tobago Street and put alone in a room. It was a successful start to what was to become an even more successful and dramatic day; three of the four boys were detained in the police station and the fourth was to be arrested later that day. The police informed the three boys individually why they had been detained. They also gave each one the legal caution that they were not obliged to say anything, but anything they did say would be taken down in writing and might be used in evidence.

Gordon Sweeney remained silent for a few seconds after Detective Constable Drummond cautioned him. Then suddenly it all came out. 'All right, I knew it would happen,' he said. 'The whole scheme is talking about it.' 'Why is that, son?' Drummond asked. Sweeney blurted out, 'I was into it, but she wasn't cut up when I left.'

When he was cautioned, Stephen Cameron immediately admitted he had been present during Carol's ordeal, but denied actually taking part in the attack. 'I saw them all getting into her, but not me,' he said. 'I thought Joe was kidding when he said he had ripped her.'

The finger now pointed at Joe. He told the police, 'You know

I fucking done it, but that cunt Thomson held her down. I'm
not taking all the fucking blame.'

Later on the three boys agreed to give the police voluntary
statements. Joe Sweeney was first. He was led into Detective
Chief Inspector Alexander Cowie's room. Mr Cowie, at forty
one of Strathclyde's youngest officers, was the head of the
Eastern CID. He introduced Joe to Constable Robert Carrigan
who was to be a witness. Sweeney started talking at 11.30
a.m. and finished twenty minutes later. Detective Chief Inspector Cowie wrote every word down. What Sweeney told the
officers was a full confession to the crime.

Five minutes later Stephen Cameron was led into another
interview room to begin his voluntary statement. Cameron
told how he had witnessed the three boys having sex with the
woman in the cabin, although he denied having sex with her
himself. He also alleged that, afterwards, he saw Joe Sweeney
running out into the street with his hands covered in blood.

The police operation was now running like clockwork. As
Cameron was halfway through his statement, the father of the
two Sweeneys, Mr Gordon Sweeney, arrived at Tobago Street.
The heartbroken man listened as his son poured out the whole
story of what had happened that night, describing how he had
had sex with the woman.

At 3.20 p.m. in the afternoon, Detective Constables Moulds,
Chatfield and Darling headed out to Paisley to bring John
Thomson in. He had been detained in a List D Residential
School for housebreaking and had been given the privilege of
his freedom for the weekend. The officers recovered the clothes
Thomson had been wearing on the night of the incident and
then took him back to Bridgeton police office. On the way, as
the car headed towards the motorway which links Paisley with
Glasgow, Thomson was informed of his rights. The detectives
told him exactly what they had been investigating. As he sat
back in the rear seat, flanked by two officers, Thomson suddenly admitted, 'The four of us screwed her, but Joe just went
too far with the razor.'

In the Eastern Division headquarters Thomson agreed to
give a voluntary statement and his married sister, Mrs Helen
McKenna, was brought to the office to witness it. In his state-

ment, Thomson admitted to having had sex with the woman
and claimed that he saw Joe Sweeney slashing her with a
razor on the back of the legs. An hour later Thomson was
locked up with the rest of the boys.

The police investigation, however, did not end there. The
detectives in charge of the case needed to get back-up evidence.
Statements from all four boys had referred to two policemen
who chased them away that night. The two officers who were
in Barrowfield on duty that weekend were located and questioned. Both recalled the incident and named the four boys
they had seen as the two Sweeneys, John Thomson and
Stephen Cameron.

But there was still much to be done before the case would
be strong enough to present to a court. As the four boys were
led to the bar of Tobago Street police office to be formally
cautioned and charged, the detectives in the case mustered
together all the productions they had taken over the last few
days. These included Carol's clothes found at the scene, phials
of blood, the locks of her hair, and clothing and shoes worn by
the four boys that night.

Carol had been released from the Royal Infirmary earlier
that Tuesday. Shortly after 5 p.m. she was brought in – a
policewoman helping her to stand up – to view an identification parade. The four accused boys took the first four positions
on the parade, followed by ten stand-ins, all young men aged
between fifteen and twenty who had been brought in from the
street. Carol picked out five people. One was Gordon Sweeney,
the others stand-ins. The four boys were then locked up. The
next morning they were fingerprinted on official Scottish
Criminal Records Office forms and their photographs taken.
They were escorted by detectives, just before lunchtime, to be
processed through Glasgow Sheriff Court and to be given the
services of the duty lawyer through the Legal Aid scheme.
During the brief court appearance, all four were refused bail
and were remanded, pending their next court appearance a
week later for full committal.

On the Tuesday morning all the possible forensic clues were
gathered together and sent to scientists at the Strathclyde
Police laboratory. The fingerprints obtained from the boys,

together with the one found on the old gas fire outside the container, were submitted to experts at the Fingerprint Section of the Scottish Criminal Records Office. It would be up to these two agencies to look for supporting evidence for the Crown case against the youths.

5 The Ordeal

After her four days in hospital Billy took Carol to his mother's house to allow her to recuperate. She crooked an arm in his and limped painfully to the waiting cab. Through the corner of his eye Billy saw her face contort in agony. He thought about the row on Friday night. He was partly to blame. 'I'll look after her, no matter what,' he vowed to himself.

Billy's family had prepared a welcome for Carol on her return. During a quiet moment with his mother he told her, 'She will be all right in a few weeks. Then we'll return to our own house. Things will soon return to normal.'

In the weeks that passed everyone could see that the wounds on Carol's face were healing. But there were also invisible wounds gnawing away at her mind, consuming her with revulsion for herself and fear of what lay outside the front door. The scars on her flesh would heal with time, but those on her mind were to take very much longer.

Carol had first felt this onslaught lying in the half-light of the Royal Infirmary's casualty ward. She had been temporarily patched up and wheeled to the ward, the bed screened by curtains, her thigh injuries protected by a cage. The initial medical treatment and police questioning completed, Carol was alone with her thoughts, unable to move because, whenever she did, the pain which racked her body increased a hundredfold.

She lay there imagining figures of the boys who had abused her. Four voices echoed in her memory. She heard them laugh; saw the glint of a razor; heard herself pleading. Much of her

ordeal had been blotted out as if brain cells were anaesthetized
by nature, clouding her memory to spare her the shock. She
was physically aware of the wounds but she could not recall
being raped. Carol *knew*, however, that these youngsters had
been within her sexually. She thought of them, 'Just children
. . . just boys . . . ,' and she tried to visualize herself lying on
the floor of the dark cabin being defiled; being assaulted in-
decently; being raped.

How could they have done it to her? Pictures of Billy junior,
who was about the same age as the boys who had stopped her
in the street, and of her own twelve-year-old son, started to
flash in her mind's eye. She tried to imagine these two youngsters, so dear to her heart, raping an older woman. It was
incomprehensible. The thought made her shudder. Yet boys
the same age as Billy, and just a little older than her own son,
had done it to her. Carol had done nothing wrong but, nevertheless, she felt dirty and degraded.

Lying in the ward during the early hours of the morning she
flashed back to the night, twelve years before, when she had
been raped by her boyfriend. She had felt desolation then, but
what she felt now was infinitely more horrifying. Carol had
covered up that incident because of shame. One half of her
wished she could cover this one up, the other half told her she
could not. 'If these boys could do that to me,' she thought, 'they
could do it to some other woman.' They had to be caught. A
nurse arrived to give her a pain-killing injection. Minutes
later the sounds of the ward turned into distant echoes.

Carol remembered very little of what happened to her in
hospital later on that morning, or the operation under anaesthetic to stitch up the injuries. Before the operation, when she
had recovered sufficiently to receive visitors, Billy arrived.

He looked at her face with incredulity. The wounds were
made even more vivid by the cap that had been put on Carol's
head to prevent her long dark hair from infecting the injuries.
Carol slowly pulled the sheet away from her legs. 'Look at
what they did to me, Billy.' Her voice trailed off into a sob.
Billy stared. He felt his head spin and he fainted. A nurse took
him out of the ward to give him a glass of water.

When he returned, Carol told him for the first time what

had happened the previous night and of the shame she felt. Pangs of guilt ached in Billy's stomach. He sat holding her hand until it was time for him to go.

Carol was able to see the injuries on her legs but she couldn't see what had happened to her face. Carol's sister and her mother, who visited her in hospital over the next few days, told her how bad it was. She lay there, imagining what it was like.

Monday came and she was allowed out of bed for the first time. Carol knew that there could be a mirror in the toilet at the end of the ward. Carrying the intravenous drip and bottle still attached to her, she took her first few tentative steps towards the washroom. There *was* a mirror. Carol anxiously positioned herself in front of it.

Her face was twice its normal size. Her eyes were blackened. She saw the slash wounds yellowing at the edges with black stitches. 'It can't be me,' she tried to tell herself. She took a second look. It was her. The sight of herself that day was so traumatic that, eighteen months later, she could not bear to see her reflection. After leaving hospital Carol learned how to brush her hair and put on make-up without the aid of a mirror.

On 4 November Carol was allowed home. Holding Billy's arm she walked into the daylight where there was a taxi standing by. When they reached Billy's mother's first-floor tenement flat in Parkhead, Billy tenderly helped her out. She was indoors in seconds. Sitting in the living room, Billy's mother, Agnes, and her daughters tried to reassure Carol that the scars would eventually vanish and she would be able to face the world again in a few weeks when she was stronger.

The door-bell rang early in the afternoon. It was the police. They were apologetic. 'We're sorry to bother you, Carol,' said one of the detectives. 'We know what you've been through, but we have four boys in custody and we want you to view an identification parade.' Billy snapped at them. 'Look at the state she's in. Can you not see she's had enough.' The officers, however, were insistent. It was urgent unless she wanted to see the boys who had assaulted her remain unpunished.

Carol nodded. 'OK,' she said quietly. 'I'll go.' 'Are you sure

that you will be all right?' asked Billy. She half smiled, but
inside she began to tremble.

Carol was taken to Tobago Street police station. Before viewing the parade Frances Adamson, a young policewoman, reassured her. She led Carol into the parade room. Carol had
difficulty in walking and, halfway through the parade, her
legs gave way. Frances had to support her bodily for the remainder of the time spent viewing the line-up.

The police drove her home afterwards and it was to be
months before Carol dared venture out again. Later that afternoon the door-bell rang once more. This time it was a police
casualty surgeon. He asked Carol if he could take samples of
blood, head and pubic hair. Carol thought that it was an in-
dignity but not as harrowing as the one she had faced in the
Royal Infirmary where doctors had examined her internally,
taking swabs in an effort to detect seminal fluid.

Carol swallowed tranquillizers and sleeping pills that night
and, from then on, she found that drugs could provide her with
temporary relief for body and mind.

During the next visit from the doctor – her general practitioner – a few days later, Carol confided in him her dread that
she had contracted venereal disease from one of the boys. He
gave her a test and, to her relief, it proved negative.

Carol spent the next four months in Billy's mother's home,
doped for the first few weeks with painkillers and stupefied
every night with sleeping pills. The injuries healed well but
Carol's mental condition, instead of improving, became worse.

In the first few weeks, relatives visited to lend support and
encouragement. One of Billy's sisters brought her daughter,
an attractive blonde-haired toddler, to see her. 'You've got a
funny nose, Auntie Carol,' the child innocently observed. She
had spotted the vicious scar across the tip of Carol's nose. The
remark, even from one so young, rooted Carol to the spot,
brutally reminding her of her disfigurement.

For days on end she couldn't care to dress herself, moping
about the house in nightwear and dressing-gown. Billy and
his mother constantly tried to persuade her to get out for some
fresh air. But Carol refused. She was consumed by an illogical
but uneasy dread that the minute she left the cocooned safety

of Billy's home it would all happen to her again. Carol was convinced that boys were waiting for her outside. She confided her fears to Billy. He tried to convince her that such a thing could never happen to her again, but Carol could not be convinced. Hardly a day passed when she did not relive the attack in her imagination.

Carol had always been a slim seven stone but, although she was eating normally, she began to lose pound after pound and then stone after stone. She turned into a living skeleton weighing only four stone twelve pounds. She spent hours alone in her bedroom, brooding. Novels would be brought in for her to read; Carol would start a book, only to discard it halfway through, sometimes even after a few pages. She could not concentrate on anything. When she appeared to be watching television, only her eyes would be fixed on the screen, her thoughts and fears a quarter of a mile away in the darkness of the cabin.

The idea of suicide started to creep into Carol's mind, slowly at first, but gathering momentum as the weeks went by. She would sit for hours thinking about herself, her life, what had happened to her and Billy. 'I'm no use to anyone,' she thought. 'No use to Billy, no use to my family, and no use to myself.'

Then with Christmas only weeks away, she made a final decision to end it all. She sneaked into the bathroom when no one was looking, took one of Billy's razor blades and turned the cold tap on. 'It will wash the blood away,' she thought. Carol drew the razor across her left wrist and the blood began to spurt and pump. She was just about to repeat the process with the other wrist when Billy, sensing that something was wrong, rushed into the bathroom. He saw the blood, grabbed Carol's arm, made her drop the blade and wrapped a towel round the wound. Billy phoned for an ambulance.

Carol was kept in the Royal Infirmary for a few days, each hour that passed a grim reminder of her visit to the hospital the previous month. By this time the strain was affecting Billy too, and he was forced to take time off work. He constantly worried that Carol would try to take her own life again, and attempted to coax her out of herself, but to no avail.

At nights Billy would wake up sensing Carol's restlessness.

She couldn't sleep. Carol's first nightmare scared him. She had broken out into a cold sweat, her screams rousing him instantly. Gently trying to bring her back to reality Billy asked her, 'What are you thinking about, love?' He knew what it was but he wanted Carol to get it out of her system by telling him. Carol, however, just sat in bed staring into the darkness, refusing to answer. Billy asked her again. 'Are you dreaming of those boys?' It took a few more minutes to get a reply, but eventually Carol admitted that her nightmares had been about her attack in the cabin and seeing the razor glinting overhead. There were to be many similar episodes in the long nights to come.

The frequency of the visits from the police decreased and Carol was told that, in due course, she would hear from the Procurator Fiscal who would ask her to give a precognition, legal terminology for a statement. A trial date would then be fixed and she would be notified by means of a witness citation.

Carol had always been generous with her praise for the way the detectives involved in the investigation had treated her. She felt reassured by their gentle manner. Her psychological anguish, however, was changing her entire personality. She had always been an easy-going woman but now she found herself flying into a temper for the most trivial reasons. One day Detective Constable Drummond arrived to give her an official form, an application for Criminal Injuries Compensation. Carol just screamed at him, 'I don't want your bloody form. I don't want money. I just want to be left alone.' She felt ashamed later at the needless abuse she had screamed at the detective who, after all, was only trying to help.

The time came for Carol and Billy to move back into their own flat. It was February, just over three months after the attack; only once in all that time had Carol stepped foot outside. The trip to their own little top-flat home was just six or seven hundred yards. Nevertheless, Carol asked Billy to hurry. She was plainly terrified. Once she crossed the threshold she wasn't to pluck up the courage to see the outside world again for another two months.

If the pressures were building up for Carol, they were also increasing for Billy. She was constantly nagging and rowing with him over nothing. Frustration also built up because they had no sex life. Billy feared that if he suggested sex it would make the incident in the cabin come back into her memory. Consequently he drew back. Unknown to him, Carol went to bed every night nervous to make the first advance herself. Her dread was that Billy would turn his back on her, repulsed by the knowledge that the last time she had sex it had been involuntarily with three strangers. It was five months before Billy and Carol made love and, when they talked about it afterwards, they both realized for the first time what had been going on in each other's minds and laughed about it.

But there was little laughter in Carol's life. She obsessively relived her ordeal and constantly thought of the new one to come in the witness box. Then one morning, towards the end of March, the postman popped through her door an official On Her Majesty's Service buff envelope marked 'Procurator Fiscal'. Carol opened it nervously. It was the letter that she had been warned about, asking her to attend the Fiscal's office to give a statement at the beginning of April 1981 – some five months after the attack.

When the day of the appointment finally arrived, Carol couldn't face it. She told Billy she wasn't going to go. 'You will have to,' he impressed on her. 'Don't worry about anything. I'll be with you. You've just got to tell the truth. Tell what happened.'

They got a taxi to the Procurator Fiscal's office, an imposing building at Customs House Quay facing a landscaped walkway which stretches along the Clyde, past the Broomielaw. Once pleasure paddle-steamers had plied nearby, taking trippers 'doon the watter' as it was known in Glasgow.

Carol again had cold feet. But Billy persuaded her to go inside. She sat in the waiting-room dreading the invitation to step into the office of the precognition clerk who was to take her statement. The pleasant young man introduced himself and began to ask her questions about the night of 31 October, writing it all down on official notepaper. When she had re-counted her ordeal, the quiet, easy interview suddenly ended. Carol found herself facing a tirade of accusations spoken in a loud voice.

'You went with these boys deliberately,' said the clerk. 'You
let them have sex with you. You wanted to have sex with
them.' Carol burst into tears. Billy in a rage protested. 'Don't
talk to her like that,' he shouted. 'What right have you to
suggest things like that? We thought that you were here to
help us.' The young man's attitude suddenly changed. 'I'm
sorry, Carol,' he said, 'but I had to do it. That is what it is
going to be like in the witness box, to be cross-examined by
the defence. They will show no mercy. I have to give you an
idea of what it will be like so that you can be prepared for it.
If I had them here just now I would castrate the bastards.'

The bizarre and brutal dress-rehearsal over, Carol returned
home, dreading the thought of having to go to court, to confront
the boys and, above all, to face their lawyers and their questions. That night she began to ponder over the futility of her
life and, for the second time in four months, the thought of
suicide entered her head. She spent three days wrestling with
her conscience. Should she take her own life? Should she try
to soldier on? Carol could see no way out and, on the night of
the fourth day after her visit to the Procurator Fiscal's office,
she finally made up her mind to take the last, irrevocable
step. . . .

She found the ideal moment when Billy asked her, 'Do you
mind if I go out for a drink?' Carol tried to sound enthusiastic.
'Go and enjoy yourself,' she said. It was 9.30 p.m. She had it
all planned. Billy would stay till closing time, come home
drunk and never notice her. He put on his jacket. 'Don't worry,
darling. I'm only going for one. I'll be back in an hour.'

As soon as the front door closed Carol ran over to press her
ear against it, listening to the sound of Billy's footsteps echoing
down the flights of stone steps as he made for the close entrance below. She ran to the bedroom window in time to spot
him in the street. He was heading in the direction of the
Clansman Bar in Springfield Road, his favourite pub. As Carol
watched Billy disappear from sight she knew she would never
see him again. She thought of his devotion, looking after her
virtually twenty-four hours a day. It had been a strain for
him. He, too, deserved a rest. On the bedroom table was a
bottle of pills, prescribed by the doctor to help her sleep. Carol

unscrewed the top and emptied them into the palm of her hand, then walked through to the kitchen to pour out a glass of water. In a few gulps the pills were gone. Carol was clever enough to hide the empty bottle in the waste bucket. 'He'll never find them there,' she thought.

Slowly Carol returned to the bedroom. Before she settled down to die, she looked at her face in the dressing-table mirror. It was the first time since staring at herself in the hospital washroom that she had gone near the mirror. She lingered at the dressing-table for a few seconds. The scars were still there. 'Goodbye,' she said to herself. Goodbye to her scars, her pain, her life. . . . To Billy as well.

She turned away from the mirror and lay down on the bed, making herself comfortable. For a while she thought of Billy, her parents, her children, her life. But it all came back to the same thing. She was no use to anyone any more. Carol closed her eyes. 'If I'm going to die, this is the way to do it,' she thought. She never felt the drowsiness overtake her.

Billy was true to his word. Exactly an hour later he arrived home from the Clansman Bar, expecting to see Carol sitting in the living room in front of the television. She wasn't there. Billy looked at the living-room clock. 'Half-past ten,' he mused. 'She's gone to bed early tonight.' He walked through to the bedroom and switched on the light. 'That's odd,' he thought. Carol didn't stir. He gently nudged her on the shoulder. Carol didn't move. In the time it takes to blink an eye, Billy saw that Carol's sleeping pills were not in their proper place on the bedroom table and realized that she had taken them.

The nudges turned into frantic shakes. Carol still did not move a muscle. She was unconscious. Billy felt dread, fear and nausea. His stomach cramped, his head exploded, he shouted, '*Jesus Christ*,' and dragged Carol from the bed, pulling her through to the living room. He shook her like a limp rag-doll. He pleaded. . . . He shouted. . . . He blasphemed. It took an eternity but gradually Carol started to come back to life again. Billy walked her round and round and round and round, talking to her, slapping her face. If he said it once, he said it a dozen times: 'Don't go to sleep, Carol. *Stay awake.*' He sat her down on a chair and searched the flat for the empty bottle of sleeping pills. Eventually he found it, hidden in the kitchen waste bucket, and put it in his pocket.

There was no telephone in Billy's house. He propped Carol up on the chair and ran the few hundred yards to his mother's where he phoned for an ambulance. Billy had never run so fast since he was at school. When he got back to the flat, totally out of breath, Carol had slumped off into semi-consciousness again. Once more he began the process of reviving her. His mother followed him – as breathless as she was alarmed. Half an hour had elapsed and the ambulance had still not appeared. Leaving Carol with his mother, he dashed out into the street and hailed a passing taxi. Carol was taken back to the Royal Infirmary Casualty Department. 'What's she done?' asked the nurse. 'She tried to kill herself.' 'Have you any idea what she's taken?' Billy fumblingly pulled the empty pill bottle from his pocket and thrust it into the nurse's hand. He was ushered out of the casualty room while the medical team battled to save Carol, pumping the drugs from her stomach.

Thanks to Billy, thanks to the taxi driver, thanks to the magnificent medical team at the Royal Infirmary, Carol recovered.

At the beginning of May, Carol's ex-husband arrived unexpectedly with their two children. He was now living in Newcastle and he had picked up the children, a boy of eight and a girl of seven, from his mother's home in the south of Glasgow where they had been staying.

Carol was delighted. She had not seen her children for over a year. When they had taken up together, Billy had asked Carol if she wanted to bring the children to live with them. But rightly or wrongly, Carol thought it best that they stayed with their grandmother. They were happy with her, happy at school and Carol did not want to destroy their new-found life. The last thing she wanted was to have the children moved about from pillar to post. She also did not want to make her mother-in-law unhappy by taking the children away. The grandmother doted on them. There was also another reason. Carol was apprehensive that, if her ex-husband knew the children were with her, he would pester her. It was a wrench for Carol and she purposely stayed away from her mother-in-law's.

When her ex-husband arrived that day he asked Billy if he objected to Carol going with him and the children to Edinburgh Zoo. Billy did not mind and Carol left, promising she would be back in time to go to the cinema as they had planned.

They went to the zoo and afterwards took the children back to their grandmother's. Carol's ex-husband asked her to go out for a meal and a drink; the real purpose of this visit to Glasgow, she was soon to learn, was an attempt at a reconciliation. 'It's not for me,' he explained. 'It's for the sake of the kids. My mother is getting too old to look after them. I'm living in Newcastle now. I've got a new house and would like you to come down. Please, Carol, let's give it another try.'

Later that night they discussed it again with the children's grandmother and, on the spur of the moment, Carol decided. 'OK,' she told her ex-husband. 'I'll give it a try, but only for the kids' sake.' Hours later they were in Newcastle without telling Billy. Carol felt terrible. She wrote to him that night, crying all the time as she tried to explain why she had left him. She knew within herself that she had let him down badly.

In the week that followed Carol was to find out that the reconciliation was not working out as she had hoped. She suspected, too, that she was pregnant, Billy being the father. She wrote a second letter to Billy asking if she could come back and saying she would get his answer on her return to Glasgow. She also told him she might be expecting his child.

In the meantime, the police in Glasgow were anxious to trace Carol to serve a citation for her attendance at the High Court trial of the three youths. A date had been set, 12 June. The full process of the Scottish legal system had taken its proper course. Justice would be done and manifestly so.

The police had arrived with the official form at Billy's; he disclosed that Carol had left him to go to Newcastle. The local police were contacted and visited Carol to tell her about the trial date. Carol got the train that very day back to Glasgow.

Billy welcomed Carol with open arms. May passed, June arrived and, with the trial only a matter of days away, the

familiar feeling of terror was beginning to gnaw away at Carol
once more. For the third time she thought of suicide. Billy was
in the bedroom and, on the spur of the moment, Carol opened
the living-room window and prepared to climb out. She looked
down . . . it was three flights up from the street. Billy heard
noises and ran through, just in time to drag her back.

The morning of Friday, 12 June, arrived. Clutching the
pale-blue piece of paper which was her official citation to attend court as a witness, Carol arrived on Billy's arm, nervous,
worried, apprehensive . . . but there.

6 The Prosecution System

The Advocate Depute rose from his desk and walked across the large room in the heart of Crown Office where the vital decisions affecting criminal prosecutions in Scotland are taken.

The Crown Office then occupied part of the top floor of Edinburgh's historic Parliament House which also contains the country's Supreme Courts – the High Court of Justiciary, the Court of Criminal Appeal and the Court of Session.

The Advocate Depute made for a large, oblong, dirty brown box, the nondescript and incongruous receptacle into which the briefs relating to all Scotland's major criminal prosecutions are placed. For the Advocate Depute and his colleagues, who prosecute all the High Court cases in the country, the selection of their next job of work is a totally random process – a case of first come, first served. He put his hand in the box and plucked out the bundle of documents, tied together with a ribbon, which sat on top of the pile.

Was it an assault from Dundee, a murder from Edinburgh or perhaps a bank robbery from Glasgow? As he walked back to his desk the Advocate Depute glanced at the backing. He had landed a case of attempted murder and rape – Her Majesty's Advocate against Stephen Cameron, Joseph Sweeney, Gordon Sweeney and John Thomson.

The Advocate Depute settled down at his desk, opened the papers and began to read, lending his years of experience and knowledge of the law to the case.

It was through this system that the evidence gathered by

the police in connection with Carol's grim ordeal was scrutin-
ized under a legal microscope and processed. The case had
already been studied by the Procurator Fiscal in Glasgow. The
Advocate Depute, or Crown Counsel as he is sometimes known,
would now direct operations.

The post of Advocate Depute is a part-time appointment and
the man chosen acts as one of twelve assistants to the Lord
Advocate; he must be a member of the Bar and proven as a
capable, experienced and articulate advocate. On his appointment he must, for the term of his appointment, forfeit all right
to defend in a criminal court. He does, however, retain his
civil practice but he is liable, at any time, to be called to
prosecute at High Court circuits throughout Scotland.

Scotland has a prosecution system which has long been the
envy of the Western world. Visitors to the United Kingdom
are surprised to learn that Scotland and England have two
separate and disparate systems of law, and two very different
methods of prosecution. It is one of the finest and most jealously guarded traditions of the Scottish legal system that the
prosecution system is totally independent, power and freedom
stemming from the unique and important post of the Lord
Advocate who is responsible to no one save the Queen and
Parliament. This position of highest privilege was created
some 400 years ago by a statute of 1587.

In earlier law books the Lord Advocate is described as 'Counsel for the Crown'. The first instance of the title, Lord
Advocate, being marked on case records was during the trial
of Arnot of Woodmilne, held in 1598. Even in those days the
Lord Advocate could pursue all crimes and, for those of a
public nature, he was the only prosecutor.

He was given the right to complain in His Majesty's name,
as guardian of his laws and morals, and to insist on the proper
'chastisement of the offender'. The Scottish legal tradition
grew so that the King's Advocate could not be deprived of his
right to prosecute by 'any collusion between the panel [the
accused] and the family of the deceased'.

It was from these early days that the independence of the
Lord Advocate's office took strength; a series of cases in the
seventeenth and eighteenth centuries firmly established that

the victim of assault could not absolve an accused person or reach a financial arrangement with him not to prosecute. The independence of the Lord Advocate was maintained and he was entitled to prosecute whatever the position between the parties.

At the same time as he was given an absolute right with regard to his decision to prosecute he was also given an absolute right on his decision not to prosecute. No individual, not even the Supreme Court, could exercise control over him. To have allowed that, it was suggested, would have allowed the judges to become prosecutors.

In England the situation is different. First of all there is a well-established system of private prosecution whereby an individual may prosecute another citizen for what he alleges is a crime. One motorist may prosecute another for careless driving or one individual may raise a prosecution for a crime which he or she holds to be offensive; for example, an allegation of a mercy killing. Such procedures are unknown in Scotland.

The second main difference between Scottish and English procedure lies in the method of public prosecution. In England a large majority of criminal prosecutions are conducted by the police. They either conduct the prosecution personally or instruct local solicitors or, at times, an official prosecuting solicitor. Particularly grave and important cases are conducted by the Director of Public Prosecutions who can also take over the prosecution on behalf of a private individual. In Scotland all prosecutions are handled not by the police but by the independent Lord Advocate. His appointment is a political one as is that of the number two law officer in Scotland, the Solicitor General. Both have to resign when the Government changes but the rest of their staff can stay on.

To prosecute all the crime in Scotland the Lord Advocate's department is necessarily large. The civil servant in charge, quaintly called the Crown Agent, reaches the top job after entering the system as a solicitor in the Procurator Fiscal's service. He is responsible to the Lord Advocate not only for the allocation of work between the Advocates Depute but also for the system of prosecution in respect of lesser cases in the Sheriff Courts. Scotland is divided into six Sheriffdoms, each

of which has its own Procurator Fiscal's department and each
of which represents an arm of the independent prosecution
system. The Procurators Fiscal running these departments are
all qualified lawyers and may appear in court. The police
report cases to the Fiscal's department which, in turn, studies
them and, in serious or tricky cases, reports to the Crown
Office for advice and a decision.

It was the work carried out in the Procurator Fiscal's office
in Glasgow – in Carol's case – which resulted in the brief being
studied by the Advocate Depute. All the statements taken by
the police were examined by an assistant given the task of
calling the witnesses into the office for further and fuller statements – called precognitions in Scotland – to be taken and
typed out. It was some months before all the appropriate work
was carried out: all the productions sent to Crown Office; all
the labels checked against the productions; and all the experts'
reports relating to blood and blood grouping collated with
those productions so that the case could be assembled in logical
and manageable form.

The assistant Procurator Fiscal in charge of the case, or
Depute as he is known, prepared a case summary with his
recommendations and sent it off to Edinburgh to be left in the
wooden box for the scrutiny of the Advocate Depute.

As the Advocate Depute ran his experienced eye over Carol's
case he realized that there was a shortage of evidence to prove
either the attempted murder or rape. He looked at the voluntary statements given by the accused; he looked at Carol's
statement; he looked at the forensic evidence. He concluded
that it would be difficult to get a conviction against Stephen
Cameron and decided to use him as a Crown witness, guar-
anteeing him immunity from prosecution in return for his
evidence. With Stephen Cameron's evidence there would be a
much stronger case against the other three.

Accordingly, he marked these instructions on the papers and
returned them to Glasgow. He did not sign his name on the
instructions, a tradition of Crown Office. Decisions do not come
from an individual but from the Office.

Work on Carol's case began again in Glasgow and, as a
result, Stephen Cameron agreed to give evidence and a full

statement was taken from him. The papers were then sent back to Crown Office to be studied once more by the Advocate Depute. He decided it would be difficult to prove attempted murder and, after due consideration, marked his new instructions on the brief: 'Proceed with rape and assault to severe injury and danger of life. High Court.' The crime of rape is such a serious one that it must be taken in the High Court. The penalty is unlimited, the court having the power to order a life sentence.

In May 1981 an indictment was served on the three boys ordering them to present themselves at Glasgow Sheriff Court so that a plea of guilty or not guilty could be recorded. If they denied the charges the trial would start in May before a judge and jury in the Glasgow High Court in the old Saltmarket. Again, Scots law demonstrates its independence and difference from English law in such a simple matter as the number of jurors who form a criminal jury. For the last 350 years the number of jurors has been fifteen and yet the reasons for choosing that number are both unclear and vague. Legal historians conclude that the need for standardization of the system of justice required a fixed number of jury men. The actual number was relatively unimportant but a rule had to be laid down for the sake of uniformity.

From the thirteenth century onwards the number varied considerably from town to town, court to court and, indeed, from case to case. In Stirling numbers ranged from fifteen to twenty-one, in Selkirk from seven to twenty-six and in Inverness from nine to twenty-one. From 1512 onwards, Wigton, a small town on the southern tip of Scotland, led the way towards modernity, having fifteen. In early days there was a definite preference for odd numbers which would permit a majority verdict in every case. By 1530 the common practice was to have juries of fifteen. There was never any legislation on the matter, no enactment in Parliament. It was practice that made the law. It is fair to say that perhaps the only conscious attitude taken in the history of Scots law was to avoid English influence because of the deep enmity between the two countries since their conflict in the War of Independence. Perhaps, therefore, chauvinistic considerations weighed heavier than legal ones in avoiding the English number of twelve. The majority system in Scotland means that a person can be found guilty if eight out of the fifteen so determine. In England, until a few years ago, juries had to be unanimous although, nowadays, ten out of twelve is a sufficient number to convict. Even so it would appear that a criminal in Scotland has less chance of acquittal than his counterpart in England.

There is, however, a counter-balancing feature in Scots law which is unique – the existence of a third verdict of not proven, again stemming from centuries-old tradition.

In the early seventeenth century juries constructed their verdicts on the basis that they found certain facts proved and certain facts not proved, the actual implication of guilt or lack of guilt being left to the judge. Accordingly, a jury verdict was simply proven or not proven.

By the eighteenth century, however, verdicts of guilty and not guilty began to reassert themselves and the findings of proven and not proven slipped into decline. It was generally accepted that it was much simpler to find guilt or innocence rather than have a separate verdict on a lengthy series of facts to be held proven or not proven.

In the best traditions of the Scottish legal system, however, the verdict of not proven did not entirely disappear. It had made a lasting impression on the minds of laymen and, as a result, is still used but with a different meaning.

As Scotland's foremost legal commentator, Hume said: 'Not uncommonly the phrase "not proven" has been employed to mark a deficiency only of lawful evidence to convict the panel; that of not guilty to convey the jury's opinion of his innocence of the charge.' When, therefore, a jury is in doubt about the guilt of an accused person, but shrink from a finding of not guilty, they can take refuge in the third verdict of not proven.

No doubt these verdicts were being explained to the three accused by their solicitors and counsel. As the preparatory work for the Crown finished with the service of the indictment, the preparatory work for the defence began in earnest. All the witnesses whose names and addresses were attached to the indictment had to be seen by defence solicitors. They would also prepare briefs with full statements from each of the accused boys to be given to their respective counsel.

The case was one of many serious cases taken in Glasgow High Court at that particular sitting. There was no sense of anything extraordinary or unique in the minds of the Advocate Depute or the defence counsel as they approached the old building of the High Court on 12 June.

7 The Breakdown

On the day of the trial Carol arrived with Billy. They were early and the court seemed strangely deserted. As they reported to a police officer they were told, 'This case is not going on today. In fact it won't be on this week. Please come back next week, Monday.' Billy was angry, knowing as he did the effect of another week's waiting. He stole a glance at Carol who was trying to put a brave face on the situation.

Although Carol and Billy did not appreciate the fact at the time, they were victims of industrial action caused by a civil service dispute. The Glasgow Sheriff Court had ground to a halt and, initially, the High Court was also affected. No cases were to be called that day. Accused persons, witnesses, solicitors and defence counsel were simply told to come back. Carol and Billy, along with the others, went home confused and sad.

Seven days later Carol stepped out of the taxi to see crowds of people massing outside the three entrances of Glasgow High Court. She thought that they were spectators queuing for a place in court to listen to her evidence. In a panic she broke free from Billy's arm and ran across the Saltmarket into Glasgow Green. Billy chased after her, caught up with her and tried to reason with her. But Carol would not listen. 'I am not going,' she sobbed. 'I don't want all those people watching me.'

Billy had to drag Carol back across the road and up the steps into the court. He explained to the police sergeant how she had tried to commit suicide a few days before and that she was scared about giving evidence. The sergeant took them into an anteroom and arranged for a cup of tea to be sent in to them, alerting the senior fiscal in charge of the High Court. Ian Carmichael was an experienced fiscal, urbane and gentle. He put trembling Carol at her ease. 'Don't worry,' he said. 'Calm yourself down. The trial may not be going ahead today.'

The fiscal explained that he had to make certain arrangements and asked Carol and Billy if they objected to waiting in the court a little longer. 'Can we get another cup of tea anywhere?' Billy asked. 'Yes, there's a cafeteria upstairs,' he replied. Billy took Carol upstairs where they stood in the queue along with police and civilian witnesses, waiting for the assistant behind the counter to serve them. When Carol was handed her cup of tea, the cup and saucer began to rattle, tea spilling over until her shaking hands couldn't hold the cup any more. Everything crashed to the floor. The buzz of conversation in the cafeteria stopped and those who looked up saw a terrified woman on the verge of a nervous breakdown.

A detective who knew Carol ran down to tell the fiscal what he had witnessed. It was decided, there and then, that, for her own safety, she should be taken to see a psychiatrist. The policeman took Carol and Billy home and arranged to return at 2 p.m. to drive them to Carswell House, the outpatient clinic of Glasgow's Duke Street Psychiatric Hospital. Carol was still shaking when a detective and policewoman arrived to pick them up. She didn't want to go. But again Billy, as he had done so many times in the past, persuaded her.

The psychiatrist, Dr Raymond Antebi, saw before him a pathetic bundle of skin and bone – Carol was only four and a half stone at that time. She poured out her heart-rending story, breaking down in tears frequently. Dr Antebi reassured her that the court would be cleared of the public. He told her that he would make arrangements personally. It went some way to calming her but she was still extremely nervous.

After the interview, Carol asked to go to the toilet before the police took her home. To her horror she discovered that she was bleeding. She was miscarrying the baby she was expecting in six-and-a-half-months' time. She was driven immediately to the Royal Infirmary where she was detained. Doctors discovered that her baby was growing in a Fallopian

tube. The foetus would have to be removed by surgery and
Carol was admitted for the operation.

Despite her ordeal Carol had made up her mind that she
was going to give evidence, that she would go through with it.

The Advocate Depute received a verbal report confirming
Carol's mental state and he decided to desert the case for the
time being. This is a course which is open to all prosecutors
when an important witness is absent, or for some other com-
pelling reason. He particularly states that the case is being
deserted *pro loco et tempore* (for the time being) so that he has
the right to raise it again when circumstances so allow.

The Advocate Depute knew that an up-to-date report on
Carol's condition would be sent to Crown Office so that a
decision could be made about the future of the case, away from
the heat of the court and in the cool atmosphere of the
Advocate Depute's room. Accordingly, the case was dropped
and the Procurator Fiscal was asked to submit an up-to-date
report on Carol's condition, along with the original case
papers.

When the psychiatric report arrived it was attached to the
brief and then dispatched from the Procurator Fiscal's office
in Glasgow to Crown Office. The papers were then placed in
the Advocate Depute's large wooden box, waiting for the
Advocate Depute – again anonymous.

During the months that followed Carol and Billy heard
nothing about the case. Nearly every fortnight, during the last
months of 1981, Billy visited the lawyer Adrian Tonner who
was handling Carol's application for criminal injuries compensation. Billy would ask, 'How's Carol's case? When is it coming
up?' The answer was always the same. 'I don't know . . . I have
had no word.'

A different Advocate Depute plucked out Carol's case from the
box in Crown Office and, as he read the papers, he considered
the interests of justice, the interests of the victim and the
interests of the accused. The interests of justice demanded a
prosecution. A woman had been attacked, probably raped and
certainly scarred. Three boys had admitted that they were
present during all, or part of, the attack. One, if not all, was

at least partly responsible. Yet the interests of the victim required to be taken into account. A psychiatrist, Dr Raymond Antebi, well-known and trusted by the Crown, had stated it would be dangerous for the woman's health if she gave evidence. Would it therefore be unconscionable for the Crown to prosecute and thus perhaps drive Carol to suicide? This was the Advocate Depute's major consideration and, consequently, in reviewing the case he asked himself whether it could proceed without Carol's evidence.

In a rape case the evidence of the victim is essential to prove that sex took place and without consent. The court is always cleared for the victim's evidence and the press are always instructed not to identify her. The Advocate Depute considered that such safeguards would not be sufficient to counteract the very real dangers expressed in the psychiatric report.

Could the case proceed on the basis of serious assault alone? As he scanned the papers and considered the matter the Advocate Depute formed the view, later supported by his chief in another court, that the rape and the assault were so intermingled and intertwined that justice could not be served by prosecuting for assault alone.

Should the Crown request the opinion of another psychiatrist? The Advocate Depute considered that a further psychiatric examination would require Carol to relive the memories of the past. There was no indication that any other psychiatric opinion would be different from Dr Antebi's; there was, therefore, no justification for submitting Carol to a further ordeal.

The Advocate Depute asked himself the final question. Should the papers be put in cold storage for two or three months in the hope that, as was hinted by Dr Antebi, Carol would recover sufficiently to give evidence? The Advocate Depute, rightly or wrongly, exercising the discretion available to him, decided that, in this particular case, the interests of justice would not be served by keeping the matter hanging over three youths; there was only a faint hope that Carol would be able safely to give evidence. As he considered all the aspects of the case he found the courage of his convictions and marked the papers with two vital words: 'No Proceedings.'

As soon as these instructions were recorded, the set of papers were dispatched to Glasgow. The Assistant Procurator Fiscal in charge of Glasgow High Court indictments was Mr Nicky O'Brien – experienced, able and administratively thorough. When he received the instructions from Crown counsel he knew what to do. On 15 September he sent a letter to each of the three accused saying that, on the instructions of Crown counsel, there were to be 'no further proceedings'. In Scots law such an intimation from the Crown is final. After that letter has been sent there can be no further proceedings. The Crown cannot change its mind even if fresh evidence comes to light. The matter is concluded. With the authority of the Lord Advocate proceedings have been terminated although, in Carol's case, the Lord Advocate was not told about the decision taken in his name and neither was the Solicitor General.

The accused boys read their letters with a disbelief that turned to delight after a quick visit to their solicitors' offices confirmed their understanding of the letter – they were free for all time from this charge. The case of Carol X would merely become another statistic in Crown Office records.

But no one had told Carol. No one had told the press who had widely publicized the assault and the arrests. As a result of an explosive culmination of events Carol's case was not designed to become another bald statistic.

The letters were sent out in September 1981. The New Year arrived and Carol went to stay with her parents for a few days. She was beginning to forget about the trial and was putting on weight. On Monday, 11 January 1982 a controversial television programme showing how the police interrogate a rape victim was to be screened. Even the idea of the programme brought back memories to Carol, although she never criticized the police because she felt they had treated her fairly. Nevertheless, Carol refused to watch it and switched to another channel.

She was still waiting for the new date for her case.

8 Power of the Press

It was 11 January, four days before the opening of the salmon-fishing season on the River Tay in Perthshire. Some newspaper reporters escape the pressures of their demanding existence by attacking an innocent white ball with a variety of clubs. Others indulge in the profession's other national sport and, every night after the end of the working day, chat together in the pubs under the shadow of the nine-storey *Daily Record* building: the Off the Record, the Copy Cat and the Montrose. These are waterfront pubs bordering Glasgow's famous Broomielaw which runs along the River Clyde. Inside the talk is of office politics, the news stories of the day and current gossip. Whatever journalists do in their spare time is designed to anaesthetize the mind from telephones ringing relentlessly, the constant pressure to research news and the need to clatter it out on the typewriter before going on to the next story.

Arnot McWhinnie, fifteen years chief crime reporter of the *Record*, and weighing a stone for every year, loved the vigorous, colourful tabloid bought by almost threequarters of a million Scots every day. He had his own form of escapism. When he was wading out into the middle of the fast-flowing River Tay, standing up to his waist in water, casting a home-made salmon fly with barbed hook over a hopefully productive lie, the pressures seemed to evaporate. But on this day McWhinnie was fishing for something else. He had detected the strangest scent of a story which, if true and if he could break it, would make major news for his newspaper.

A simple note in his desk diary was to point McWhinnie in the right direction: 'Check the Glasgow razor rape case.' For more than eighteen years the thirty-nine-year-old journalist had reported most of the major crimes in Scotland. Years of experience had blurred his memory of the crimes he had investigated, but he remembered this one well. The Glasgow razor rape case had been a particularly sadistic crime.

McWhinnie walked through the busy open-plan newsroom on the third floor and hurried down a flight of stairs to the library on the floor below where the *Record* kept its vast archives of newspaper cuttings. Four large, electronically operated banks – leviathans of machines, each of which contains tons of newsprint – housed the all-important cuttings. The crime section is vast, its thousands of cross-references spanning the whole gamut of crime from murder to rape, incest, treason, theft. Every lawbreaker, whose case had been reported in the *Record*, had his name entered in this vast storehouse of information.

The trays moved up and down, occasionally creaking, sometimes groaning, until they stopped at the section: 'Crime: attempted murder'. The library girl thumbed through a batch of salmon-pink folders and plucked one out headed 'Crime: attempted murder – Stephen Cameron'. The file contained only five clippings. Two of them referred to the police investigation of the incident. A detective had described it as one of the worst he had ever seen. The investigation was centred in Glasgow's tough East End. If a detective from there says a crime is bad, it must be. Another clipping referred to the arrest of the boys and the remaining two to their first court appearance and full committal a week later. There the file ended but the *Daily Record*'s investigation had continued.

Over the months McWhinnie and his colleague, Charlie Beaton, had made sporadic checks on the Glasgow razor rape case. For years both journalists had learned to rely not only on their memories but on a carefully developed system which combined the desk diary and a special background book in which details of every major incident were lodged. Both reporters had spent years researching the background to crimes, tracing and visiting relatives and friends of those accused, in a bid to obtain not only information but what is known in newspaper slang as a 'collect' – a snapshot of the accused. Background investigations also included colourful details of the crime, the accused and the victim.

None of this material could, of course, be used until a plea of guilty had been entered, or a trial concluded with a guilty verdict. But, nevertheless, it had to be prepared in advance. Journalists remembered the days of old when the High Court, Scotland's premier court, was ruled by Lord Clyde, the Lord Justice General. He was a stern, crusty man who frowned on press activities to the extent that any reporter risked proceedings for contempt of court by even speaking to a witness before a trial. Nevertheless, research had had to be done – but very carefully and very quietly. Sometimes, when police had found out that a witness had been approached before a court case, the luckless journalist would be summoned to appear before the head of Glasgow's CID, on the instruction of the Procurator Fiscal, to be given a strict warning of the dangers of breaking Lord Clyde's rules. With the passage of time, however, and the appointment of a new Lord Justice General, Lord Emslie, things began to change. Lord Emslie was a much more liberal man, more understanding of the needs of modern society. He redefined the often grey areas between contempt and genuine newspaper activity, to build an important bridgehead between the law and the press, so vital in a changing era.

McWhinnie turned to the background book. A page in a small, black, loose-leafed volume would reveal details of the offence, the name and addresses of the victim and the accused, the instructing lawyer, dates of court appearances and what research had been carried out.

The Glasgow razor rape case had been entered into the book, revealing that Carol's boyfriend had been contacted by Charlie Beaton early in 1981 and had refused to give an interview. It also disclosed that the trial had not taken place.

Glasgow Sheriff Court, reputed to be the busiest in Europe outside Hamburg, had been in chaos for months because of the civil servants' strike. There was a tremendous backlog of cases and both journalists were aware that, with the routine disturbed, a case could be slipped through at any time.

On that cold, bleak morning of 11 January McWhinnie decided to visit his contacts in an effort to find out the current state of the razor rape case in its passage through the courts. Over the years he had developed a wide range of informants, although he did not like the use of that particular word. It implied something underhand. McWhinnie's contacts were men who gave him information, not for reward but because they felt they could trust him with a confidence. They were from the police and legal professions, lawyers, fiscals, advocates and even sheriffs. Often information would be given to him on the strict understanding that it was non-attributable. In other words, you could use it but not quote the source.

McWhinnie left his office overlooking the frozen River Clyde. It had been the worst winter since 1947 and most people had never seen the river so iced up. The office car, a bright-red Ford Cortina complete with telephone and driver, took him into the city.

An investigation for a newspaper can often be a hard slog. Luckily, within half an hour, McWhinnie's inquiries turned up some of the answers, though not all. What he found out made him realize he was approaching a sensational story.

Over a coffee his first contact told him there would be no Glasgow razor rape trial, because of the victim's state of health. 'On the day of the trial she was taken to see a psychiatrist,' he said, 'and, as a result of that, the Crown Office decided they couldn't risk putting her through the witness box in case she tried to commit suicide again.'

'Had she already attempted it?' asked McWhinnie. 'Yes, she cut her wrists and took an overdose.'

Later that morning a second contact who knew more about the case bluntly described it as a 'bloody scandal'. He declared, 'The Crown Office was given a cast-iron case. There was enough evidence, at least against one of the boys, to convict of assault a hundred times over.' The contact revealed that there was also a 'voluntary' confession and that one of the boys originally charged had signed a statement describing what he had witnessed that night – although he denied taking part in it. The charges against him had been dropped and he had turned Queen's evidence. The contact talked at length about the victim having 'noughts and crosses' style wounds, her medical treatment and other details of the crime. It was all on the record though not for quoting, the stipulation being that the source be not revealed.

There were, however, other provisions. 'For God's sake,' he pleaded, 'don't name me and under no circumstances mention the voluntary statements. Knowledge of these is limited to only a few sources and I don't want any comeback.' Without hesitation McWhinnie agreed to the contact's request, adding his own proviso: should someone else from another source volunteer the same information without binding him to confidentiality, he would be free to use it.

The journalist headed back to the office excited by the information. He had a gut feeling that it was a story of incalculable proportions – rape and horrible assault – which the authorities had successfully investigated to the stage that four youths had been charged and brought before the court. Yet there was a suggestion that there would be no trial. Before the investigation could go any further it was vital to find out if the case had been abandoned for all time or only temporarily.

McWhinnie took the news editor aside. Fergie Millar, a mercurial character, had been a news editor for longer than anyone else in the country, including Fleet Street. It was a tribute to him that he had managed to last the pace for so long. Even after decades of seeing the same type of story every other week he refused to allow his enthusiasm to be dampened by the 'we've seen it all before' attitude.

Millar firmly believed his paper had the right to 'stick its neb' into everything, even if it sometimes meant living dangerously. 'Newspapers are the guardians of free speech and fair play,' he would preach, 'and if injustices are done it's our job to uncover them. Our rights in a free society involve an understanding of our duties towards that society.'

Fergie Millar could hardly believe it when his crime reporter briefed him on the development in the razor rape case. 'What a story!' he said. 'What do you plan on doing next?' They both agreed that the next step would be an official phone call to the Crown Office in Edinburgh's Parliament Square, where all major decisions affecting prosecution under the criminal law of Scotland are made.

Not all that long ago, when a reporter was required to contact Crown Office for an official statement, he did so with a feeling of trepidation. Even QCs and solicitors treated it reverently. In the fifties and sixties the Crown Office rarely deigned to give the press comments about anything, save to say 'No comment.' Those who worked behind the brass plaque on the oak door of the Crown Office were now freer to talk to the press. They had learned not only the wisdom of commenting to newspapers, but also giving off-the-record, non-attributable background information, which often helps a journalist to obtain a more balanced and responsible approach to his story.

As the heads of all editorial departments went into the morning conference that day McWhinnie was phoning Crown Office. He got through to Mr Ian Dean, the Deputy Crown Agent, a former Procurator Fiscal of Dumbarton, a man known for his caution but also for his courtesy and his guidance. Mr Dean could only vaguely recollect the Glasgow razor rape case. Was the charge deserted temporarily? Or had the trial been abandoned for all time? Mr Dean replied, 'I cannot say at the moment because I honestly don't know but I will look out the papers and come back to you tomorrow.'

As 11 January drew to a close McWhinnie and his editor, Bernard Vickers, agreed that, while the Glasgow razor rape case was a major story in its own right, it would assume even greater proportions because of a controversial rape case in Ipswich the previous week, during which Judge Bertrand Richards had fined a rapist £2000 rather than send him to prison. He had told the court he was doing so because the seventeen-year-old victim had contributed to her ordeal by thumbing a lift from passing strangers late at night.

The 12 January was cold and bleak as ever. McWhinnie contacted Ian Dean. The Deputy Crown Agent still had no information but promised to ring back. Five hours later he did. 'I have to tell you,' said Mr Dean, 'that this case will not be proceeded with.' The obvious question was 'Why? Is it because of the woman's mental health?'

Mr Dean replied, 'You should know the position by now. I cannot discuss reasons behind any decision in an individual case. I can reveal, however, that the woman's health was taken into consideration. We can also confirm that the case was eventually marked "No Proceedings" after a great deal of consideration and a lot of investigation by Crown counsel.'

Mr Dean also explained in layman's terms the law in relation to rape. In the majority of cases it was necessary for the victim to give evidence to show that penetration had taken place and had occurred without her consent. That statement immediately begged the question: if the Crown could not prove rape without the woman's evidence why had it not proceeded on the razor assault charge? If the woman had died would there not have been ample evidence for a murder trial? This time Mr Dean refused to make any comment whatsoever.

So, there it was at last: official confirmation that the three youths accused of rape and assault had escaped prosecution because their victim was so mentally affected that she had to be spared the ordeal of giving evidence.

Mr Dean's statement, however, as frank as his masters allowed it to be, left a series of questions unanswered: Who made the decision not to proceed? Was it justified? Could the prosecution be reinstated? Could anything be done to ensure that the boys did not escape scot-free? Could this ever happen again? All these questions would have to be answered.

The key to unlock such a controversy has always been to prime an MP to write officially to the appropriate government department, demanding an answer. That afternoon McWhinnie contacted David Marshall, the Labour MP for Shettleston, Glasgow, whose constituency included Barrowfield.

In the evening the *Daily Record* editor, Bernard Vickers, called a meeting with his deputy, Jim Wilson, and with McWhinnie and Fergie Millar. As editor he had an immediate problem: what stance should the paper adopt in the Glasgow razor rape case? Should the *Record* print a leader criticizing the Crown Office? In the absence of any answers at that early stage of the investigation it was decided not to print any comment. The story stood on its own merits. Perhaps the paper and the public would obtain the answers they sought from angry MPs. The next day, 13 January, the *Record*'s exclusive was carried on page 5. The disappearance of the Prime Minister's son, Mark Thatcher, in the Sahara during a car rally, had knocked the Glasgow razor rape case off the front page. Nevertheless, the story made an impact.

Wednesday, 13 January 1982: *Daily Record*

Rape Case Boys Go Free – Ordeal of Woman Victim: Exclusive by Arnot McWhinnie, Record Crime Reporter

Three teenagers, alleged to have committed one of Scotland's most violent rapes, will not be prosecuted. . . . Today I can reveal that the Crown has dropped the charges. . . . The move followed reports from a psychiatrist called in by the Crown. . . . Mr David Marshall, the Labour MP whose Shettleston constituency takes in the area where the victim lived, said, 'It's the most horrific story I have ever heard – I cannot understand why the Crown did not go ahead with a trial without the woman's evidence. . . . Would the charges have been dropped if she had been murdered or driven into such a state of insanity that she would have been incapable of giving evidence anyway? . . . It worries me that the others might realize that the way to escape scot-free is to put their victim into such a state that she cannot give evidence.'

Mr Marshall continued, 'I will be writing to the Lord Advocate or the Solicitor General asking for an explanation.'

The day before, Scotland's controversial and colourful Solicitor General, Nicholas Fairbairn QC, MP, had prosecuted another rape case at the High Court in Glasgow. It was then that he heard about the Glasgow rape case for the first time. Fairbairn was tipped off about the *Daily Record*'s interest by the fiscal at the High Court, Nicky O'Brien, who was aware that the Crown Office had been in touch with his own department.

'What's it all about?' asked the nonplussed Solicitor General. 'It's about another rape case,' O'Brien told him. Fairbairn received only sketchy and second-hand information that day.

When the story appeared in the *Record*, Fairbairn was later to claim that he contacted the Crown Office asking for the papers on the case to be made available to him the following day.

Part Two

9 The Mole

The sleeping giant of Fleet Street was beginning to awaken. That morning, 13 January, the *Daily Record*'s sister paper, the *Mirror*, used the rape story in its London and Manchester editions; other newspapers, sensing the drama, followed it up.

Every journalist in Britain wanted to interview Carol but she had gone to ground. During his initial inquiries two days earlier, McWhinnie had failed to trace her. She had vanished. Her neighbours were either protecting her or had no idea where she was. Police contacts could not come up with an answer. She had not been seen for months and the word was that she had gone to take up her life again in Newcastle with her ex-husband.

Thursday, 14 January: BBC Radio Scotland

Rape Charges Storm
There has been considerable disquiet over the Lord Advocate's decision not to proceed with charges of attempted murder and rape. ... Tonight two women's groups and a Labour MP said they would be investigating the matter. ...

On 14 January Fairbairn's rape trial at the High Court in Glasgow finished. He succeeded in obtaining a verdict of guilty against the accused. Feeling pleased with himself – it had been a very difficult prosecution – Fairbairn travelled back to Edinburgh. He expected the papers on the Glasgow rape case to be lying on his desk in the Crown Office. Fairbairn was

furious when he discovered they were not there and even more
angry when he found out that the Crown Agent was away on
business and there was no one else available to discuss the
matter with him. The Crown Office would be closed the next
day, Friday, so he demanded that the papers be sent down to
him on Monday in the official sealed bag which carries mes-
sages from Edinburgh to all Scottish government ministers in
London.

That day, the 14th, McWhinnie received a telephone call
from Ron Bailey, the legal officer of an organization called
Safe Women's Transport. 'We want to raise a private prosecution against these three teenagers ourselves,' said Mr Bailey.
'We will do it for the woman and, if necessary, pay all the
legal expenses.' Mr Bailey disclosed that the Labour MP for
Bootle, Mr Allan Roberts, who was closely associated with the
organization, had instructed him to examine the possibilities.
'Women in London', explained Mr Bailey, 'have been appalled
by the Glasgow rape case and are demanding some action so
that the three teenagers will not escape punishment.'

Minutes before catching a plane for Europe that morning,
Mr Roberts wrote to the Lord Advocate and the Solicitor General, demanding that the Glasgow prosecution be reinstated
– or the youths privately prosecuted.

Safe Women's Transport, an organization which had applied
for charity status, was seeking to persuade local authorities
and central government to finance mini-buses to taxi women
about after dark in London and Liverpool. McWhinnie promised to contact a leading Scots criminal lawyer for the best
advice he could get. Private prosecution was virtually unheard
of in Scotland and the legal machinery required to raise one,
a Bill for Criminal Letters, was archaic.

McWhinnie phoned Ross Harper, a Glasgow solicitor. 'It is
an incredible situation,' said Harper. 'I have never heard of
anything like it before. There is obviously a strong and un-
derstar.dable public feeling that the Crown made a major
error.'

'Could an MP raise a private prosecution?' asked McWhinnie. Harper's answer was curt, definite and decisive. 'No – not
a hope, not a prayer.'

The lawyer's advice was not based on a nationalistic reaction to an English MP's desire to enter the lists of the Scottish law courts, but founded on settled law. 'Before a person can raise a private prosecution he must obtain the permission of the court,' explained Harper. 'A court will not grant permission unless he can show a special interest.'

'When did that last happen?' Harper was stumped. He said, 'I cannot recall with certainty. It was about the turn of the century. But I do remember there was a case a few years ago when somebody tried to bring a private prosecution against the publishers of a book he claimed was obscene. That was unsuccessful because he failed to show any interest. There have been several other attempts, some involving allegations of perjury.' 'When was the last successful application?' 'Certainly well before my time,' said Harper.

For the next ten minutes the lawyer and the journalist chatted about the case. The women's organization Rape Crisis had been pressing for changes in the law to allow rape victims who could not face the ordeal of entering the witness box the facility of giving written evidence. 'Would this be possible for exceptional cases under the existing law?' asked McWhinnie. Harper referred to Section 32 of the new Criminal Justice (Scotland) Act which gives the power to the prosecution in a criminal trial to apply to the court to take evidence in 'commission' from witnesses who were either too infirm to attend or were abroad. 'To be fair,' he said, 'when the Act was going through Parliament during its various stages, the Solicitor General explained that he did not envisage that Section 32 would apply to the victims of crime.' But Harper said, 'This was comment, and comment does not make our law. The people who determine our law are the judges in the courts. It is possible that the Crown could have at least attempted this manoeuvre, but their chances of success would not be too high. It would have had the effect of showing the public that they had tried. Do you want to know what I would have done if I was a Crown Office official? I would have halted the case temporarily, pending further psychiatric examination of the woman to determine when she would be fit to give evidence. If she had recovered, there would have been no impediment on the part of the Crown to prevent it raising the prosecution again and going on with a trial. There was no way the case could have been time-barred.'

Harper also answered one of the most important questions in the whole controversy: having sent the three accused letters saying the prosecution had been dropped, could the authorities charge them again with the same offences? The short answer was no.

The deciding case involved a High Court of Criminal Appeal in Scotland in 1975. A man called Thom, the former Town Clerk of Brechin, had been accused of embezzlement, only to receive a letter two months later from the Procurator Fiscal stating that 'having made further inquiries' he was not going to proceed any more on the charge.

Consequently, Thom was told he could uplift his bail. The move was announced through local newspapers. But four months later the luckless individual found the police knocking on his door once more. They charged him with exactly the same offence. He went to trial, was found guilty and received a two-year prison sentence. The lawyers acting for Thom decided to appeal on the grounds that he had already received a letter from the authorities saying the charges had been dropped. During the appeal, the three judges agreed that he should never have been charged again – and immediately set him free.

'As a result of this case,' said Harper, 'it is certain that the three teenagers in the Glasgow razor rape case can never be brought to trial by the Crown.'

McWhinnie asked Harper if he could put his thoughts down on paper over the weekend for a feature in the *Record* on Monday morning.

As McWhinnie put down the phone the TUC's General Secretary, Mr Len Murray, was writing to Lord Hailsham, the Lord Chancellor, calling for an urgent review of the law on rape, sparked off by the Ipswich case and now by the Glasgow Rape case.

'It is extremely alarming that a case of such importance should be dropped because the victim cannot give evidence,' wrote Mr Murray. 'I know that you will agree that the increased incidence of rape is very worrying and women must be able to rely upon the prosecution of the law against such physical assault.' He told Lord Hailsham that the TUC would be urging unions to raise the matter with its sponsored MPs.

Friday, 15 January: London *Times* editorial

The Double Ordeal of Rape
   When a victim of a particularly brutal rape is so badly affected by her ordeal that she is unable to give evidence at the trial of her alleged attackers and the case against them is therefore dropped, there is a conspicuous failure of justice. The decision of the Scottish prosecution authorities to discontinue proceedings against the three youths accused of rape and attempted murder appears to suggest that the more horrible the experience of a rape victim, the greater the rapist's chance of getting off. The charges ought to have been allowed to lie in the file with the possibility of them being revived at a later date.

   The Lord Chief Justice, Lord Lane, travelled into London on the morning of the 15th to listen to four appeals by convicted rapists in the London Appeal Court. He dismissed the four appeals and, referring to the controversy which had landed on his own doorstep – the furore over Judge Richards and the rapist who got off with a fine – Lord Lane laid down firm guidelines for all judges in England when dealing with rape cases. He said, 'Rape is always a serious crime and other than in wholly exceptional circumstances it calls for immediate custodial sentences.'

Sunday, 17 January: 'Agenda' – a BBC Scotland Television Political Affairs Programme

Rape Controversy Grows
   Mr Donald Dewar, Labour MP for Glasgow, Garscadden and Labour spokesman on Scottish Legal Affairs said,
The public has a right to be satisfied that everything possible was done to bring to trial anyone who may have been responsible. I don't have all the facts in my possession and I find it difficult to make any comment apart from general statements of the law. . . .

As Mr Dewar spoke on television that Sunday, a man who did know all the facts listened – and was frustrated. He knew that one of the youths had confessed to the police to ripping the woman with the razor; he knew there was an important Crown witness who had seen the boy running away from the hut with a razor in his hand, shouting, 'I ripped her, I ripped her'; he knew that police officers had seen the boy run away from the vicinity and had chased him; he knew that one of the boy's fingerprints had been found outside the hut; and he knew that people were saying that the Crown must have been correct all along.

As he watched television that afternoon, the man struggled with his conscience. 'Does the public have the right to know?' he asked himself. 'Do I have a duty to tell them?'

Monday, 18 January: the *Daily Telegraph*

MP Queries Rape Case Decision

A Glasgow MP is to ask the Lord Advocate about the case in which charges against three teenagers accused of rape and attempted murder have been dropped. . . . After a visit at the weekend to talk with officials of the Glasgow Rape Crisis Centre, Mr David Marshall said that he would be having discussions with his colleagues in Parliament to see what changes or new measures in law would give assistance in the preparation of cases involving rape.

The Crown papers did not arrive on Fairbairn's desk in London on 18 January as promised and he phoned Edinburgh to find out why not. He was told the Crown Agent would personally bring them down later in the week.

At lunchtime on Monday the phone rang on Arnot McWhinnie's desk in the *Daily Record* office. He mildly cursed as he picked up the receiver. The phone had been going for most of the morning and he was just about to go to the office canteen for lunch with some colleagues. 'Is that Arnot McWhinnie?' asked the unfamiliar voice on the other end of the line. 'Yes, what can I do for you?' 'We don't know each other, but I think I can help you on the background of the Glasgow rape case. Would you be interested in meeting me?'

McWhinnie asked who was speaking. The man identified

himself. 'If you mention my name I'll tell you nothing,' he said. The journalist agreed to preserve the man's anonymity. 'Did you know there was a confession in the case by the youth who used the razor?' asked the man. 'Do you also know that one of the youths turned Queen's evidence and gave the police an eyewitness account of what happened in the later stages of the incident?'

McWhinnie explained that he did, but not in any detail, and disclosed that he had promised a contact not to use this information. 'You can keep your promise to him,' said the man, 'but you need not give me any undertaking except of anonymity. I will let you see the lot.'

McWhinnie was speechless. It is once in a lifetime that such an opportunity is afforded to a journalist. When he recovered he asked to meet his informant immediately. 'I can't just now,' said the man, 'but meet me later in the afternoon, say about 4.30 p.m.' They arranged to meet in a coffee lounge in the centre of Glasgow.

The next three hours were amongst the longest McWhinnie had ever faced, apart from three dreadful occasions when he had to wait in the High Court before giving evidence. He thanked his good fortune that he had not gone for lunch at his usual time that day. The man might have taken cold feet and never phoned back. All these things were running through his mind that afternoon. He mentioned nothing to anyone except the editor, Bernard Vickers, who tried not to display his excitement. His immediate reaction was, 'What could happen to us if we publish such details?'

McWhinnie had already considered the position carefully. 'If we name the youths and publish details of confessions then we could face an action for defamation,' he was forced to admit. 'But would any lawyer recommend such a move to a client, knowing that there would have to be a proof in a civil action and incriminating evidence would be revealed? No lawyer would take such a risk. If these boys have escaped a criminal trial, they are not going to risk a civil one.'

McWhinnie suggested to his editor that, in any event, the paper might not wish to name the accused boys. By holding back, the *Daily Record* could not be accused of staging a trial

by newspaper. The *Record* could not be held in contempt of
court because the prosecuting authorities had sent letters to
the accused boys stating that the charges had been dropped.
There was no court of which to be held in contempt.

By having access to documents which had been part of the
prosecution evidence in a trial, the mystery man might be
breaching the Official Secrets Act. He had every right to pos-
sess the documents, however, and the crime of theft did not
enter into McWhinnie's worries. Nevertheless, he took an
opinion from a legal source. The verdict was that he was in
the clear. The Official Secrets Act had nothing to do with it.

It was exactly 4.30 p.m. in a city-centre coffee bar when the
'mole' met McWhinnie. He had a bulky file in a large manilla
folder. He opened it and took out a three-page handwritten
document which McWhinnie immediately recognized as a
photostat copy of a court production. It was the official police
statement of a seventeen-year-old, Joseph Sweeney, the youth
who, it was alleged, had committed the slashing.

The mole then brought out another sheaf of papers. He
looked round to make sure that no one was watching before
slipping them over the coffee table. McWhinnie saw the
voluntary statement of Stephen Cameron, the boy against
whom the charges had been dropped in return for a promise
that he would give evidence on behalf of the prosecution. He
saw statements from the police who cautioned the three boys
in the Eastern Division Police station. Phrases like 'I had a
razor, so I gave it to her and came out,' ... 'My hands were
all blood,' ... 'He had a razor in his hand. He said he had
ripped her,' ... leaped from the page. 'Keep them,' said the
man. 'They are only photocopies.' 'Why are you doing this?'
asked McWhinnie. 'I told you over the phone. I'm doing it
because I think the public has a right to know the full facts
about this case. If there isn't going to be a trial, then perhaps
the *Daily Record* will be this woman's last refuge.'

Before disappearing into the tea-time rush of office workers
heading home, the man made McWhinnie promise again that
he would never reveal his name. McWhinnie went back to the
office, knowing it was a promise he would have to keep, even
if it meant going to jail. It took him a little over ten minutes

to get back to his desk. 'What's the score?' asked the editor. 'I was right after all,' said McWhinnie jubilantly. 'The police had a pretty convincing case at least against one of the boys. I've got the whole story.' He sat down at his desk, nerves jangling, to write it. The 'exclusive' was completed forty-five minutes later.

At the same time the *Daily Record* editor, its chairman, Derek Webster, and the leader writer, huddled together composing a comment piece. The editor also had to consult with the newspaper's legal adviser. The *Mirror* was also planning to publish details of the confession. McWhinnie's copy had already been wired down south and lawyers from both papers wanted to know whether the Crown had written official letters to the accused boys, advising them that the charges would be dropped. The Crown had done this and so there was no legal impediment in the way of the story. A buzz went round the office that night. There was talk of the biggest *Daily Record* exclusive for a decade.

Tuesday, 19 January: *Daily Record*

Rape Teenagers Alleged Confession – the Case the Crown Decided to Drop
   Today the *Daily Record* can reveal that the Crown Office had a full and dramatic alleged confession to one of Scotland's most violent rapes . . . and that they had a full voluntary alleged statement from another teenager claiming he had witnessed the rape . . . he also claimed that a third teenager had boasted of slashing the victim with a razor . . . yet, in spite of these alleged confessions, the Crown Office decided to drop the case. . . . Mr David Marshall, the Labour MP for Shettleston, Glasgow, said, 'If the Crown Office had possession of this evidence why didn't they prosecute the youths?'

The front-page story in the *Record* in Scotland and in the *Daily Mirror* in England had consequences throughout the country. Radio and television broadcasts on Wednesday morning and afternoon, unable to get any other sources to confirm the story, quoted the *Daily Record*. Reporters from almost every national newspaper in Britain converged on the East End of Glasgow, hunting for Carol. Her story, if they could get it, would be the big follow-up for the next day. As they scoured the dingy streets of Parkhead and Barrowfield the Crown Office in Edinburgh refused to comment on the confession story. All a spokesman would say was, 'The Lord Advocate is in Luxembourg and we cannot make any comment until he returns.'

The Crown Agent ordered an inquiry to find out if any of his staff had fed information to the *Daily Record*. In Glasgow, Detective Chief Superintendent William Morrison, a Strathclyde CID officer, ordered a similar inquiry in a bid to determine whether the leak had come from any of his men.

In London, Fairbairn once again phoned asking for Crown Office and demanded the papers. There was still no sign of them. In the meantime the Deputy Crown Agent, Ian Dean, read the contents of the papers over the phone.

In 10 Downing Street the Prime Minister, Margaret Thatcher, ordered a report into the background of the controversy.

Later on that afternoon in the Commons, Mr Alan Beith, the Liberal MP for Berwick, asked Mrs Thatcher if she was aware of the enormous public concern that had arisen over sentencing in rape cases, following the failure of the Crown to proceed in the Glasgow case. 'Will she say whether she is prepared to carry out a review of the application of the law in rape cases?'

The Prime Minister replied, 'It is vital that women should have confidence in the ability of the law to protect them against this violent, detestable – and I use the Honourable Gentleman's word, odious – crime, and to ensure that persons are found guilty should they commit it.'

Fairbairn had been left to face the flak alone because his chief, the Lord Advocate, Lord Mackay, was at the European Court in Luxembourg on Tuesday and Wednesday, having been asked personally by the Attorney General to represent Britain during two important cases. Before flying out with his entourage of advisers and civil servants Lord Mackay had spent days doing paperwork in connection with the cases. Like Fairbairn he had first heard about the Glasgow rape case before publication in the *Daily Record*. The Deputy Crown

Agent had informed him the day before publication that the newspaper was examining the case and asking for a statement. The Lord Advocate had told Mr Dean that he could release a statement providing it was accurate. At that point Lord Mackay did not have a full brief on the case. It was just another rape case to him – one which the press were looking at.

He first realized its significance on the Tuesday in Luxembourg when his lunch was interrupted by a telephone call from a *Daily Mail* reporter looking for a statement. The Lord Advocate told the journalist that he hadn't had a chance to study the case papers himself and, in any event, could not make any comment until he had replied to the MP, David Marshall, who had written to him with a series of questions on the case. That night he instructed his private secretary to contact Fairbairn. The Lord Advocate's secretary spoke to Fairbairn's private secretary on the phone and passed on a message that he (Fairbairn) was to issue no statement until Lord Mackay got back from Luxembourg to approve it himself. Lord Mackay wanted to ensure that any statement he did make could be backed up with accurate facts and would also be honest in every detail.

Back in Glasgow that Tuesday evening Carol was tracked down by the press. A huge queue of journalists waited their turn to interview her in her top-floor flat. Television interviews on the nine and ten o'clock news that night showed her – silhouetted in order to protect her anonymity – and millions of viewers all over Britain heard her words. Carol revealed that she had not known that the charges had been dropped until she read the *Record*, and that she had always been prepared to give evidence so long as the court was cleared.

In Parliament MPs, incensed by the news, wrote a series of letters to both the Lord Advocate and the Solicitor General. That night Fairbairn decided he would have to prepare a written statement for release to the press the next morning. He would also have to be questioned on it. Fairbairn tried to contact the Lord Advocate in Europe but could not reach him. Eventually he received a message through his superior's pri-

vate secretary: 'Don't release your statement until the Lord
Advocate arrives in Britain.'

Arrangements were made for the papers to arrive in London
the next morning, Wednesday – at long last. Fairbairn started
drafting out the statement and continued his Parliamentary
duties. In the early hours of the morning of Wednesday, 20
January, he returned exhausted to his London flat. It was 2
a.m. when he got to bed.

10 The Fall of Fairbairn

The shrilling telephone shook Fairbairn out of a deep sleep. He looked at the alarm clock. It was 6 a.m. 'Who on earth is this?' he muttered, his hand groping at the green bedside receiver. 'I'm sorry to bother you,' said the caller. 'It's the *Evening Standard*.'

Nicholas Hardwick Fairbairn, QC, Baron of Fordell, a Scottish estate overlooking the River Forth, had spent much of his professional and political life in a blaze of publicity and controversy and was no stranger to early-morning telephone calls from the media.

When he was appointed Solicitor General in May 1979 the Prime Minister, Margaret Thatcher, knew that her new law officer was an MP noted for his outspoken habits. Five years earlier he had succeeded former Prime Minister, Alec Douglas-Home, as the MP for Kinross and West Perthshire.

Before becoming an MP Nicholas Fairbairn had been a colourful, highly successful man, specializing in the defence of criminal cases in Scotland's High Court. He was a household name, known for his broad sense of humour, sardonic wit and cutting tongue. His mind was intelligent and inquiring and he combined the exactitude of a scientist with the breadth of an artist. He was also articulate and, at the same time, sensitive.

Although he was a bold and outspoken supporter of Conservatism, Fairbairn was no respector of the establishment, although he looked the part, dressed immaculately in Edwardian clothes, a square topper on his head and a snuff box to hand.

His boldness often brought him trouble and plunged him into controversy. His supporters claimed he was a generation or two, or even three, ahead of the more stuffy and conservative traditions of the law. His ability, however, was unquestioned and his sense of humour unparalleled. For instance, he listed his hobbies in *Who's Who* one year as 'bunking and debunking', the next year as 'upholding what's right and demolishing what's left', and 'making love, ends meet and people laugh' in the third year.

The son of a world-famous psychoanalyst, William Ronald Dodds Fairbairn, he originally started a medical course before changing to the law. His mother's family had connections with the Dukes of Gordon, which added an aristocratic touch to his breeding.

In the 1960s Fairbairn bought a dilapidated castle, Fordell, near Inverkeithing, Fife, and, at great cost, restored it for his new bride, the daughter of Baron Reay. He did much of the work himself, landscaping the grounds and manhandling huge blocks of stone to create walls. His wry sense of humour was apparent to any visitor who clambered up the flight of spiral stairs leading to the main drawing room. At the top Fairbairn had dressed an alabaster bust of Caesar in a bowler hat, spectacles, a dark coat and an umbrella. It stood there like a silent butler, beckoning guests to enter.

In 1979 his marriage broke up and Fairbairn returned to the castle after the divorce, a lonely man, separated from his wife and three daughters.

In London, Fairbairn was described by a political commentator as 'one of the most intelligent fools' at Westminster. 'Dandy Nick' was another name given to him by his opponents. He designed his own clothes and, one day, raised scores of eyebrows in Parliament when he arrived wearing an overall. Unabashed, Fairbairn explained that it would prevent the seat of his trousers from becoming shiny, sitting long hours on leather chairs in committee.

In December 1981 Fairbairn had been involved in the biggest controversy of his political career. Newspapers were full of sensational accounts of how one of his lady friends, a former secretary at the House of Commons, had tried to commit

suicide, allegedly by hanging herself from a lamp-post outside
Fairbairn's London home. Fairbairn never revealed the truth
– in order to protect her. He had been in Scotland at the time.
The incident almost ended his political career and there were
calls for his resignation from a handful of furious MPs.

The journalist who phoned Fairbairn at 6 a.m. on Wednesday, 20 January, was full of apologies. He explained he was
working on the Glasgow rape case story and wanted a first-
edition story for the *Evening Standard.* Fairbairn gathered his
senses. 'I'll be giving a statement about that later on in the
day,' he told the reporter. 'Contact my office and they'll tell
you when to collect it.'

The journalist, however, was insistent. 'Did you see the television last night?' 'I did not.' 'Well, the victim was on and she
claims she was prepared to give evidence all along, despite
what was said about her medical condition.'

'I find that extraordinary, as you will hear in the statement
later on,' Fairbairn replied. But when pressed further, he told
the reporter that the woman had been found unfit to give
evidence. He knew that this was so (because of her attempted
suicide), but refused to disclose the reasons to the journalist.

The Solicitor General's next comment made the reporter's
ears prick up and he noted it down in shorthand. 'The excel-
lence of the Scottish legal system had been impugned by misunderstanding,' said Fairbairn. 'How come?' asked the
Standard journalist. Fairbairn replied, 'The overriding factor
which finally decided the matter was the simple, inescapable
fact that the prosecution did not have sufficient, competent or
available evidence to stand any chance of gaining a conviction.

'By presenting the true facts which I established from a
thorough personal inquiry, I sincerely hope that I will allay
public anxiety. The person involved was a responsible Crown
official. He acted in a perfectly proper and just manner. I
believe the decision was a correct one.

'However, there is no doubt in my mind that the matter of
this unfortunate woman's mental stability was irrelevant.'

'Thank you for your help,' said the reporter. 'I am sorry
again to have got you up so early.' Fairbairn put the phone

down, not for one moment realizing that the last alleged nineteen words of his interview were to start a process which would
help destroy his ministerial career.

Later that morning an official Government car took Fairbairn to Dover House in time to attend the Scottish Secretary's
weekly meeting with his ministers at 9 a.m. During the meeting Fairbairn was told in no uncertain terms that he was to
abandon the idea of putting out his own statement because
the whole affair was becoming too parliamentary. MPs had
the right to be first to hear what the Government had to say
about the Glasgow rape case. Fairbairn was reminded that
Members of Parliament had written to himself and the Lord
Advocate. Any reply would have to be made from the floor of
the House and the Speaker was subsequently given notice that
Fairbairn would address the Commons on the afternoon of
Thursday, 21 January.

The repercussions of the 6 a.m. phone call were soon apparent. Fairbairn's comments were published in the *Evening
Standard* and also in the *Evening Times* of Glasgow. When
Mrs Thatcher heard about them she was said to be furious.
She had given instructions that there were to be no statements
on the Glasgow rape case until the Lord Advocate got back
from Luxembourg to discuss it with her. She sent one of her
aides to seek out Fairbairn and, in what must have been an
uncomfortable few minutes, he received a dressing-down on
the Prime Minister's instructions. He was ordered not to say
anything again to the press about the case and, for the rest of
the day, he locked himself in his office, refusing to take phone
calls from newspaper men anxious to find out when his statement would be coming. They were politely told by a secretary
that there would be no statement and that, instead, Fairbairn
would be addressing the House the following day.

In the meantime papers relating to the case were flown
specially with the Crown Agent from Edinburgh to London
and the Solicitor General was able to see them that day for
the first time.

As the London *Evening Standard* and the Glasgow *Evening
Times* hit the streets MPs complained bitterly that Fairbairn
had abused and insulted Parliament by giving a statement to

the press. In politics, it is bad enough to disobey the order of an immediate chief; it is even worse to flout Parliament. When an MP asks questions of a Government minister, he is entitled to have a written or an oral reply. He does not expect to read it in the columns of a newspaper. This is a fundamental and jealously guarded parliamentary tradition – and Parliament does not easily forgive those who breach it.

As the day wore on MPs, disturbed by the Glasgow rape case, became even more furious about Fairbairn's statement. They were also confused. The crux of the case, they had been led to believe, was that the trial had been abandoned because of the woman's mental condition. Yet Fairbairn claimed in the *Standard* that this was irrelevant. He had also concluded that, despite the fact there had been confessions in the case, there was not sufficient evidence to justify a conviction.

Mr David Marshall, the Labour MP for Shettleston, who had originally asked for an investigation of the case, said, 'I find it the height of arrogance that Nicky Fairbairn should pre-empt the Lord Advocate's reply to my questions.'

Labour Scottish Legal Affairs spokesman, Mr Donald Dewar, the MP for Glasgow Garscadden, said, 'Mr Fairbairn has abused Parliament and almost certainly confused an already complex situation.' The morning papers on Thursday, 21 January, were to be full of comments about Fairbairn's impertinence to Parliament.

That Wednesday the Lord Advocate completed his business in Luxembourg and, unaware of the looming parliamentary storm, intended to return to London on the 7 p.m. plane. Luxembourg, however, was fog-bound and, as they sat in the airport, Lord Mackay and the other passengers could hear the plane circling overhead unable to land. The plane flew to Brussels and the passengers were bussed there to catch it. They arrived back at Heathrow at 11.30 p.m.

Lord Mackay was met at the airport by a photographer and a reporter who asked if he could make any comment about Fairbairn's statement in the *Standard*. The Lord Advocate did not know that Fairbairn had issued a statement. It came as a complete surprise to him. He had ordered him not to make any statement. The official car waiting to pick him up and take him back to his London flat contained the Glasgow rape case papers. Lord Mackay studied them into the early hours of the morning, preparing the statement he would give to the House of Lords and which Fairbairn would also give to the Commons later in the afternoon.

The Lord Advocate had also received a report that Carol had said on television that she had wanted to go to court all along. When drafting out his statement Lord Mackay thought of private prosecution as the answer. He had been researching private prosecution in relation to another matter and knew that, while he might be accused of using the idea as a shield to hide behind, it was his duty towards the woman to suggest it. He was also well aware that no private prosecution would get off the ground if the Lord Advocate denied it.

On the morning of the parliamentary debate he arrived at his office at Fielden House at 9 a.m. He met Fairbairn for the first time round about 10 a.m. Lord Mackay seldom gives way to anger but he voiced his displeasure forcefully. He paced round the room raising his voice. 'I asked you not to give any statement and you have – to a newspaper.'

The Crown Agent, the Lord Advocate's private secretary and other officials looked on in embarrassment as Lord Mackay rebuked his number two for flagrantly defying his order. Fairbairn, so used to speaking in the defence of others, rose to his own defence. 'I spoke to a journalist because I thought it right and important that the public, who are anxious about this case, should have their misunderstanding about the affair authoritatively corrected. If Mrs X told the press that she had always been ready to give evidence, why did she take an overdose of drugs? Why was she in a state of collapse in the High Court?'

'That's not the point!' thundered the Lord Advocate. 'I told you not to make a statement until we were in a position to go over it together.'

Fairbairn took the statement he had prepared and thumped it down on the Lord Advocate's desk. 'That's the statement. I didn't issue this statement to the press. I corrected a misunderstanding.'

As Lord Mackay read it, he automatically reached for his

pen to alter a phrase here and a phrase there. Fairbairn resisted. 'We don't have time for that,' he protested. In any event the Lord Advocate decided his statement was the one to use; it was tidied up and sent away to be retyped and copied.

The meeting between Scotland's senior law officers ended and they both departed, Fairbairn to the House of Commons and Lord Mackay to a cabinet meeting. The Prime Minister was anxious to hear details of the statement which had to be issued in both Houses. Lord Mackay assured her that everything was in order and that he was back in command of the situation. As a woman, Mrs Thatcher was horrified by the details of the case and, as a politician, she felt acute embarrassment for her party which had campaigned for law and order. She was especially impressed to learn from her top Scottish law officer that the three accused boys might face justice via a private prosecution. It seemed an ideal solution to a very delicate problem.

There was one problem, however, left for the cabinet – what to do about the storm of protest over Fairbairn talking out of turn to the press? It was decided that the then Leader of the House, Francis Pym, would apologize to Parliament if the Labour Party looked for an apology. Lord Mackay left 10 Downing Street satisfied that the Prime Minister was happy with the direction of events.

The Lord Advocate returned to his office and, in the meantime, Fairbairn, who lunched in the Commons with the Crown Agent, was still totally unaware of the stormy passage he was about to have in the debate later that afternoon. He had been told that he would have to apologize to the House but he believed that, when he did so, most MPs would accept it. 'All ministers speak to journalists,' he thought. He still believed the newspapers were to blame for stirring the whole matter up. They wanted to keep the Glasgow rape case alive.

The House, which was packed, commenced its sitting at 2.30 p.m. It was Prime Minister's Question Time and Fairbairn heard Mrs Thatcher answer questions on violence in Liverpool, a proposed merger involving the Royal Bank of Scotland, the Trident missile project, magistrates courts and British Rail.

The questions ended with one about the bugging of public telephone boxes.

After Question Time, Mr Michael Foot asked the Leader of the House, Mr Francis Pym, to state the business for the following week. He followed his question with a thrust: 'The matter I wish to raise concerns the conduct of the Solicitor General for Scotland. I gather that he is to make a statement later today, but he has already made statements on the same subject to the press. I gather that the Prime Minister has already issued a reprimand to him today but, in my view, the Honourable Learned Gentleman should come to the House himself and apologize at once for what has occurred.'

As Fairbairn, flanked by the Home Secretary, Mr William Whitelaw, and the Scots Secretary, George Younger, heard that statement, he realized that what he had thought of as just a 'little local difficulty', an intrusion into the sacrosanct affairs of the Crown Office, had become a matter of national importance.

Mr Pym rose to his feet. 'My answer to the Right Honourable Gentleman's comments about the Solicitor General for Scotland is that I am mindful of my responsibilities as Leader of the House towards every Member of the House, and of the need for the House to be informed at the first opportunity on matters of public importance. That did not happen on this occasion. I regret it very much and, as Leader of the House, I should like to apologize to the House for that. I ask the Right Honourable Gentlemen in the House to await the statement that my Honourable and Learned friend will make later.'

Fairbairn, who was totally unaware of the arrangement for Pym to apologize on his behalf, felt betrayed. He knew that when he apologized it would look as if he had been ordered to.

The House was strangely silent as he rose to deliver the long-awaited statement.

'With your permission, Mr Speaker, I should like to repeat a statement being made in another place by my Right Honourable and Learned friend, the Lord Advocate.

'Before reading that statement, may I make a personal apology to the whole House? Certain remarks were attributed to myself and reported in the press yesterday and repeated this morning. Any remarks I made were made before matters developed to the point at which it was obviously the wish of Honourable Members that a statement should be made in Parliament about the case. If anything I may have said showed any disrespect to the House, then I wish to apologize unreservedly, as that was furthest from my intentions. I shall now read the statement. . . . With Your Lordships' permission I should like to make a statement. . . .'

The House exploded in a mixture of anger and amusement, with MPs rising to their feet to try to interrupt. Who were 'Your Lordships'? Did Fairbairn think he was still in court? Did he not remember he was in the House of Commons? The Speaker had to call the House to order. In fact, Fairbairn was only reading verbatim from the Lord Advocate's statement which Lord Mackay would also read out in the Lords. However, many MPs thought it was an incredible gaffe.

Fairbairn continued, 'The Lord Advocate is answerable to Parliament for the conduct of criminal prosecution. It is, however, the practice not to divulge any details of evidence in particular cases. This is intended for the protection of all the parties involved and it is particularly important in the present case where it is possible that the complainer at some future date may make an application to the High Court of Justiciary to bring a private prosecution.'

MPs realized immediately that this not only opened the door to a private prosecution for the victim, but also allowed Fairbairn to shelter behind a suggestion that to give too much away at this stage could affect the chances of such a private prosecution. In the knowledge that law officers are accountable to Parliament and cannot shelter behind the notion of ministerial secrecy, confidentiality or public interests, Fairbairn conceded, 'Subject to these restraints, I wish, however, to be as frank and open as possible about this matter to the House and to the public on account of the anxiety aroused by the case.'

There was hardly a whisper as the Solicitor General outlined the background to the controversy and how, on the day of the trial, Carol was taken to see a psychiatrist.

He continued, 'In the interests of the woman, I would not

wish to reveal the details of the psychiatric report, save to say that her medical history since the events complained of caused the psychiatrist to conclude that a court appearance at that time would be detrimental to her health, and carried a hazard of suicide both before and after the trial, whatever the result. Accordingly, the case was not called.'

Fairbairn indicated that a decision had had to be taken as to whether the trial should be further postponed, whether the Crown should proceed with the whole or part of the indictment on the strength of the complainer's evidence, or whether the case should be dropped altogether. 'In arriving at the decision, Crown counsel was principally influenced by the likely effect on her health of the prospect of having to give evidence.'

Added Fairbairn, 'Given that the complainer was not at that stage able to give evidence, the difficult decision arose whether, on the remaining evidence available to the Crown, the Crown should proceed with both or one of the charges. The view was taken by Crown counsel that, in the light of all the circumstances, in the absence of the complainer, it would not have been proper to proceed on the whole or any part of the indictment.

'In the light of the information available to them, Crown counsel considered that the prospect of sufficient improvement in the complainer's health to alter the situation was not enough to justify keeping the proceedings alive any further and, accordingly, instructions were given that the case should be dropped. Once that has been done in Scotland at the instance of the Lord Advocate, no further prosecution at his instance is possible. Crown counsel exercise their independent professional judgment in coming to decisions on matters such as those I have referred to, but in cases of difficulty they may, and do, refer questions for his decision.'

Fairbairn's statement ended with an announcement of new and important changes in Crown Office procedures. 'The Lord Advocate has decided to instruct that no decision to drop proceedings altogether, in any case of murder or rape, should be taken before the hearing of evidence has begun, without the question being referred to him for decision.'

No sooner had he finished than Mr Bruce Millan, speaking

as Shadow Secretary of State for Scotland and thus underlining the importance the Opposition paid to the whole matter, castigated the statement as 'wholly unsatisfactory'. He paid tribute to his fellow MPs for raising the matter and also to the Scottish newspapers, particularly the *Daily Record*, for pursuing the matter with 'such persistence'.

In full flow, the mother of Parliaments can be extremely ruthless, as Fairbairn was to find out. One observer said later, 'He was subjected to a cross between a political gang-bang and the closing stages of a stag hunt. It was not a pretty sight, and few of the participants can have felt proud of their afternoon's work. Poor Mr Fairbairn, one of the most intelligent fools at Westminster, was well aware before he stood up that he had already been abandoned to his fate by his political betters.'

Mr Millan recalled Fairbairn's statement in the *Evening Standard*: 'There is no doubt in my mind that the matter of this unfortunate woman's mental stability was irrelevant.'

He reminded the House that the statement it had just heard from Fairbairn had revealed that the reason the prosecution had not gone ahead was the condition of the victim herself. This was 'completely incompatible' with his statement to the *Evening Standard*. Was Mr Fairbairn aware of the confession statements quoted in full in the *Daily Record*? Was he aware that the woman herself had said that she was willing to give evidence? Was he aware, therefore, that to the layman it looked as if there was a considerable amount of evidence available which would certainly have justified a prosecution? 'Nothing that has been said this afternoon will in any way allay the considerable public anxiety in Scotland on this matter.'

Fairbairn's announcement of the new procedures to be adopted in the Crown Office, said Mr Millan, called into question the competence of the Crown Office and, indeed, the competence of Fairbairn himself.

Mr Millan suggested that the reference to a private prosecution was a 'red herring'. The last successful application had been in 1909. 'Yet the Honourable and Learned Gentleman tells us this afternoon that this woman, who is not apparently fit enough to give evidence in a normal public trial, is potentially fit enough to bring a private prosecution. This is absolute nonsense and the Honourable and Learned Gentleman knows that it is!'

Mr Millan continued, 'Public confidence in the law officers and in the Crown Office is at a very low ebb indeed in Scotland at the present time. We cannot allow this matter to rest on the basis of this statement this afternoon. What we demand is a full judicial inquiry into this extremely worrying and horrifying affair.'

In replying, Fairbairn helped to sow the seeds of his own destruction. Having apologized to the House for the statement which he made to the press, and having heard Mr Pym apologize to the House for that statement, Fairbairn proceeded to deny its truth or accuracy.

'May I make it absolutely plain to the House that I never, at any time, said to anyone, or held the view, that the mental state of this woman was irrelevant. Her mental state was absolutely critical and it was in consideration of the interests of the woman, above all, that the decisions that were taken, were taken.

'I am astonished that it may be that this unfortunate woman, who underwent these terrible events, wishes now to give evidence. All I can say is that Crown counsel, having to consider her health and her future in the light of her medical history, took the view that it would be improper to force her to give evidence at this time.'

Other MPs jumped to their feet, forcing the Speaker to call for order. He ruled he would only allow another twenty minutes for questions. First to catch the Speaker's eye was Mr Michael Ancram, leader of the Conservative party in Scotland. He threw a life-line to Mr Fairbairn. Mr Ancram accepted that Conservative members shared horror and disgust over the circumstances of the case, but did Fairbairn agree that the disturbing failure to fulfil the public interest was due not to an error in the administration of the law but to the limitations of the law itself? 'Does he agree that there is a case now for referring questions of rape to the Scottish Law Commission so that it may look at the matter of evidence in rape trials to see whether rape victims can be further protected in future?'

This was a way out for Fairbairn to take – don't blame the lawyers, but blame the law. Fairbairn, however, ploughed on. 'Regrettably, I can see no circumstances in which one can say that the victim should not be put through a further ordeal in court, because I can see no way in which, out of fairness to those who were accused, one could conduct the trial in her absence.'

Mr Russell Johnston, the Liberal MP for Inverness, echoed the thoughts of thousands of people throughout Britain. 'If this poor wretched woman had died as a consequence of the assault, a case would have been brought without question. Because she was reduced to such a condition that she could not be in court, the people who did it go free. To the layman that seems incredible. Does the Honourable and Learned Gentleman agree that, in this case, the media have virtually acted as a review body and brought the matter to us? Can he assure us that, if a private prosecution is brought, the Crown Office will offer no impediment whatsoever?'

Fairbairn answered Mr Johnston by stating quite categorically that the Crown Office would put no impediment whatsoever in the way of the victim. But he stressed that, if the woman had died, there could have been no prosecution for rape. He further added that to try the attempted murder charge, and not rape, in the absence of the complainer was not considered to be a proper process.

Mr David Marshall, the Glasgow MP who instigated the Commons controversy, jumped to his feet. 'Is the Solicitor General for Scotland aware that this pathetic statement will not restore public confidence in the law? Was there an alleged confession? Was there an eyewitness account? Were there other incriminating statements? Was there forensic evidence? Will the Honourable and Learned Gentleman tell the House the name of the person who decided to drop the charges? Has that person ever been disciplined? Has that person ever been involved in any other controversial cases? Will the Honourable and Learned Gentleman recommend to the Government that an all-party select committee be set up to look into all aspects of the law and procedures relating to cases of rape?'

Finally, Mr Marshall suggested, 'As the Honourable and Learned Gentleman now has no credibility left, will he resign?'

Fairbairn refused to name the person involved, to a chorus of angry 'Why nots?' from MPs. The decisions, he said, had been taken by responsible and highly qualified Crown counsel in the very difficult circumstances of the case, acting in what they believed to be the best interests of the woman and the interests of justice.

MPs were queuing up to question the beleaguered Solicitor General. Conservatives were becoming noticeably frosty and, as the strain told on Fairbairn, the verbal slips and gaffes came. Mr William Hamilton, MP for Central Fife, could not resist recalling the speech made by Fairbairn in July 1979 when he said that rape was not a problem in Scotland and was a 'normal activity'. 'In view of those opinions which he expressed then and presumably holds now, does he think he is a fit person to hold the position he does?'

Fairbairn accused Mr Hamilton of trying to mislead the House as to the meaning of his words. 'What distinguishes sexual offences from offences such as murder, stabbing, theft and the like, is that they involve a human relationship and are not necessarily purely criminal activity. That is why the crime of rape is so difficult. . . . I have long experience of it, I can assure Honourable Members.'

The House erupted in laughter. Mr Gordon Wilson, the Scottish National Party member for Dundee East, captured the mood, prefacing his question with, 'At the risk of allowing the Solicitor General for Scotland to put his foot in it once more. . . .'

Mr Donald Dewar, the Labour MP for Glasgow Garscadden, pressed relentlessly on what he thought was a vital matter. Fairbairn had been quoted in the evening press the night before. Was the report accurate? If not, why did Fairbairn apologize? Mr Fairbairn repeated his denials about the accuracy of the press. 'At no time have I said that the mental state of the woman was irrelevant to anyone. It was essential to every consideration. At no time have I suggested that there was insufficient evidence where the complainer had given evidence. The Crown did not desert the case temporarily because the woman would have continued to be under the expectation and fear of giving evidence.'

Mr Harry Ewing, the Labour member for Stirling, Falkirk and Grangemouth, rubbed the matter home. The Leader of the House had apologized generously for Fairbairn's indiscretions; Fairbairn had apologized too. Now he had made a statement that was a complete contradiction of everything that appeared in the press. 'The House cannot function properly on that basis,' declared Mr Ewing.

The debate on the Glasgow rape case was over and, with that, the House went on to discuss Zimbabwe.

In the House of Lords, Lord Mackay received a more gentlemanly reception to the same statement. The Lord Advocate told Lord Ross that the reason he could not go into details about the evidence was that he had to take into account the interest of the victim and any possibility that might exist of proceedings in the future. 'So far as I am concerned, I have nothing whatsoever to hide.'

As proceedings in both Houses finished, it became clear that Nicholas Fairbairn supported the individual decision in the case and was intent on justifying it. Lord Mackay, however, was intent on justifying the system as a whole, saying that it would be strengthened because, in future, no cases would be dropped without his own personal sanction.

As he left the House that evening Fairbairn felt that he had acquitted himself reasonably well in difficult circumstances. These sentiments, unfortunately, were not shared by others. One prominent member of the Labour Party turned solemnly to his companion and said, 'I do not know what this row is all about, but I don't think that we will be seeing much more of that young man in the Government team.'

Fairbairn walked from the House, a few of his friends murmuring, 'Well done,' 'Congratulations,' 'Bad luck.' As ever an optimist, he hoped that the Glasgow rape case was buried for good. He sat in his Commons office ready to engage in the immediate correspondence of the day. It was 5 p.m. He was ordering his thoughts for future business, checking his diary for the evening, when there was a tap on the door. The Prime

Minister's Private Secretary, Mr Ian Gow, a very close friend of Fairbairn's, had arrived to see him. Somewhat diffidently, Gow questioned him about the background of the case; Fairbairn told him all he knew. He asked how the row had blown up. What had happened? Did he speak to the press? Were the press accurate? He was obviously preparing a brief.

Twenty minutes later Gow left to report back to the Prime Minister. He returned to Fairbairn's office in the Commons about 6 p.m., looking glum. Fairbairn was no fool. He knew Gow's position. He knew what Gow was doing and he knew that his own performance was now open to question. When Gow asked him what his feelings were, Fairbairn knew that the end had come.

'This thing has gone sour,' said Gow, 'and everyone is blaming you. Have you considered resignation?' Fairbairn paused for a second and lowered his eyes. 'Yes, I have,' he said. 'What are you going to do now?' asked Gow. 'I think I should resign,' replied Fairbairn. 'It would be a public act of purification. Rape has become a very political and emotional issue. The department for which I am responsible has made a very serious mistake. I never said that publicly but it was an appalling blunder, quite contrary to anything I would have sanctioned and, as the person who has been criticized for it, I think that I should take the blame. I will resign.'

Fairbairn then wrote out his letter of resignation to the Prime Minister.

My Dear Margaret,

I have been considering my position following the apology which preceded the statement I made to the House this afternoon about the Glasgow Rape case.

I wish to make it abundantly clear that I am entirely satisfied that the Crown Office and Crown counsel handled the delicate proceedings in the Glasgow Rape with total propriety. However, I appreciate that in my dealings with the press, I may have made errors of judgement. In the circumstances, I have decided that I ought no longer to remain in office as Solicitor General for Scotland.

I would like to thank you most sincerely for having given me the honour of serving as a Scottish law officer during the past two-and-

a-half years, but much more of having the privilege of serving in
your government, which is devoted to our national survival.

I will do all in my power to support you and your administration
in the House, and in the country, in your unflinching dedication to
the salvation of our country.

Yours sincerely,

Nicholas

Fairbairn gave the letter to Gow who immediately took it to
Mrs Thatcher. Soon afterwards he returned with the Prime
Minister's reply.

My Dear Nicholas,

It is characteristic of you that you should have written as you did.
I believe that you have come to a responsible decision which accords
with the highest traditions of office. In accepting your resignation, I
want to thank you most warmly for all that you have done as a
Minister and as a law officer since the administration was formed.

I am glad to know that we shall continue to have your loyal support
in the future, as we have had in the past. I send you my personal
good wishes.

Yours ever, Margaret

At 7 p.m. Fairbairn was taken by Gow to see Mrs Thatcher
in her Commons room. It was L-shaped and impressively
Gothic with two large windows on either side of a polished
redwood drinks cabinet. At one end of the room was a Victorian
writing desk and, at the other, the conference table at which
Government policies had been formulated over the decades.

As he entered he heard the kindly words from his Prime
Minister, 'You look shattered, Nicholas. I can see it in your
eyes.' Tears had been welling up as he was led in to meet her.
He sat down alone on one of two sofas facing each other. Mrs
Thatcher sat on the opposite sofa with the Chief Whip, Mr
Michael Jopling. Gow was hovering around in the background.

So far as Fairbairn could see the Prime Minister seemed as
upset as he was. She asked him if he wanted a drink. Fairbairn
nodded and the Prime Minister motioned Gow to pour them
all drinks. She expressed her immediate concern for Fairbairn
and was extremely sympathetic. He knew her words of sym-

pathy were genuine. Mrs Thatcher told him that the press were massing at Downing Street, having got word of his possible resignation. 'Would you like to phone your family before the news breaks?' she asked. 'Or your agent?'

The meeting lasted only ten or fifteen minutes and Fairbairn, still numb from his sudden resignation, realized the privilege which had been accorded to him. Mrs Thatcher instructed Gow to take Fairbairn to dinner so that he could escape the attentions of the press. He barely remembered what he ate that night, but was grateful someone was there to help him escape from himself and, to some extent, share his misery. For the next three or four days Mrs Thatcher phoned several times to ask how he was.

Fairbairn was visited only by his friend, Mr Malcolm Rifkind, then a junior minister at the Scottish Office, at a secret address, the house of a dear and valued friend. The headline, 'Fairbairn under Fire', became 'Fairbairn is Sacked' the next day. For ten days he disappeared from view.

Arrangements to address dinners all over Scotland were subsequently cancelled. Fairbairn returned to Fordell Castle, refusing to speak to the press and gaining moral support from the thousands of letters which flooded in. One was from Lord Home whose constituency he had taken over. The most bizarre was from a Great Train Robber who sent him a potted begonia.

Ten days later, on 31 January, Fairbairn agreed to face the television cameras on BBC's 'Agenda' programme. Viewers saw a weary man almost breaking down when talking about the drama of the previous couple of weeks. The interviewer, James Cox, the BBC's political correspondent in Scotland, asked him if he thought that he had been made a scapegoat. 'Let those who watched it judge,' said Fairbairn. He continued to defend the Scottish system of prosecution. 'I would be horrified if it led to any loss of confidence in the law,' he told Cox.

Fairbairn felt that the Crown counsel who was in charge of the case ought to have referred to the law officers before making his decision. Cox pursued the issue. 'Had you seen the papers do you think you would have made a different decision?' Fairbairn told him, 'I might have – and I might not have.'

Cox then asked if part of the reason why he resigned, or was required to resign, was to restore public confidence. Fairbairn said, 'Well, I hope that my resignation has the effect of restoring confidence in the law ... resignation of a minister is a purification of the system. It is a matter of public purification.'

Cox asked if his flamboyant lifestyle, which had become irksome to some of his more traditional colleagues, had contributed to his resignation. Fairbairn agreed that it was a view that many people had formed. Was it an accurate view? 'Probably.'

Cox continued, 'In other words, as I think someone said in one of the papers, they got you with a second barrel from the shot-gun.' Fairbairn, irreverently and inventively, replied in only two words, 'The dullards.' He described what had been a very difficult time: 'A public humiliation, insult, everyone trying to get you, to photograph the body, ask whether it enjoyed the sacrifice.'

As thousands watched, seeing tears in Fairbairn's eyes, hardly one of them could have failed to feel a tinge of regret. He was a ruined man. Was his resignation forced on him because of his previous eccentric habits? Did he upset too many people? Was it because he talked to the press? Was it because there was an error in his department? Was it a matter of public purification? Or was it because he felt ministerial responsibility? Was it because he denied what he said to the press? Was it a combination of all these matters?

The position is best described by Fairbairn in his interview with James Cox that Sunday afternoon. When he was asked whether he jumped or whether he was pushed, Fairbairn the brave, Fairbairn the sentimental, said simply, 'I fell.'

11 A Ray of Hope

The nine days of high drama which began with the publication of the first story on the Glasgow rape case and ended with the resignation of Nicholas Fairbairn left Carol in a daze. She felt genuine sorrow for the plight of the deposed Solicitor General, but was bitter about the decision made by his office to drop the charges against her attackers.

The news that the youths were free of all charges had been broken to Carol by Billy. On the morning of 13 January, just as he was about to go to work, Billy had glanced at the *Daily Record*. Flipping over the papers he saw a headline: 'Rape Case Boys Go Free'. He looked closer. Disbelieving, he recognized the names. The case was Carol's.

Carol was still at her parents' home but Billy, expecting her home that day, decided not to go to work. He wanted to be on hand when Carol arrived so that he could break the news to her.

When she returned and heard the news Carol stared at the article in disbelief. 'But I wanted to give evidence,' she told Billy. She read through every word of the article. The youths, she learned for the first time, had been freed in September. Her next reaction was anger. 'How come they can tell the *Daily Record* the charges have been dropped,' she asked Billy, 'and yet they haven't been near me? I have had to read it in the papers.'

Carol felt bitter. She felt rejected. She felt neglected. These youths had been walking the streets without a stain on their character, yet she had been living for all these months in fear of having to go to court to give evidence against them.

For the next few days the young couple kept in touch with the ensuing row mainly through the columns of the newspapers and their television set. She read of MPs writing to the Lord Advocate and the Solicitor General furiously complaining about the way the case had been handled.

On 19 January Billy learned from an official letter that his divorce in England had come through. Carol was in the other room as he excitedly read through the letter. 'I'm divorced,' he shouted. Carol was at his side in seconds. 'Congratulations,' she smiled. Then he looked at her. 'Let's get married,' he said. Carol nodded, 'OK.' She added, 'When's the date?'

That morning the news broke in the *Record* that the youths had made statements to the police. The news did not dampen their plans for an engagement celebration that night.

Both of them knew that the press were on their tail. Billy had met two reporters in a pub and had refused to lead them to Carol. Journalists from almost every paper in Britain were trying to locate her. Gordon Airs and Bill Corke from the *Daily Record* had been searching for her since the previous evening, following a tip-off to the news desk that she had been seen in Glasgow, despite the story circulating that she was living down south. With no definite leads the two journalists decided to visit local pubs, asking for Carol by name in the hope that somebody would know her and reveal where she was staying. They were faced by a solid wall of silence. There were also dangerous moments in pubs with staff and customers – the East End is known for its 'hard men' – challenging the two reporters over their motives for trying to locate Carol. Menacing groups of stockily built men, some bearing the marks of previous encounters, were asking, 'Why the hell do you want to bother the lassie? Why don't you leave her in peace? She's had enough and now you're trying to dig it all up again. Get lost.'

In one pub an irate man who knew Carol personally swung a punch at Corke who, in the best traditions of newspapers, didn't take up the offer of further violence, made an excuse and left.

That night they met three men, each of whom claimed to be Carol's boyfriend. Each one refused to lead them to her. What Airs and Corke didn't know was that, while two of them were impostors, one was Billy.

The following morning reporters from Scottish and English newspapers joined the hunt for Carol. They were getting nearer and nearer all the time. The first two to actually track her down were Joe Quinn of the Press Association and George Philips of the *Daily Mail*. Billy invited them in and Carol spoke for the first time to a complete stranger about her ordeal. It made her feel better to talk to somebody else. The two journalists sensed her outrage and deep shock at the fact that the boys had been freed and she had not been informed by the Crown Office. She also said that 'they should be castrated'.

Airs and Corke arrived at Carol's flat hard on the heels of the first two reporters and, within half an hour, representatives from newspapers, radio and television were queuing up to interview Carol. She had just washed her hair, ready for her big engagement celebration night out and had a towel round her head, turban style. All those who saw her that night noted Carol's attempts to turn away her face or look down at the floor to prevent anyone from seeing her scars.

The engagement celebration was cancelled and, late that night, exhausted by their interviews with the media but nevertheless thrilled with the support they were getting, Carol and Billy went to bed.

For the next two days journalists from all over Britain sought to interview Carol. By that time she was thoroughly disenchanted and wanted a break from the spotlight of publicity. They went to Billy's mother's home to escape the attentions of the press who were almost camping outside their own flat. In the small hours of the Friday morning, and at the end of their tether, Billy and Carol phoned the *Daily Record*, hoping that the newspaper which had broken the story might be prepared to take them away for the weekend. Billy asked for Gordon Airs who had interviewed Carol previously. But whoever answered the call refused to give him the reporter's home telephone number.

Early that morning reporter Jim Taylor and photographer

Ron Burgess, both from the *Scottish Daily Express*, climbed the stairs to the top floor to give another routine knock on Carol's door. They had been tipped off by a neighbour that the couple's pet budgie was still in the flat and that someone would have to return to feed it. That someone called out, 'Who's that?' Billy and Carol had sneaked back to feed their budgie at 5 a.m.

'You're lucky to catch us in,' said Carol. 'We only came back to clean out the birdcage, grab a few clothes and get away from all the publicity. My nerves are at breaking point and I am chain-smoking.'

The couple treated the two *Express* men with suspicion at first but, after some pleasantries were exchanged, they asked if they could use their car to take them away from the city. 'I don't care where we go,' said Carol. 'Take us somewhere in the country. Just get us out of here and we'll give you our story for nothing.' The two journalists put Carol and Billy in the car which zigzagged through several East End streets to shrug off possible press cars following them.

All Carol wanted was a bit of rest and some country air. She confided in Taylor and Burgess that she was going to contact a lawyer to take out a private prosecution against the three boys. 'Can you help us contact him?' she asked. Taylor mentioned the name of one Glasgow criminal lawyer whom they knew, but Carol and Billy shook their heads. 'We'd rather go to Ross Harper,' she said. 'We would have confidence in him.'

Carol and Billy soon found themselves being driven along Loch Lomondside to the picturesque town of Inveraray, sixty miles from Glasgow. They booked into a quiet country inn and, after settling down, went out together hand in hand for a quiet stroll. The young couple enjoyed every minute of their stay. It was a breath of fresh air after months of misery in the East End.

The following morning as they shopped in Inveraray's main street, Carol confided in the two *Express* journalists that she and Billy had decided to get married in February. Later that evening they moved from Inveraray and booked into another hotel at Carrick Castle where Carol, a bit of a tomboy, mingled anonymously with the customers in the bar, playing pool, darts and dominoes. Taylor was surprised at how adept she was. Carol was used to playing pub games. From the age of sixteen her father and her uncle had taken her into pubs and, while they were drinking, Carol played the games. She recalled how once a man came up to her father saying he should be ashamed of himself for having taken her into a pub. He told him, 'At least I know where my daughter is. Where's yours?'

In the meantime the *Express* team had located Mr Harper and they told Carol that he had agreed to see her. The thought of a private prosecution excited her. It wasn't so much revenge as the possibility that justice could be seen to be done. It was a ray of hope for the future, to which Carol clung.

12 The Private Prosecutor

Ross Harper returned to his office at five o'clock and saw on his desk the terse message: 'Please phone Gordon Hay, *Scottish Daily Express* . . . urgent.'

Harper had had a busy day at Dumbarton Sheriff Court. It was 22 January, only a few days after Scottish legal and political circles had been sent reeling with the gruesome details of the Glasgow rape case and the resignation of the Solicitor General. During the previous week lawyers had debated not only the controversy but possible changes in the law. Harper's views on the issues raised in the case did not attract unanimous agreement in the legal profession. In a television debate he had been joined by one of his well-known colleagues, Joseph Beltrami, who had argued the case that the Crown was right.

Harper reached for the telephone. A minute later Gordon Hay of the *Express* was on the other end of the line. 'I've been trying to get you all day,' he said. 'Miss X says she wants to start a private prosecution and she's wondering if you might take the case. But that was at 10.30 a.m. and we were unable to contact you. I don't know if her position has since changed. If it is still on, would you be interested in acting for her?' Harper indicated that he would.

Later Hay phoned back to say that Miss X did wish to consult with Harper. Harper suspected that the *Scottish Daily Express* were in some way controlling Miss X and voiced these fears to the reporter, but Hay, an affable Aberdonian, was insistent that Carol had actually asked the *Express* to take her away. He was obviously delighted at getting a scoop over his paper's arch rival, the *Daily Record*, but he pointed out that Carol, at her wit's end, had wanted to escape the attention of the media and the *Express* had been there fortuitously when she finally made up her mind to leave Glasgow.

Arrangements were made for Harper to obtain a lift in an *Express* car on the Sunday. The car came as promised. Harper told his wife he would be back for lunch, but to his surprise the car headed out of the city past Loch Lomond into Argyll. The journey lasted two hours, and, at its end, he found himself in the picturesque village of Lochgoilhead on the windswept shores of a lonely sea loch. The car pulled up outside an attractive little hotel only a stone's throw from the sea.

As Harper stepped inside he wondered what to expect. He had read how Carol had tried to kill herself and how in the opinion of a psychiatrist, she would be in danger of suffering from further psychiatric harm if she were to expose herself to a court. Did she really want to raise a private prosecution, a case from which she would derive no particular benefit? Alternatively, was the two-hour journey part of a 'media plot', designed to exploit a poor victim for the sake of a few lines of publicity? Within the next few minutes he would know.

Harper was ushered into the hotel lounge. There, sitting by a cheerful, blazing log fire, was his prospective client and her fiancé. Carol was introduced to him. Harper noticed immediately that she was unsure of herself, always stealing a look at her fiancé for comfort and confidence. He was a man of the world. He was sure of himself and he knew that the weeks, months and years ahead were potentially fraught with danger, stemming from Carol's uncertain life and made more fragile by her assault. He was a typical Glasgow East Ender. Not the East Ender of the gangs; not a layabout, not work-shy, but a skilled tradesman confident in his abilities. Travelling abroad in pursuit of work to Portugal, Spain, France, he had obtained a knowledge of the world and an ability to analyse objectively. Yet he retained a respect and a liking for his own city of Glasgow. He felt a deep sense of shame that someone from Glasgow could have committed such an offence against his girl.

Carol was nervous and uncertain. Billy was her crutch and support. But both were sure of one thing: that those who were alleged to have perpetrated this assault had not been brought to justice, and that in their hour of need they had been let down. Not let down by the police, not let down by the Fiscal, but let down by a system or an individual. Her case had been dropped. She had not been told. She had wanted to give evidence. She still wanted to give evidence. Yet the accused were still walking the streets not only free, but untried.

Billy explained that his family were clients of Harper's firm. He had discussed the matter of a private prosecution with Carol and Carol wished to obtain Harper's advice. Accordingly Harper proceeded to discuss the case with her. Was it a matter of vengeance that she now wished a private prosecution? Carol said it was not. She felt she had been wronged and she did not think it was right that the accused boys should be free in the East End of Glasgow without going on trial. If there was a remedy which she could obtain at her own hands, then she would wish to exercise that remedy.

After some time Harper agreed to accept instructions from her, provided she agreed to cooperate in a further psychiatric examination so that it could be ascertained whether the ordeal of a private prosecution – and he explained to her that it would be an ordeal – would be detrimental to her health. 'There's no point in making legal history if the cost is twenty years of misery to you,' he told her. Carol readily agreed.

She also made a special request. Would Harper deal with the press at all times, tell them what was happening and make sure they did not approach her for any information? She was happy to talk to the two *Express* reporters but not to some thirty or forty others.

Harper made one final check. Was Carol taking any money from the *Express* newspaper? Carol said that some of her hotel bills were being paid by the *Express* but Billy was standing round for round with the *Express* reporters in the bar, refusing to let them buy every drink. They were not looking for charity and they were not taking charity.

Harper explained that if she were to accept money from the newspapers to finance and mount a private prosecution, she could be open to criticism. The courts did not relish cases being taken as a result of outside influences and, indeed, the entire private prosecution could be put at peril were there any suggestion that the *Express* was financing the matter. Carol must be a free agent, counselled Harper. Immediate expenses or advice could be covered under the legal-advice scheme. Harper would investigate the possibility of legal aid for a private prosecution. While he was doubtful about that, he was sure that the absence of finance would not be a barrier for such an important case.

In Carol and Billy's presence Harper drafted out a statement indicating that instructions had now been given to investigate the possibility of raising a private prosecution. He then returned to Glasgow.

From that moment on, his home was under siege from journalists wanting to know what was happening. When would the case be started? Who would be paying for it? All he could confirm was that he had received instructions.

On the Monday morning when Harper arrived at his office he realized that, in view of the massive interest in the matter, the sooner the case got into court the better. Then it would be under the protection of the court. Before that, however, preliminary work was required to be done and done speedily. He telephoned the Lord Advocate's office and a meeting was arranged that afternoon to see the Crown Agent, Mr William Chalmers. Before the meeting Harper engaged Mr Kevin Drummond, one of Scotland's brightest young advocates and a very experienced criminal practitioner. Drummond closeted himself in Harper's office that morning, researching the background to private prosecutions.

During the meeting in Edinburgh that afternoon, the Crown Office officials could not have been more helpful. They gave Harper and Mr Drummond the Crown witness list from the previous occasion and told them they could start to take statements immediately. It was apparent that the Crown Office wished not only to help but to be seen to help. Officials assisted Harper and Drummond to prepare a statement for the fifty to sixty journalists who were waiting outside for news of the latest developments. When Harper met them outside, the questions flowed. Had counsel been instructed? Who would pay the fees? What would the next step be? Was he confident of success? What were the merits of the case? Answers could be given to some of these questions, though not all. It would be totally wrong, for instance, to discuss the evidence or speculate on the chances of success – that was a matter for the court.

Harper could not discuss Mrs X's state of health. But he could read the statement prepared at Crown Office. Another question, to which he had no answer, was on the subject of fees. Harper had not had time to ask the Law Society whether funds would be made available from the legal-aid system or whether Carol would have to find the money herself. Harper was aware that the image of the law in Scotland was being tarnished by criticism from English MPs. Here was a chance to remind the world at large that Scots law was founded on the basis of lawyers providing their services for free when the need was greatest. He told the reporters of this great Scottish tradition and indicated that he was quite sure that counsel would provide their services for free when there was a need. His remarks were appreciated by the older members of the Bar and older solicitors. It was not understood, however, by the younger members who had not lived through the days when this tradition was at its highest.

The next day Harper telephoned the clerk to Mr Charles Kemp Davidson, QC, the Dean of the Faculty of Advocates, Scotland's top QC, to ask if he would take the case. England has its barristers and Inns of Court. Scotland has advocates who gather together under the Faculty. Each year the Faculty of Advocates elects, by due and democratic process, a man acknowledged by the majority of members as being well and truly above his peers – a man to represent junior advocates, senior advocates, eminent silks.

The Dean of the Faculty carried with him not only a tradition lasting several hundred years, but certain rights and privileges. He could address any court at any time, whether he was briefed in the case or not. History recalls how he could travel through the circuits of Scotland representing luckless advocates who were perhaps unjustly berated by cruel and capricious judges. 'Send for the Dean,' was the cry of any

advocate who thought that justice in Scotland was being er-
oded by a capricious bench. When the Dean arrived the court
was silent and he could stand at the bar of the court and
demand to be heard.

Scotland had been lucky, or wise, in its choice of Deans over
the centuries. Each and every Dean since the sixteenth century had been appointed to the bench after his term of office
expired.

When Mr Harper contacted the present Dean, Mr Charles
Kemp Davidson, he readily agreed to take on the case. That
afternoon Harper and Drummond travelled to Edinburgh to
see him. Not only did Mr Davidson agree to prosecute for
Carol, he agreed to charge no fee whatsoever if the state did
not assist. The case was one of public interest. Carol herself
had no means to pay. It would not have been appropriate for
the bill to have been paid from outside sources – possibly
pressure groups. In such a case as this, there had to be no hint
of outside influence. Already baseless rumours had been building up that the *Scottish Daily Express* was providing £60,000
for Carol's legal expenses.

The complicated process of raising a Bill for Criminal Letters – the Scots legal term for an application for a private
prosecution – began in earnest. The team of lawyers was working in a legal no-man's-land. Several meetings were arranged
with Mr William Howard, the principal clerk to the Justiciary
Office. As the senior clerk he was able to bring many years of
experience to the problems faced by the private prosecution
team. However, even he did not have experience of the last
successful case – in 1909! The records of the Justiciary Office,
however, proved to be good and true. It was not long before
Mr Howard was able to lay his hands on all previous cases,
precedents and, most important of all, the style in which the
Bill would have to be presented.

The Crown had provided a list of witnesses but not the
statements themselves. Harper's precognition officer was
instructed to put everything aside and, aided by a team of
four assistants, swept into action. One of Harper's staff, an
ex-detective sergeant who had graduated in law, was
appointed 'Chief Executive Officer' to coordinate events, while

Mr Graeme Warner, the Edinburgh partner, personally super-
vised the procedures and liaised with counsel. Within a short
space of time a full brief with statements from all the witnesses
had been prepared for counsel. The Crown productions and the
photographs of the scarred woman were examined.

The scene of the crime was visited. Carol was taken to a
psychiatrist and the report revealed that, subject to a further
check before the trial (if it took place), she would be fit to give
evidence. The original Crown productions were taken from the
High Court in Glasgow and put into a strong-room in Harper's
office.

While all this activity was taking place, Kevin Drummond
prepared draft after draft of the application for a private prosecution. He had to investigate the law relating to all private
prosecutions this century and the last. The defence, in objecting to a private prosecution, would argue that the three youths
could not possibly get a fair trial because of the widespread
publicity. As a result Mr Drummond had to study every con-
ceivable case relating to the effect of newspaper publicity on
criminal trials.

The team was a strong one: the Dean, the top legal brain in
Scotland; Kevin Drummond, arguably the busiest defence
counsel in the country; backed up by Harper's efficient organization. But there was one thing missing. No one on the team
had ever prosecuted. Harper had nightmares, anticipating the
private prosecution being allowed to go ahead, the trial starting and some simple mistake ruining it all.

There could be no mistake. Planning had to be immaculate.
Accordingly, it was decided, with the Dean's consent, that the
team should be strengthened. Approaches were made to Mr
Alastair Cameron, a very experienced QC, now in private
practice; he had formerly held the post of Advocate Depute. As
a Crown prosecutor he had built up a reputation for toughness
and commonsense. He knew the prosecution process inside out
and his enlistment to the team was of great importance. Mr
Cameron responded to the call, knowing also that no payment
might ever be made.

After weeks of careful preparation and countless meetings
the private prosecution team was ready. A date for the hearing

to decide whether Carol would be allowed to take the three youths to court was fixed for 16 March. It would be heard by three judges: Lord Emslie, Scotland's Lord Justice General, and Lords Cameron and Avonside. The hearing was expected to last at least four days.

The Bill which was to be presented to the court was couched in medieval legal language. It was addressed to 'Elizabeth II, by the Grace of God, of the United Kingdom of Great Britain and Northern Ireland, and of Her other Realms and Territories, Queen, Head of the Commonwealth, Defender of the Faith', and to the 'Sheriff Principals of the Lothian and Borders, of Glasgow and Strathkelvin, to Chief Police Officers, Governors of Prisons, and Messengers at Arms'. The Bill asked the court to hold that 'true it is and of verity' that Joseph Sweeney, Gordon Sweeney and John Thomson were guilty of 'Crimes of heinous nature' and, by the laws of 'this and every other well Governed Realm', should be severely punished. It also asked the court to bring the three youths to trial at Edinburgh High Court on 24 May so that they could be 'Punished with the Pains of Law'.

13 Private Prosecutions

Jamie was poor and born of poor parents on a cold winter's night. It was 27 November, the year 1809. He grew to be a big boy, simple, but never in the least aggressive. One day in his early teens Jamie failed to return at nightfall and his mother was concerned for his safety. She bolted the door of the house and went out to search for him. While she was looking, Jamie came home tired and hungry and burst open the door. He looked for food and, in so doing, pulled down a cupboard full of his mother's best crockery. When she returned she was very angry; so angry that she chastised Jamie with a leather strap with such ferocity that the boy would never afterwards stay with her, but instead lived in the streets of Edinburgh.

As he went round the streets he was tormented by young boys who called and shouted after him, 'Daft Jamie . . . Daft Jamie . . .'

When Jamie was eighteen he met an Edinburgh citizen, a Mr Burke and, after talking a while, Mr Burke invited Jamie to a lodging house owned by his good friend, a Mr Hare. They were very friendly and Jamie, unable to credit his good luck, gratefully took the pleasing drink offered to him. When he had had a surfeit, Messrs Burke and Hare lay on top of him, as a result of which he died. There were no marks, no bruises. Jamie had died of suffocation. His body was sold to an un-questioning member of the medical profession. It would be used for dissection.

Edinburgh is renowned throughout the world for the skill of

its surgeons. Edinburgh University and Edinburgh Royal Infirmary are highly respected as training grounds for surgeons who practise not only in the capital of Scotland but take their skills to remote parts of the world.

In the early nineteenth century the practice of anatomical research was growing. Doctors were discovering more and more about the human body. But for doctors to pursue their researches, for students to learn and practise, they needed bodies – and there was a shortage of these.

Where better to find dead bodies than in graves? Grave robbing became a serious and lucrative profession. No questions were asked. The citizens of Edinburgh were shocked. Fear besieged the city as the prowlers scoured the graveyards, trying to dig up bodies to sell to the school of anatomy in Edinburgh. Graveyards became closely protected. Recently buried bodies were guarded by iron cages which were put over graves to avoid the depradations of the body snatchers.

As a result of these precautions bodies were in short supply and, when an old pensioner died accidentally in William Hare's lodging house, a fiendish plot was conceived. A certain doctor Robert Knox, who wanted to practise his dissection techniques, happily, and without question, purchased the body of the pensioner. A new business was created.

Unknown travellers were enticed into the lodging house. They were regaled with drink, then suffocated in such a manner that no marks of violence appeared on their bodies.

Aided by the bold Mrs Burke and Mrs Hare, the intrepid two murdered no less than fifteen persons for the sole purpose of selling their bodies to the equally unscrupulous Dr Knox.

Up the close and down the stair
But and Ben wi, Burke and Hare
Burke the butcher, Hare the thief
Knox's the boy that buys the beef.

When the authorities finally discovered the murders and tried to prosecute, their problem was one of evidence. They decided to prosecute Burke and cite Hare as a Crown witness. In accordance with a principle of Scots law, once Hare had been cited and given evidence as a Crown witness he could not be prosecuted at the instance of the Crown.

Janette Wilson did not relish the prospect of seeing Hare escape – as she would put it, 'scot-free'. Janette was the mother of daft Jamie and was a determined woman. Even though Jamie had been wandering the streets away from home she was determined to try to bring Mr Hare to justice. She tried to start a private prosecution. By the early nineteenth century the Lord Advocate was well and truly in charge of all prosecutions, if the courts consented. A full-scale legal hearing took place in Edinburgh and the court decided not to let her prosecute Hare privately because of the immunity he had been granted by the Crown. More than a century later judgments in the Hare case were to be quoted extensively in an effort to stop a private prosecution by Carol X.

The courts at that time had available to them, as had the courts in 1982, the volumes of Baron Hume whose writings played such an important part in the recording and development of Scots law. Writing in 1800 Hume stated quite clearly that His Majesty's advocates prosecute for the public interest in the name of His Majesty as guardian and administrator for all his people of the laws which secure 'their tranquillity and welfare'.

As the law of private prosecutions fell more and more into disuse it was assumed by some legal writers in the twentieth century that private prosecutions were a thing of the past. The last-recorded case of a private prosecution being successful was in 1909 when a well-known firm, J. & P. Coates Ltd, prosecuted a coal supplier for fraud. Since that time other applications to the court for private prosecutions were all unsuccessful.

Chartered accountant Charles McBain, in 1961, endeavoured to take proceedings against a bookseller who sold D. H. Lawrence's *Lady Chatterley's Lover*. Mr McBain alleged that the contents were 'lewd, impure, gross and obscene and contained passages devised, contrived and intended to corrupt morals especially those of young people'. The Lord Advocate had refused to prosecute and Mr McBain made a vain attempt to persuade the court to allow him to mount a private prosecution. It was held that he had not shown substantial personal interest which is 'necessary to ensure proceedings'.

Ten years later a Dr Trapp presented to the High Court a Bill for Criminal Letters in an effort to mount a private prosecution. He alleged that, in an inquiry into reasons for his dismissal as a headmaster, two witnesses had committed perjury. He asked for permission to prosecute. The Lord Advocate refused to prosecute and, again, the court refused the application.

Paddy Meehan was convicted of murder and sentenced to life imprisonment in 1969. He alleged that Crown witnesses had committed perjury at his trial and he presented, in 1974, a Bill for Criminal Letters seeking a private prosecution. Although Meehan was subsequently pardoned, the court in 1974 once more emphasized that a prosecution for such a crime as perjury should be left to the independent decision of the public prosecutor. The 'broad' consideration of the public interest and public policy must normally outweigh the private interest which an individual may seek, stated the court.

Throughout all these cases the courts emphasized their complete satisfaction in the independence of the prosecution system in Scotland; it was sufficient to serve the needs of the community, they said. An important factor in considering a petition for a private prosecution was the position of the Lord Advocate. Did he agree with the private prosecution? If not, why not? If he did agree, surely he could and should prosecute on behalf of the Crown. Therefore it could be argued that there was no need for a system of private prosecution.

The case of Carol X, however, was to open new considerations that had never been anticipated by any of the authorities over the previous 400 years.

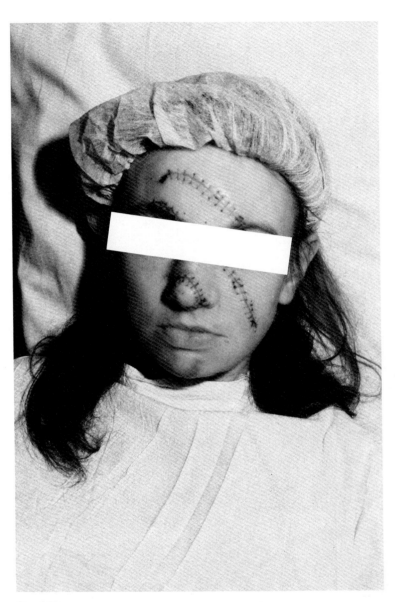

Carol X

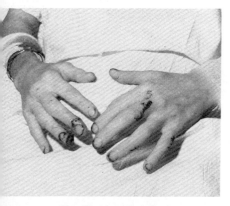
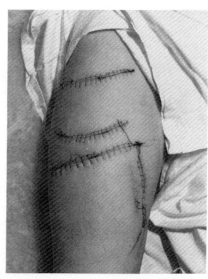

Carol's wounds after
stitching

The container in which Carol was held

Above left Nicholas Fairbairn QC, MP, the Solicitor General for Scotland

Above right Lord Mackay, the Lord Advocate

Left David Marshall, the first MP to raise the issue in the Commons

The Four-Day Debate

Lord Justice General Emslie,
Scotland's senior judge

Lord Cameron

Lord Avonside

George Penrose QC,
for the defence

The Trial

Lord Ross, presiding

The Prosecution

The Dean of Faculty,
Charles Kemp Davidson,
QC, leading

Kevin Drummond,
Advocate

Alastair Cameron, QC

The Defence

Donald Findlay,
Advocate, acting for
Joseph Sweeney

Donald Macaulay, QC,
acting for Gordon Sweeney

Hugh Morton, QC,
acting for John Thomson

Detectives involved in the case

Detective Sergeant
Adam Drummond

Detective Chief Inspector
Alex Cowie

The Accused

Joseph Sweeney

Gordon Sweeney

John Thomson

Prosecution witness
Stephen Cameron

Ross Harper and Arnot McWhinnie

14 The Wedding

As preparations for the private prosecution got under way Carol and Billy readily accepted Harper's advice that they move, temporarily, out of the East End to avoid contact with any of the three youths. In addition, they would be able to escape from the press. Accordingly, they moved from the East End to a rented flat in the West End which a member of Harper's staff had located for them. Gratefully, they spent the first week or two secluded in their hideaway. No one knew their address apart from their solicitors and very close friends.

Carol and Billy still met an *Express* journalist who had befriended them but who told them, somewhat ruefully, that he was unable to help them financially. The *Express* staff had direct orders from London that they were not to become financially involved in the case. There were other people in Britain, however, who wanted to help and who could help. Several sent anonymous donations to the Chief Constable and the Lord Provost of the city of Glasgow and these were passed on to Carol through her solicitor. An organization, Women against Violence, telephoned Harper, asking if they could assist with the legal expenses and offering to make a nationwide appeal. Harper demurred. At that time there were indications that the State might pay the expenses but, in any event, Harper did not want any pressure group to be associated with the case. He held that it would be wrong for Carol to be the subject of a nationwide charitable appeal.

The association, however, offered a small street collection in Liverpool to help Carol; all in all, about £250 was collected

from this source and other donations. Carol was overjoyed at
the generosity of citizens from many hundreds of miles away.
The wedding date had already been set for 11 February. The
extra money could not have come at a better time. The notice
of marriage was displayed on the public noticeboard in the
registry in Martha Street, Glasgow. The couple were terrified
that the newspapers would spot their names and another hunt
would begin. Their worries were idle and 11 February dawned
a beautiful, sunny winter's day. Billy took Carol, wearing an
ice-blue, two-piece outfit with a lace fringed top and a white-
brimmed hat, to the register office for the ceremony. Billy, in
a grey pinstripe suit with a carnation, held Carol's hand as
they repeated the vows before the registrar.

Now man and wife, they walked out into the winter sunshine
to accept congratulations from their friends and relatives. Two
of Billy's shipyard workmates were standing outside and the
three-year-old daughter of a friend ran towards them and
handed over a lucky silver horseshoe for Carol. It was a gesture
that meant more to Carol than to the ordinary bride, especially
with the prospect of court proceedings.

The wedding reception was in a hotel outside Dumbarton,
overlooking the Clyde. They were joined by ten friends and
relatives who toasted their health in champagne. Carol was
filled with happiness. Life had a new meaning for her and she
knew she could rely on Billy's support for what lay ahead. It
would be a testing time for the two of them but they were
determined to make it together.

15 Four-Day Debate

On the morning of 16 March 1982 at 10.30 a.m. precisely, Scotland's top judge, Lord Emslie, with two of his senior colleagues, made his way in single-file procession through the stone-floored corridors of Parliament House, Edinburgh.

From their chambers to their destination – the High Court where the law of Scotland is determined and which has been the stage for the enactment of many famous trials – the three judges, all in step, followed the black-robed macer who bore the official instrument of justice over his right shoulder.

The appearance of the judges, wearing cream silk robes slashed with red crosses, was heralded by a booming warning to spectators and lawyers alike to stand up: 'Cou . . . rt'.

Lord Emslie, the Lord Justice General, Lord Cameron in his eighties, the oldest judge in Scotland, and Lord Avonside, one of the law's most forceful personalities, had arrived to focus their brilliant legal minds on a plea by Carol, an ordinary Glasgow housewife, for justice to be done.

Below the tassled, purple-velvet-covered bench, where the judges bowed before sitting, was an array of Scotland's foremost legal experts. Appearing for Carol: the Dean of the Faculty, Mr Charles Kemp Davidson, QC, Mr Alastair Cameron, QC, Kevin Drummond, advocate, and Ross Harper and Graeme Warner, solicitors. For the three youths she was seeking to prosecute: Mr George Penrose, QC, Mr Donald Macaulay, QC, Mr Hugh Morton, QC, their three junior advocates, Alan Rodger, Hamish Stirling, Frank Lunney and the three defence solicitors, Desmond Finnieston, Frank McCormack and Brian Fitzpatrick.

The Lord Advocate, Lord Mackay, the senior Advocate Depute, Mr Ranald MacLean QC, and the Crown Agent, Mr William Chalmers, had also gathered for the hearing.

The scene was set for the historic proceedings to begin. The atmosphere was heavy with the expectancy of drama. Suddenly a telephone rang. It was the only concession to the twentieth century in a court, unchanged in appearance for 100 years or more.

Embarrassed, the clerk of the court, William Howard, picked it up and, after a few whispered words, put the receiver down. Someone had got a wrong number while operating the court's internal phone system and the phone in the court had not been switched off!

The moment of comic relief over, Lord Emslie asked the Dean to start the proceedings which were to last four long days, the result of which will be recorded in Scotland's law books for centuries to come.

Opening the hearing, the Dean outlined the history of the case; the trial of the three youths not taking place in June 1981 because the indictment was never called; the Lord Advocate intimating, by letter to the accused, that no further proceedings were to be taken, on 15 September; and his confirmation of this in Parliament.

Mr Davidson then told the three judges that, according to the Hansard report on the Lord Advocate's statement in the Lords, the critical factor behind the decision not to prosecute was the woman's health. He flourished a sheaf of papers as he announced that he had a medical report on her present condition, compiled by a lady consultant psychiatrist in January. 'The sum and substance of it is that, in the psychiatrist's opinion, the complainer is now fit to give evidence, but she would wish, if any trial take place, to re-examine her one week before.'

The Dean told Lord Emslie that Carol's evidence in any trial which might take place was a vital part of the case. Lord Avonside peered over his spectacles, 'You mean, I take it,' he growled, 'vital for the rape charge – but not for the assault?'

'Well,' replied the Dean, 'particularly for the rape.' He also informed the judge that one of the main witnesses upon whose evidence Carol was going to rely was someone he could only describe as a criminal associate. That was Stephen Cameron.

'It is her intention to grant him immunity from prosecution,' he added. 'So far as he is concerned, she is prepared to grant him an undertaking that the Bill will not be applied for in respect of him.

'It is for the court to decide whether to allow the private prosecution on the evidence known today and not on what has gone before. The court must make its decision on the broad grounds of justice,' he urged.

Dealing with an anticipated defence objection that it would be oppressive, after such a delay, to allow a private prosecution, the Dean claimed it would not be unjust. He turned to the question of whether they could get a fair trial after what Lord Emslie had described, by way of interjection, as 'saturation coverage' of the case by the media in general.

'The question still remains in any case as to whether the court, on the material available to it, considers it would be possible to obtain a fair trial subject to appropriate directions in law given by a trial judge,' said the Dean.

He reminded Lord Emslie of a recent judgment he himself had made from the bench. In it, the judge had come to the conclusion that the public's memory of recent newspaper articles and broadcasts and their detailed contents was 'notoriously short'.

The Dean said it was not even known yet when any private prosecution trial, if it was allowed, would take place. This got a swift response from Lord Emslie who commented, 'Does it really matter where or when it takes place in the light of this publicity? It is inconceivable that this trial will take place except in a further blaze of publicity. It is simply a factor which is to be borne in mind. I am not saying it is fatal, but it is a feature of this case which might make it more difficult.'

The Dean submitted that there was no material produced which could persuade the judges to say that the trial had been prejudiced to the extent that the Bill should not be passed. He conceded, 'If your Lordships were to pass the Bill there would have to be a sufficient lapse of time so that the publicity in January faded to such an extent that a jury carefully and properly directed could put it out of their minds.'

The Dean sat down and the moment everyone in legal, political and newspaper circles had been waiting for was at hand – the first public pronouncement on the case by the Lord Advocate since his statement in the Lords. Was he going to resist the idea of a private prosecution – or back it? There was no doubt in the mind of anyone at the hearing that, if Lord Mackay urged the judges not to grant a private prosecution, his political life would be in jeopardy.

He was invited to address the court by Lord Emslie. A small, stocky but purposeful figure, he got to his feet, a carefully prepared statement in his right hand, and began to read from it. Lord Mackay repeated his opening remarks twice to reinforce and emphasize the point he wished to put over.

'The Crown's position is and always has been, since this case was first considered by the Crown counsel, that, on the assumption that the applicant is available to give evidence at a trial, there is a sufficient case against the three persons in respect of whom Criminal Letters are sought, to justify a prosecution on the two charges against them proposed by the Bill.'

Nothing could be clearer than that. Lord Mackay then gave the official Crown version on the background to the controversy. It had been on the basis that there was sufficient evidence that the Crown raised the two indictments against the three youths. They had been called to plead at the pleading diet and had pled not guilty, although one of them entered a request for some form of separation trial.

'It has been said that neither of these indictments was called at the High Court. In respect of the first, in April–May, the applicant had moved to England and service of the citation was not effective for the trial in June, and the Crown was ready to proceed to trial intending to do so.

'At that time the applicant attended at the court voluntarily, having been contacted in England, and arrangements were made for her to be examined by a consultant psychiatrist on behalf of the Crown.'

Lord Mackay then handed the judges the confidential psychiatric report and quoted only one section of it, the section relating to Carol's fitness to give evidence for the prosecution.

The psychiatrist had written:

As to her fitness to give evidence she gave me two reasons why she dreaded a court appearance. Firstly, she does not want to relive again the experience she was subjected to, and secondly, that she did not want to see her assailants. There is no question that the effect on her behaviour of this traumatic experience which took place in 1980 has left a very deep psychological wound which so far hasn't healed.

I am of the opinion a court appearance at present would be detrimental to her health, and would be hazardous and may lead to pre-trial suicide attempts, but more disturbingly, even after the trial whatever the outcome would be.

The psychiatrist also suggested that, if the woman gave evidence, the court would have to be cleared, with a minimum of lawyers present. The report went on:

Cross-examination at this stage is only likely to produce a severe block in her communication which could lead to her retreating into silence.

It is difficult to foresee an improvement in her state over the next two to four months as her history reveals a general attitude to the court case which has not improved since November 1980.

One must never forget this woman has been severely and psychologically traumatized, and any further pressure on her will only cause more unhappiness, despair and isolation.

Lord Mackay told the judges that, when Crown counsel received this report, it was decided it would not be right to ask Carol to give evidence in court. Accordingly, the indictment was not called in June. He went on, 'In the light of this information it was considered that the prospect of sufficient improvement in her health was not enough to justify keeping the proceedings alive, and accordingly it was intimated to the three persons in question in September 1981 that no further proceedings would be taken.'

Lord Mackay also pointed out that two of the three youths were fourteen at the time of the alleged offence and the other was sixteen.

Lord Avonside, himself a former Lord Advocate, interrupted
Lord Mackay to ask why a letter had not been sent to the
woman informing her the proceedings had been dropped, when
letters had been sent to the accused.

'It is my understanding,' said Lord Mackay, 'that up till now
it has not been the practice to write to alleged victims, and I
regret it had not been done at the time.' Lord Avonside mildly
chided him and pointed out that, if the woman had known this
in September, she might have been able to start private prosecution proceedings much earlier.

Lord Mackay went on to reveal that the latest psychiatric
report on Carol, which said she was fit to give evidence,
stressed that the alleged rape happened at a particularly difficult period in her life. 'There is now a change in her circumstances,' he said, 'and there is now a good deal of support and
reassurance for her.'

By this stage in the proceedings the Lord Advocate had
admitted that, with Carol's testimony, there was enough evidence to justify putting the three youths on trial: the decision
not to go ahead had been based on humanitarian grounds,
both for Carol and the accused. He also admitted that he had
erred by not revealing to her the fact that the proceedings had
been abandoned. However, he had still not touched on the
question which was vital to the private prosecution application. Was he going to oppose Carol's bid? And was the action
she was taking proper?

Lord Mackay did agree that, having sent the youths letters
on 15 September, he had given up his right to prosecute on
behalf of the Crown. 'In that situation I consider that it is not
open to me to concur as Lord Advocate in this private prosecution. It is for Your Lordships to consider the situation – and
I agree with the Dean – to consider it at the present time in
the light of the information you have.'

It was Lord Avonside who came straight out and asked him
the crucial question. 'Are you opposing the Bill?' 'I am not,'
replied Lord Mackay.

Lord Avonside's next question was equally searching. 'If, as
Lord Advocate, you had thought the Bill incompetent, would
you have considered it your duty to oppose it?'

Lord Mackay's answer was equally as honest. 'Had I considered it to be incompetent I would have drawn it to your
attention. My view of the matter is that the Bill is competent.
This is a highly exceptional but competent way for a matter
of this kind to be brought to the attention of the court, so that
the court has an opportunity to review the situation, and so
that the court, if it thinks it appropriate in the circumstances,
can allow the case to go to trial. A private prosecution is the
only way I know of to achieve this.'

It was a major concession by the Crown and those on the
defence looked shaken by the official pronouncement.

But Lord Avonside still had the bit between his teeth. Why,
he asked, had the Crown not taken a second psychiatric
opinion about the woman at about the time it was decided to
send the 15 September letters to the youths? This had been
one of the major criticisms against the Crown in its handling
of the case. Lord Mackay answered the question. He admitted
that, at the time the letters were sent, the period covered in
the psychiatric report still had some time to run, but he drew
to the court's attention the problem of asking the woman to
relive the details of the alleged attack.

Lord Avonside put another controversial question to Lord
Mackay, one which MPs and newspaper leader-writers had
been pressing with vigour. 'Did the Crown ever consider going
ahead with the assault charge alone, even though the victim
could not give evidence?' Lord Mackay answered, 'This was
considered, but Crown counsel decided that the charges were
so closely bound together that it would be difficult to establish
one charge without the other.'

The first day of the great debate was over. Pundits in the
press benches awarded round one to Carol.

Over the next two days the three defence counsel were to
counter-attack. They had decided to split up the legal objections amongst each other. Mr Penrose would argue against the
Bill on the grounds that it was legally incompetent. Mr Macaulay had selected to fight on the grounds that the three
youths could never receive a fair trial because of the extensive
publicity. Mr Morton would urge the judges to veto the appli-

cation because such a move would be legally oppressive, vindictive and unfair.

Mr Penrose began on the Tuesday morning. His task was the most difficult of the three and demanded constant referral to legal textbooks. There were two aspects to Mr Penrose's submission. The first dealt with the historic and exclusive power vested in Scotland's Lord Advocate, the right to accuse and to raise indictments in his own name. Mr Penrose maintained that the exclusive power of accusation exercised by the Lord Advocate when he raised the first indictment against the three youths had ended such rights as Carol might have had in a private prosecution.

The second aspect of Mr Penrose's argument was based on the letters sent to the three youths on 15 September. When they had been told that no further proceedings were to be taken, the boys had automatically obtained a protection from prosecution, not only at the hands of the Lord Advocate upon whose authority the letters had been issued, but also, he argued, at the hands of any private prosecutor.

Mr Penrose quoted extensively from the Burke and Hare case. The Dean had used the saga of the notorious Edinburgh body snatchers in his argument that Carol was entitled to grant Stephen Cameron immunity if he gave evidence on her behalf.

Mr Penrose was to use the case to his own advantage. Hare, he submitted, had given evidence against Burke on only one murder charge. However, when the mother and sister of another victim, 'Daft Jamie', attempted to prosecute him, six judges, by a majority of four to two, dismissed their application.

Linking Burke and Hare to the present case, Mr Penrose submitted that, as a result, if the Lord Advocate raised an indictment and it failed for any reason, there could be no other trial, not even at the instance of a private individual.

Mr Penrose revealed to the three judges that he had researched the history of private prosecutions since the Burke and Hare case. 'In 153 years I can find not one case where private prosecution has been proposed after the public prosecutor has initiated proceedings.'

When Mr Penrose finished his demanding and precise legal submission Mr Macaulay entered the arena with what was probably the most powerful argument against a private prosecution.

The QC, who was on first-name terms with many of Scotland's leading journalists – as a struggling young advocate he had been a legal adviser on the *Daily Record* – was to attack the press relentlessly for the way it had publicized the case. To reinforce his argument, Mr Macaulay was armed with three large boxes containing every edition of every newspaper which had published details of the Glasgow rape case. The defence had also spent weeks gathering transcripts of television and radio material.

The *Daily Record*, the *Glasgow Evening Times*, the *Scottish Daily Express* and *Sunday Times* had files of their own. They were handed to the judges. Every story used by each of these four newspapers had been photographed on huge, glossy, tabloid-size prints and bound together. The *Daily Record*, Mr Macaulay was to claim, contained the most significantly prejudicial and offensive material.

Mr Macaulay opened his argument by telling the three judges that it was his opinion that, because of the publicity, the youths would be unable to have a fair and impartial trial anywhere in Britain. He said that, if an individual could get permission to prosecute privately, the post of Lord Advocate would become useless. He argued, 'There wouldn't be much point in having the post of all.' If complainers were going to be allowed to challenge every decision of the Crown, the courts would be opened to floods of Bills such as this and be overwhelmed by people, saying, 'I don't like the decision of the Crown Office.'

Lord Emslie interrupted, with a smile, to tell Mr Macaulay, 'They would get very short shrift if they tried that.'

Mr Macaulay then went on to deal with the widespread publicity. 'It would be impossible for these boys to get a fair trial,' he said. A statement coming from the solicitor, now acting for the woman, that any further publicity could be prejudicial, had come too late to affect the risk of prejudice.'

For the benefit of the three judges Mr Macaulay outlined the background of how the controversy had come to light.

'The case has been discussed in a welter of publicity with some information and some not so well-informed material,' continued Mr Macaulay. 'Some of the claims have been extravagant in the extreme, but there is nothing I would like to say at this point to criticize what the press did in bringing the fact of no further proceedings to light. It was legitimate investigative journalism.' The real effect of the publicity was that a wave of public sympathy had been created for the woman – and, with it, unfair animosity towards anyone who contributed to her distress.

'There must come a point where, no matter how well directed a jury is, it will be impossible to say with any certainty that the trial which would proceed in the light of this publicity would either be fair or impartial. No matter how hard the judge may try to impress on the jury that they should ignore what they had read elsewhere, it is almost impossible to envisage that any juror in Scotland could possibly put out of his mind the publicity which attended this case.

'Unless someone has been on a trip to the far side of the moon from January 13th till the month thereafter, anyone who has been in Scotland must know of this woman's case, and must know the inference carried in the press, and must know about the resignation of the law officer. The material has carried with it the implication that a mistake has been made. No reasonable defence could be presented on behalf of any of these three youths at any time.'

Mr Macaulay then started to read out the headlines and stories which he claimed were offensive. He continued, 'What has happened here is that there has been a public and uncontrolled review of this case, including the publishing of "crucial" evidence, photographs of the victim, her injuries and the locus, her own account in television and radio interviews, and more detailed accounts in the newspapers, her own personal reaction to events, and the effect these events have had on her life.

'Whatever the merits of this application on competency it would appear that there is no doubt at all, if the court allowed this Bill to proceed, then it would be doing an injustice to the very concept of justice itself.'

With these strong words Mr Macaulay adjourned his argument for the day and, when Wednesday morning came, he continued analysing newspaper and television accounts of the case. He referred the judges to the files on four of them: the *Daily Record*, the *Scottish Daily Express*, the *Glasgow Evening Times* and the *Sunday Times*.

He quoted extracts from various *Daily Record* articles and went on to deal in more detail with an article of 19 January which, he said, was the 'most significant piece of publicity in the whole case ... the disclosure that one of the three boys confessed his crimes to the police in a voluntary statement. The *Daily Record* actually published extracts from the boy's confession and from statements by the other two.' 'How can documents of that kind get into the hands of the press, right down to police notebooks being copied?' asked Lord Cameron, obviously taken aback at the details disclosed in the paper. 'I hope there's an investigation about that.'

Mr Macaulay was quick to spot that the judge might be on his side. 'It seems rather remarkable and extraordinary, to say the least, if any of the defence solicitors' precognitions could have got to the *Record* and put their clients in jeopardy. The source of the story must be someone on the other side of the fence. I don't know positively. It reflects that the reporter has been given access, perhaps to police notebooks.' Again Lord Cameron asked how this was possible. Mr Macaulay continued, 'That publication alone, the *Daily Record* on January 19th, by a newspaper carrying a circulation of threequarters of a million a day, would be sufficient for Your Lordship to hold the youths could not get a fair trial.

'Who is the true complainer?' continued Mr Macaulay. 'Who is really motivating it? Does the woman really want this Bill to be presented, or is there something more to it? Your Lordships will have to consider very carefully whether there is anything in the background to suggest that the woman's motivation is not a genuine one. Is there something more in the background to this case than the court has been advised of?' With this veiled allegation that the media were manipulating the woman, Mr Macaulay closed his argument. Fortunes had changed and now the press benches were forecasting that the case was swaying against the prosecution.

That Wednesday afternoon Mr Morton presented the last of the three defence objections to the legal move; this was the argument that the youths were victims of oppression.

One of these major arguments was founded on the new Criminal Justice (Scotland) Act, 1980, which limited the time-span between the service of an indictment and the trial to twelve months. If the judges agreed to a private prosecution and trial was delayed it would take place two years from the date of the alleged offence.

Mr Morton also criticized the suggestion that the State was going to give money from the public purse to finance Carol's private prosecution. The Secretary of State, he said, was giving sympathetic consideration to that, according to a reply to a Commons question.

'If the position is as I understand it to be, that the Crown is barred from public prosecution by their letter of 15 September, it would be grossly unfair for the State to get round that by the back door, paying someone else to take up the prosecution. It would be grossly oppressive for the Crown to continue to prosecute by financing the means of doing it,' he said.

The Lord Advocate, who was still in court, told the three judges that his position might have been impugned as a result of what Mr Morton had said. 'It was open to the construction that I was doing something unfair. My position is in accordance with the interests of justice. I am doing my best to serve the ends of justice as fairly as I can.'

Lord Emslie, too, told Mr Morton that he could see no suggestion of the Crown trying to prosecute by the back door. The QC felt compelled to make an apology. 'I am sorry if I, in any way, impugned the Lord Advocate's position,' he said.

Thursday, 19 March, and the last day of the hearing. It was the Dean's day. When he stood up that morning he pulled out an ace which looked as if it would win the hand.

Of course, he admitted, there was a notoriety about the case. 'But one of the most obvious concerns of the media in January was not the fact that the alleged assailants were going free but that they were not brought to trial at all.

'The difficulty in dealing with this matter sensibly is that we really have no means of telling what is the effect on the minds of jurors of pre-trial publicity.'

He referred the judges to the new Contempt of Court Act which banned any inquiry into the deliberations of juries, even for academic research. There appeared to be a cut-off in legitimate investigations into factors which might influence juries in reaching a verdict. The Dean continued, 'In this state of affairs I submit that the court is in a very difficult situation indeed. It has to put itself in the position of any ordinary lay person and it is very difficult indeed to do that. There is an element of surmise about the whole thing.'

Lord Emslie asked the Dean, 'Are you suggesting, because of the difficulty in predicting exactly what influences the minds of jurors, the proper course is to err in favour of allowing a trial to take place, see what the evidence looks like and consider in the light of that evidence whether a verdict of guilty can stand?' The Dean agreed that that was his suggestion – subject to the qualification that it was just one of the factors the judges would have to bear in mind.

The Dean then delivered his master stroke, a punch which sent all the defence legal objections reeling. 'The other consideration is – what are the consequences if there is not a trial at all? This is a matter of a quite critical importance. There is no way that I can think of, assuming the Bill is not passed, whereby this matter can be ventilated. In my submission a very important factor which has been recognized by courts in the past as being one of the fundamental principles of a civilized society is that, if crimes are committed, then they should be tried *not* by newspapers or anyone else, but by the *courts of this land*.

'This is an important factor more clear-cut than the question of whether a jury's mind might be affected by publicity. If it does come to a trial, the picture – if there is one – in the minds of potential jurors, assuming they had read the newspapers and seen the television broadcasts, will be a blur. Jurors do not have transcripts of broadcasts available to them nor do they stockpile past issues of newspapers.

'In recent years the courts have become more robustly confident in the ability of jurors to deal with matters of publicity. In this case anonymity was very carefully observed by the newspapers. The argument on pre-trial publicity rests on surmise. But against this there are certain very important considerations in the public interest, and of those I would suggest the most important is that there should be a trial through the courts of law as it would at least defuse this matter.'

Lord Emslie had listened thoughtfully to what the Dean had to say. He observed, 'One of the problems, if a jury was to hear this case, is that it would require courage and a sense of duty beyond that normally expected of a Scots jury without any preconceptions. In this case the crime achieved notoriety and, if a private prosecution does take place, it will be a unique event in this country and the jury will be aware of pressures which do not exist in an ordinary case.'

'Yes,' said the Dean. 'The whole system is on trial because the jury system is the foundation of a civilized country with a jury deciding on the evidence and nothing else. If that slips it might be suggested that the whole system of justice is a fraud. Society wants to see a fair trial.'

A few minutes later the four-day hearing was at an end. 'We will take time to consider this very unusual application,' said Lord Emslie.

Part Three

16 Well of Truth

Carol and her lawyer – the youths and theirs – had to wait twelve days for the result of the hearing.

Sometimes it is possible to gain an inkling into a judgment in advance, because a case is either so strong or so weak that pungent views are expressed from the bench. In this particular case there had been no such clues. Security was tight.

Only five people knew the truth that morning of 1 April 1982, as the press and public filed into court to await the decision – Lord Emslie, Lord Cameron, Lord Avonside (who was indisposed and could not attend), Lord Mayfield who would take his place on the bench to read out his colleague's opinion, and Mr William Howard, the clerk to the court.

The judges took their seats, Lord Emslie in the middle. The parties at the bar had changed. The Dean was on holiday in Washington, DC. Mr Alastair Cameron, QC, had to appear in another court and Ross Harper was in Florida on business. Junior counsel, Kevin Drummond, assisted by Harper's partner, Mr Graeme Warner, waited to hear the words of the judgment. Within a few moments they would learn whether all the effort had been in vain.

Carol was not in court. Neither were the three youths.

In accordance with normal practice, such judgments are always read out by each member of the court, copies to be handed out afterwards.

Lord Emslie was first. Sensing the air of expectation, he adjusted his spectacles, picked up the twenty-one-page draft and, in the clear, precise tones for which he was renowned both as counsel and judge, proceeded to read: 'This is a Bill for Criminal Letters by the alleged victim of the crime of rape, and of what appears to have been a gruesome and hideous assault in which she was grievously injured and disfigured by repeated slashing cuts of a razor.'

The court was hushed as the judge summarized the contents of Carol's application. As the pages fell away from his hand, a perfect stranger who had never heard of the case could have followed precisely what was happening. The perfect stranger, of course, would be reading this judgment at the time of the next private prosecution application, perhaps in seventy years', 100 years', even 150 years' time, and would be able to glean every pertinent fact and each, and every, reason for the decision arrived at by Lord Emslie in the Glasgow rape case, 1982.

'The history of the matter is as follows,' continued his Lordship. 'The Lord Advocate indicted the three respondents for trial . . . all three pled not guilty . . . the complainer presented herself . . . grave doubt was entertained as to her fitness . . . arrangements were made to have her examined by a distinguished psychiatrist. . . .

'In the light of that advice the very proper decision was that the indictment should be allowed to fall.'

Lord Emslie, therefore, had set his seal of approval on the original decision not to proceed with the case in the June sitting because of the unacceptable risk to Carol's health.

Lord Emslie continued by narrating the Crown's reasons for dropping the charges against the three youths on 15 September and pointed out that a public prosecution thereafter 'ceased to be competent'.

Having dealt with the history of the case, Lord Emslie continued, 'In presenting this Bill the complainer asserts that in the events which happened, she as a private individual has the right, with leave of this court, to prosecute the respondents to trial. She qualifies the necessary interest in respect that she is able to show that she has suffered injury of a substantial, particular, special and peculiarly personal nature beyond all others as a result of the alleged criminal acts of the respondents.

'The position is that the Lord Advocate, while finding himself disabled from granting his concurrence by reason of his decision in September 1981, has informed us that he does not oppose the passing of the Bill on the assumption that the court is satisfied on the material now before it that circumstances have changed materially since September 1981, i.e., that the complainer is now likely to be able to give evidence at a trial of the respondents without exposing herself to the risk of serious injury to her health.'

Lord Emslie said that, in his opinion, the sufficiency of evidence in the case appeared to depend essentially on Carol herself giving evidence, and also on Stephen Cameron, the eyewitness, who could be regarded as an associate in the crime, also giving evidence against the three accused. He added, 'We are informed that her condition has now so much improved that she appears to be capable of giving evidence in court. It is clear, therefore, that in this case, the necessary very special circumstances are present. They consist essentially of the marked change which has taken place in the complainer's health and, in the light of that change, the Lord Advocate's indication to us that he does not oppose the passing of the Bill. From what I have said so far, this is one of those very rare instances in which, unless the Bill is incompetent for reasons advanced by the respondents, or it is demonstrated that to require the respondents to stand trial now would be oppressive, this court would, in my opinion, be prepared to pass the Bill and order the issue of Criminal Letters.'

Carol had therefore cleared the first hurdle, but Lord Emslie had still to discuss the competency of the Bill and the effect of prejudice caused by newspaper publicity. The signs were hopeful. But again no one was certain. Perhaps the publicity argument produced by the defence would be sufficient to stop the case?

Lord Emslie then dealt with the three defence submissions, one by one. He complimented Mr George Penrose, QC, on his 'clarity and skill' but revealed he had no hesitation in rejecting his submission. He went on, 'The rights of a private prosecution in our system of criminal jurisprudence have grown up alongside those of the Lord Advocate and, indeed, historically

bulked larger in earlier times than those of the King's
Advocates. These rights still exist and there seem to be no
good reason in principle for saying that they should not be
available in any case in which the Lord Advocate has, for any
reason, declined to prosecute an offender to a conclusion.'

Lord Emslie also rejected Mr Penrose's submission that the
Lord Advocate's decision not to prosecute prohibited a private
prosecution. He concluded, 'On the whole issue of competency
of this Bill, therefore, I am not persuaded that there are any
good reasons in principle or authority, for holding that, in the
events which have happened, this Bill must be rejected as
incompetent. In so saying I am content to record that the Lord
Advocate, in addressing us, said that he was satisfied that the
Bill was competent and that, had he entertained any doubt
upon the question, he would have felt it his duty to so inform
this court.'

Lord Emslie then turned to the question of publicity, which
many of the pundits in court believed was the main barrier to
a private prosecution. Was it possible to have a fair trial? The
judge was forced to admit that the publicity argument put to
him by Mr Donald Macaulay, QC, was a 'formidable one' which
he had examined with more than usually anxious care.

He observed, 'It cannot be disputed that the massive publicity, and in particular the matters referred to first in the *Daily
Record* of 19th January 1982, have created a risk of injustice
in that the respondents might not receive a fair trial from an
uninstructed jury.

'The question for us is whether, in a few months' time, the
risk of prejudice as the result of the publicity, true or false,
the most damaging of which occurred before January 21st
1982, will still be so great that even careful direction from a
trial judge could not reasonably be expected to remove it.

'In this case this question is of the greatest difficulty and it
is only after considerable hesitation that I have been persuaded to answer it in the negative.

'In considering what the answer should be, I have not forgotten that, while public interest and securing fair trial of
accused persons is of the highest importance, so too is the
public interest in the fair administration of justice and the

detection and trial of alleged perpetrators of crime. Great weight must be given to this latter aspect of the public interest in this case, for the crimes alleged are of a particularly serious and horrible nature. In light of this consideration, and my assessment of the probable course which presentation of available evidence at a trial would follow, can I confidently affirm now that a fair and impartial trial of the three respondents cannot reasonably be secured?

'I have come to be of the opinion that I cannot so affirm. Trials in cases which have become notorious are not uncommon and that this case should be remembered as the notorious "Glasgow rape case" does not move me to think that fair and impartial trial of those accused by the complainer will be, on that account, impossible.

'As to the particular allegations made first in the *Daily Record* newspaper on January 19th, 1982, it must be borne in mind that public memory of the detailed content of the newspaper articles and of broadcasts is notoriously short. Having read all the relevant material for myself, I formed the distinct impression that the burden of its message is that the alleged perpetrators of the alleged crimes ought to have been put on trial, and that what will remain in the minds of potential jurors in a few months' time will be a recollection that the massive publicity between 14th and 21st January 1982 had been directed to the express public anxiety that this might not happen.

'I am prepared to accept that the particular references to alleged evidence in the *Daily Record* of January 19th 1982, are unlikely to be remembered in any detail by potential jurors and to have any material influence upon their ability to remain true to their oath and to accept faithfully and to apply the directions of the trial judge who will, no doubt, in this case, find it necessary to identify precisely for the jury the only evidential material upon which they are entitled to consider whether the guilt of any accused has been established beyond reasonable doubt.

'The risk of prejudice will undoubtedly be present inevitably in the course of many trials and our system essentially depends on the assumption that jurors will behave with propriety and exclude from their deliberation all considerations which have not been presented to them in evidence in court in the course of a trial. In this case I have concluded, although with some hesitation, that this necessary assumption can still be made.'

To the private prosecution team sitting only a few feet away the words flowed like sweet music. Lord Emslie read through another page which dismissed arguments by the third QC, Mr Hugh Morton, and then rounded off his judgment.

'I am of the opinion that we should, in this quite exceptional case, pass the Bill and order the issue of Criminal Letters. It is fortunate that this is a course which we will rarely be disposed to follow, for the great strength of our system of criminal law still resides in the role of the Lord Advocate, as the impartial and wholly independent prosecutor in the public interest.

'One final observation only follows to be made. It is obvious, I believe, that the press and the media must recognize that further publicity about this case in advance of the trial may add materially to the risk of prejudice which already exists. The situation is one of particular delicacy and it is to be hoped that, even in reporting this judgment, those who disseminate information to the public will exercise the greatest discretion.'

Scotland's top judge had allowed Carol the private prosecution. There was hardly one person in court who did not sense history in the making. But before they could be sure, the two other judges still had to speak.

Lord Cameron revealed he had read Lord Emslie's opinion and was in complete agreement with him. He added his own observations. In a sentence which summed up the problem of publicity, Lord Cameron observed, 'The well of truth can be poisoned beyond the possibility of its waters ever being purified.' At the end of the day, however, he thought publicity was not of so fundamental a character as to involve such a risk of an unfair trial which could not be overcome by proper directions from the presiding judge, 'whose directions I have no reason to think would be disobeyed or ignored by a jury fully aware of its heavy responsibilities and loyal to its oath'.

Lord Avonside, in his judgment, read out by Lord Mayfield,

also agreed that Carol should get her private prosecution. He said, 'One is faced with a delicate and difficult decision. On the one hand is the interest of the public that justice should be done and should be seen to be done and, on the other, quite properly, is the interest of the respondents in this case which I believe to be unique in the facts which surround it. In my opinion the interest of justice must be paramount.'

He continued, 'The date of the trial has yet to be fixed. It would seem, although this is only a tentative view, that it would probably be in May, some four months after the January publicity. Memory is short, and particularly so of what is written or said in the media. At worst, jurors, in my opinion, would have a vague memory that there had been some sort of publicity regarding the case before them. Details would be forgotten.'

Carol had got her private prosecution. A few seconds later Mr Drummond jumped to his feet and asked Lord Emslie to grant a warrant for the arrest of the three youths and their detention until the trial date. He told the court he had received information that the youths were planning to abscond. In these circumstances it would be impossible to serve the Criminal Letters on them and the whole purpose of Criminal Letters would be defeated by their flight.

Mr Donald Macaulay, QC, denied there was any evidence that the boys were about to leave the country. He said it would be incompetent for the High Court to issue a warrant and submitted that Carol, as the private prosecutor, in effect the fiscal, had to present a petition for the arrest of the boys to a sheriff. Lord Emslie agreed and the court was adjourned.

Seconds later Detective Inspector Philip Smythe, of the Eastern Division CID, who had been sitting in the back of the court, was phoning his boss, Detective Chief Inspector Alex Cowie, to tell him that the Bill had been passed. Within a few minutes two teams of detectives headed out to Barrowfield to arrest the three boys. By midday they were back in the Eastern Division's new headquarters in London Road, under lock and key. With the Bill in their hands, the private prosecutors instructed a team of sheriff officers to serve copies on the Chief Constable of Strathclyde, the Sheriff Principal of Glasgow and

the Governor of Barlinnie Prison. There was also a copy for
the Sheriff in Glasgow, in front of whom the three youths
would appear.

Mr Drummond dashed back to Glasgow and was present
when the three youths were charged. They were locked up in
the cells overnight, pending their appearance at Glasgow Sheriff Court the next afternoon. During their appearance, the
Sweeney brothers and Thomson were charged with exactly the
same offences as they had been accused of when they first
appeared in the same court in November 1980. Mr Drummond
failed to persuade the Sheriff that they should be kept in
custody and they were released on bail.

The three youths went back to Barrowfield knowing that, at
long last, justice was catching up with them. The date of the
trial was fixed for 24 May 1982.

17 Last-Minute Nerves

As the weeks passed and Carol and Billy stayed secluded in the West End, the first chinks began to appear in their marriage. Billy had not gone back to work so that he could look after his new bride but, living together twenty-four hours a day, seven days a week, was beginning to have its effect. They were simply getting on each other's nerves. They were missing the companionship of the East End and, as the weeks went by, Carol became edgier. She would fly into a temper at the slightest thing and rows came almost daily.

In an effort to get out and about they drifted back to their old haunts in the East End. There they were spotted by newspaper men. A reporter from an evening paper took Carol and Billy out for a meal in an hotel on the outskirts of Glasgow. Both drank too much and, when they got home, they had a fight. Carol wanted to go back to the East End but Billy wanted to stay in their hideaway flat in the West End. Carol stormed out and went to the East End, thinking all the time that Billy would relent and follow her. Billy was equally stubborn and stayed at the other flat, thinking that Carol would eventually make her way back there. Carol spent the night at their East End flat and, when Billy did not turn up, she spent further nights with friends and relatives. For ten days Billy, worried sick, did not see her. He trooped round all Carol's relatives, vainly trying to locate her. It was useless.

In the meantime arrangements were proceeding for the trial. The defence solicitors wished to interview Carol. Harper made an appointment for her to be questioned in his office. He had also arranged for her to be seen again by the psychiatrist before she gave evidence or, indeed, was called on to give evidence. But Carol had simply disappeared.

In desperation Billy contacted Arnot McWhinnie who toured round various addresses in Glasgow searching for Carol. They covered many miles, checking all Carol's friends and relatives. Eventually, through a contact, McWhinnie heard that Carol had been seen in a bar regularly at lunchtimes. Of all the bars in Glasgow it was the Mecca Bar – the same bar where the tragic story had started. On a Thursday afternoon the reporter went to the pub. The trial was due to start on the Monday. Carol was nowhere to be seen but one of the bar staff confirmed, 'Yes, she's in here every day. She came here at lunchtime yesterday but had so much to drink that eventually we were forced to send her home.'

McWhinnie asked the barmaid if she would ring him the minute Carol appeared and, true to her promise, the barmaid made contact. Leaving Billy in the car McWhinnie walked into the Mecca and there, sitting at the same table where she had sat on the night her ordeal began, was Carol with her Aunt Christine and some other friends. She was pale and trembling. 'Billy's outside waiting for you,' McWhinnie told her. 'Where have you been all these days?' 'I just wanted to get away from it all,' said Carol. 'I can't live with Billy any more, we're having too many rows and getting on each other's nerves all the time. I want a divorce.' McWhinnie was shocked and asked her if she still wished to go ahead with the private prosecution. 'Have no fears about that, I am definitely going ahead with that. But I just wanted a few days to think it all over.'

McWhinnie left the pub and ran over to his car where Billy was sitting. 'She's still a bit uptight,' he told him. 'Disappear just now, and I promise you things will work out.'

Putting all his trust in McWhinnie, Billy left and the reporter contacted Harper's office to arrange for one of the legal assistants to come down to the Mecca to collect Carol. When eventually she saw her lawyer, Carol wanted to start divorce proceedings against Billy. But a few days later Carol changed her mind and was reunited with her husband.

Harper was worried. He did not know whether it was the stress of the court appearance or of the marriage, or a combination of both, which was affecting Carol so badly. He arranged for Carol not only to see the original psychiatrist but also to see another psychiatrist. He had to be sure that the strain would not be intolerable. But Carol was insistent. Having come so far she was certainly not drawing back.

Arrangements were made for Billy and Carol to spend the weekend in Edinburgh. Harper's staff in Edinburgh promised to visit the couple and check that everything was all right. There were to be no more prolonged visits to Glasgow's East End public houses. Carol and Billy looked forward to a break in Edinburgh and, on the Monday morning, they were to be joined by one of Harper's staff, Mrs Mary Stewart, a secretary, who was under instructions to do everything possible to keep Carol calm for the moment when she would step into the witness box for the first time to face the accused.

Carol visited a hairdresser in Edinburgh over the weekend to help bolster her confidence. She was dressed in a new, dark-blue wool skirt and red knitted jersey. An Australian tourist staying in the hotel over the weekend struck up a conversation with Carol. Carol told her who she was, and was amazed to hear that the Australian tourist had, herself, read about the case in her own country. Before Carol left for court, the woman pinned a little brooch to her chest for good luck.

When Carol was collected and driven to the court she felt excited, but when taken to a private room within the court she could not hide her nervousness. Her anxious solicitor asked her, for the last time, 'Are you able to go on with it?' Carol looked up, controlled her trembling hands, concealed her tears and muttered firmly, 'I am giving evidence.'

18 The Trial Begins

Monday, 24 May, 11.30 a.m. and in Court No. 9 two rows of press benches were filled to capacity. The public benches were swollen with potential jurors drawn from the Edinburgh area, interested onlookers hoping to sit through the case and a sprinkling of lawyers and law students anxious to see legal history in the making.

The centre of attraction, however, was focused on the dock and the three youths who sat there. They had been ushered into court by a police officer and told to sit in the order in which their names appeared on the indictment. The three were flanked by two police officers wearing ceremonial white gloves and holding heavy wooden batons across their knees. Everyone in court craned their necks to capture a glimpse of the trio.

The first was Joe Sweeney, a medium-built slim boy with a sallow complexion, who sat nervously picking at his lips with his fingers. His brother, Gordon, the smallest of the three, was next to him, brown eyes wide open in awe as he searched round, hoping to recognize a familiar face. John Thomson was last, dark-haired and sullen. The three boys did not speak. They sat there with their own thoughts, rarely even looking at each other. Gone was the jaunty bravado of the typical Glasgow East End teenager. Instead, the onlookers saw three scared boys, overawed by the oak-panelled court-room and the impressive array of gowned and bewigged counsel standing before them. Gone, too, was the battle-dress of the East End – denims and bomber jackets. The Sweeney brothers and Thomson wore suits, collars and ties. They looked decidedly out of place and uncomfortable, in the type of clothes which teenagers from any working-class background in Britain wear only at christenings, weddings or funerals. The suits were ill-fitting and old-fashioned with narrow lapels. Were they borrowed or hired? One wag in the press benches, immediately behind the three, jokingly speculated about the name of the suit-hire firm they had visited. The boys also wore their hair neat and short. Perhaps they had been advised to dress smartly and invest in a hair-cut for the occasion?

QCs, advocates and lawyers for both the private prosecution and the defence were making last-minute preparations before the judge entered the court. The Dean of the Faculty, Mr Charles Kemp Davidson, QC, a striking, sombre and steely-eyed figure, sat erect in his chair, thumbing through the thick file of witnesses' statements. On his right, Mr Alastair Cameron, QC, a Crown prosecutor for many years before he crossed over to the other side, neatly arranged a pile of law books and paused now and again to have a muted conversation with the Dean. Mr Kevin Drummond, advocate, the youngest in the prosecution team, sat on the Dean's left. He leaned back on his chair to stretch his legs full out under the table, eager for the trial to begin. From time to time a smile would flicker across his face, particularly when he glanced over at the ranks of the opposition across the table. As a talented defence advocate that was where he normally sat. Behind him were Ross Harper and his Edinburgh partner, Graeme Warner, both bearded, both wearing pinstriped business suits, and both sorting out the prosecution files and productions which the jury would shortly see. Now and again Harper left the court for a few seconds to make arrangements with the court officers to have witnesses at hand.

Unlike counsel, the two private prosecution solicitors and their opposite numbers on the defence would be unable to address the court. It has always been forbidden in the High Court for solicitors to do anything else but sit on the sidelines to brief their counsel and take notes.

On the other side of the huge oak table covered with law books, briefs and notebooks, sat the defence team: Mr Donald Findlay, Joseph Sweeney's counsel, an up-and-coming young

advocate, sporting bushy Edwardian mutton-chop sideburns;
Mr Donald Macaulay, QC and Mr Hugh Morton, QC representing Gordon Sweeney and John Thomson. These two QCs,
both from ordinary backgrounds, had risen through the ranks
to become eagerly sought counsel. Mr Macaulay, from Hebri-
dean stock, and Mr Morton, six-foot plus with an impish face,
had built their reputations on skilful and, at times, uncom-
promising styles of advocacy and cross-examination.

Any moment now the judge, Lord Ross, would come into
court. Last-minute conversations were held between counsel,
one to the other, and solicitors with their clients. Suddenly the
room echoed with a booming 'Cou ... rt'. It was the macer
announcing the arrival of Lord Ross, walking slowly in step
behind him, his hands behind his back.

Everybody stood to attention, one of the court policemen
motioning the three youths and the spectators on the public
benches to get to their feet. Lord Ross, a former Dean of the
Faculty of Advocates until he became a judge, bowed. Counsel
and lawyers bowed back. As he took his seat the official mace
was placed on the wall behind him.

It was shortly after 11.30 a.m. Normally, any High Court
sits on its first day at 10.30 a.m. No one in the room knew,
save for counsel, the lawyers and the three accused, that for
almost an hour there had been dramatic behind-the-scenes
bargaining. Plea bargaining, as it is known in America, is not
practised in Scottish courts. However, it is not unknown for
counsel and solicitors on opposing sides to discuss hypothetical
bargains with a view to taking their clients' instructions.
Whatever bargains were being contemplated, whatever pleas
were being offered or suggested, the meeting came to nothing.
The trial was to proceed.

The clerk of court, Ian Smith, stood up and, in a clipped
voice, announced, 'Call the diet of Criminal Letters on behalf
of Mrs Carol X against Joseph Sweeney, Gordon Sweeney and
John Thomson.' The three youths were standing in the dock.
'Are you Joseph Sweeney?' asked the clerk. Sweeney nodded.
The same procedure followed with the two others. Mr Findlay
rose from his seat slowly to address the judge. He argued that

the trial should not be allowed to go ahead because of the publicity and notoriety attached to the case.

Two weeks earlier, Lord Ross had faced similar pleas from counsel representing the other accused at a special hearing at the High Court in Edinburgh. Mr Findlay's argument was pointless because Lord Ross had already ruled then that the trial should go ahead. He told counsel politely, 'I have already listened to two pleas to the fact that, because of the publicity which took place some time ago about this case, there was a grave risk of prejudice, and therefore the trial should not take place. As I indicated then, it should be possible for the trial to be conducted fairly by proper and careful direction to the jury.'

The court now had to hear how the three boys were to plead. The clerk motioned them to stand up. 'Joseph Sweeney, how do you plead?' he asked. Mr Findlay announced that his client was pleading not guilty and that a special defence intimating that he was blaming John Thomson for the razor charge had already been lodged in court. Mr Macaulay revealed that Gordon Sweeney, also, was pleading not guilty and that he had a special defence, blaming his brother and John Thomson. Tendering a not-guilty plea on behalf of Thomson, Mr Morton said that his client would be blaming Joseph Sweeney.

It was the first drama of the day. Joseph Sweeney was being blamed by the other two, including his own brother, for the most serious charge, that of slashing Carol. In turn, Sweeney was saying that it wasn't him who was responsible but John Thomson.

The clerk then began to select the jury, picking their names at random from slips of paper jumbled up in a large glass goblet. There were defence objections to one man and one woman who were both told by the clerk that they need not take their places on the jury. At the end of the ballot eight women and seven men were in the two rows of jury seats ready to 'well and truly try the accused and give a true verdict according to the evidence'.

These fifteen people were now poised to undertake one of the most difficult tasks ever faced by a Scots jury in view of the coverage of the case by the media. As well as the three accused being on trial, the jury and the whole jury system were on trial too. They were ordinary people from different walks of life, probably with no previous experience of sitting in the High Court; they must have felt the pressures of the weighty task that lay before them.

The others who had been called as potential jurors were thanked by Lord Ross. He turned to the fifteen selected to give them a brief outline of how the trial would be conducted. He explained that, unlike English law, there would be no opening addresses by counsel. The parties would launch straight into the evidence. Lord Ross introduced the prosecution and defence counsel to the jury and pointed out the three accused sitting in the dock.

At this point Lord Ross gave the jury vital directions as suggested by Lords Emslie, Cameron and Avonside when they allowed the trial to go ahead in March.

'You must arrive at your verdict solely on the basis of the evidence led before you in this trial and also in the light of the directions in law which I shall give you,' he told them. 'You must approach the evidence free from all preconceptions and prejudices, excluding from your deliberations all considerations not presented to you in this trial.'

Lord Ross went on, 'You will see from the charge, it is alleged that the accused raped this woman and assaulted her with a razor. Allegations of this character sometimes provoke in the minds of listeners a strong emotional reaction. You may feel disgusted or appalled at the description of what is alleged to have occurred. But you must not permit any feelings of disgust or revulsion to weigh in any way with your consideration of the evidence and the verdict you arrive at. You must not allow your judgment to be biased in any way by feelings of disgust, horror or revulsion or anything else, as the evidence unfolds.'

His warning given, the judge then allowed the jury ten minutes to settle into the jury room. When they returned to court, witness number one took the stand. He was David Thomson, a thirty-eight-year-old Strathclyde Police civilian Scenes of Crime officer.

Quietly and unassumingly the trial started. Mr Thomson told the court how he went to the container in the scrap-yard at Davaar Street where Carol was alleged to have been attacked. He took a series of colour photographs. Mr Thomson told the Dean that the pictures showed general views of the yard and the interior and exterior of the cabin. The jury saw copies. On some of them areas of blood-staining, locks of blood-stained dark hair and articles of clothing, all said to have come from Carol, were quite clearly shown.

Mr Thomson also told the jury how, with the aid of a dusting brush, he found a fingerprint on a disused gas fire just outside the cabin door. He lifted the print off with a piece of tape so that it could be preserved for experts to examine. The photographer's evidence was formal, his cross-examination by the defence designed only to clear up a few minor points.

Next in the witness box was fellow Scenes of Crime officer, Robert McLaren, aged thirty-three, who told how he took colour photographs of blood-staining at the entrance to Carol's flat. Then came Constable Ian Hogg of Strathclyde Police Identification Bureau who went to the Royal Infirmary to take photographs of Carol.

These photographs, too, were handed to the jury. One woman visibly paled and shook her head as she stared at the terrible injuries which the photographs revealed – criss-cross wounds across Carol's face and thighs. With stitches all over her face Carol looked grotesque.

The formal scene-setting evidence was over in a matter of ten minutes. Quietly, in a hushed voice, without any drama, the Dean announced, 'My next witness, my Lord, is witness number four, the complainer in this case. I call Mrs Carol X.'

19 Carol's Evidence

No matter how hard she tried, Carol had found it almost impossible to keep the trial out of her mind. The hour's delay had made matters worse. With tension mounting up, she suffered an attack of nerves, turning chalk-white, trembling and feeling a sickly emptiness in the pit of her stomach. It was a moment of extreme worry for Harper and the private prosecution team. Was she going to be fit to give evidence? Would the trial have to be abandoned again?

Carol was taken by Mrs Stewart to the ladies room. Somehow she managed to summon up reserves of strength and determination and, only minutes before she was due to appear in court, Harper asked her if she still wanted to go through with it. Carol nodded.

Meanwhile, inside the court, members of the public were asked to leave. The victims of rape are always allowed to give their evidence in private and Carol was no exception. The press were allowed to stay, however, provided that they exercised discretion in reporting and did nothing to reveal Carol's identity.

The moment had arrived. A policeman held the door open. Carol took a last look at Billy and walked in, slowly but deliberately, passing within a few feet of the accused youths as she made her way to the witness box. The jury saw a young woman, small and pathetically thin, weighing less than seven stone and wearing a pair of spectacles in an effort to disguise the scars on her face and the tip of her nose. Carol raised her right hand, tentatively, to take the oath. She was a tiny figure, only four feet ten and a half inches tall.

A woman on the jury stared at the colour photographs which showed Carol's injuries after the attack. She then looked intently at Carol, standing only a few yards away, obviously wondering if this could be the same person.

Carol looked round the court. She saw the judge in his cream silk robes, slashed with crimson crosses, sitting to her right. To put her at ease, Lord Ross asked Carol if she would like to sit down whilst giving evidence. Carol bravely declined. A voice came from across the court and she looked over. It was the Dean. Carol recognized him from photographs in the press. Up until that point she had never met him. 'Are you Carol X?' he asked. Carol nodded and quietly answered a few preliminary questions. What age was she? Where had she been staying prior to the incident? They put her at ease. Carol told the Dean she had been staying with Billy for nine to ten months before the attack and had subsequently married him. She had previously been married for six years. 'He divorced me,' she admitted frankly. The two children by her former marriage were now staying with her ex-husband's mother in another part of Glasgow and a third child, a boy aged twelve, was with her parents.

The Dean then asked her to describe what she had been doing earlier in the day before she was attacked. She told of her shopping trip to the centre of Glasgow to buy clothes for herself and Billy's son. She also described the afternoon drinking session with her friend, Babs; the row with Billy which blew up because his tea was not ready; and how she had walked out on him to end up in the Mecca Bar at Glasgow Cross with Babs. The Dean asked Carol how much drink she had taken that day. She told him that, in the afternoon, she had sipped one and a half cans of Carlsberg Special Brew lager and two glasses of Eldorado wine diluted with lemonade. In the evening she had taken two vodkas and lemonade and part of a can of Carlsberg as she sat in the Mecca Bar.

What had she been wearing that night? The Dean asked the macer to hand items of clothing, now official private prosecution productions, to Carol to identify them. She recognized the pink, green and white sleeveless top she had been wearing. She had only bought it that day. It was now covered in dark dried blood. Carol also identified her jeans, checked jacket, bra, pants and tights, all, like the top, heavily blood-stained. She was also shown a pair of red sandals. These had belonged to her too. She had been wearing them that night. The Dean asked Carol to examine the shoes. They had sustained significant damage. The rubber heels had been almost scuffed off.

The Dean asked if the shoes had been new. Carol told him they had been given to her by a girlfriend who found them uncomfortable to wear. When they were passed down they were brand new and not in their present damaged condition.

Mr Davidson took Carol back in time to the Mecca Bar and her walk home. Why did she leave the pub? 'I left because I felt remorse of conscience,' Carol told him. 'I wanted to get back to Billy again. I asked someone if I could borrow my bus fare and she gave me 15p, but no buses came and I just walked.' During the forty–forty-five-minute walk, Carol said she met no one until she neared home. 'Who did you meet?' asked the Dean. 'Two young boys. They asked me if I had a light. It was just 300 yards from my home. One of them said, "Excuse me, could you give me a light?".'

'Did you know either of them?' 'No,' said Carol. 'What happened next?' asked the Dean. Carol told how she opened her bag to get a lighter. 'I was struck from behind,' she said. 'What was the next thing you remember?' probed the Dean. 'The next thing I remember was coming to on my back and something shiny over me. I remember saying something about "Don't use that." A boy said back, "You're getting it you cow, or bitch, or something like that".'

Step by step the Dean led Carol through the crucial part of her evidence. 'Do you remember anything else?' he asked. 'Yes, I remember being dragged. I remember being dragged by the arm. But I can't remember if it was one or two. I just remember being dragged. When I wakened up it was pitch-black. Then I remember running. I ran out to where I could see light. It was London Road. I went to my home. I couldn't get an answer at the door.'

As the horror of the night flooded back to her, Carol began

to tremble and sob in the witness box. She couldn't get her words out. 'Take your time,' Lord Ross suggested. Carol reached up to the judge's bench for a decanter of water and a glass. The shorthand writer poured her a drink and passed it down to her. She nodded, took a few sips and regained her composure. The Dean had been standing across the court-room as Carol had pulled herself together. He was forced to go over her evidence again, this time asking her for more and more details.

'In the place where you were lying,' he asked, 'just how much could you see?' Carol told him she could see nothing much at all. 'Could you make out the person who spoke to you?' Carol could not. 'I could just see his outline,' she explained. 'What did you think the person had meant when he told you, "You're getting it"?' Carol paused and replied, 'He had something shiny in his hands. I remember saying to him, "You don't have to use that." I thought it was a blade, but I just saw it shine. He was bending over me. His legs were on both sides of my body.'

The Dean continued, 'Had you any idea what had happened to you? Were you aware whether you were dressed or not, or to what extent you were dressed? Were you aware of anyone else in the vicinity?'

It was obvious to the jury that Carol's recollection of the events that night was vague, in places non-existent. She answered each of the Dean's questions with a faint 'No' and shake of the head. All she could remember was running towards the lights of London Road – street lights. She ran home. 'But I couldn't knock the door. I tried to bang it with the side of my hand. It was my right hand. My fingers were all cut.' 'Were you aware of that injury happening to you?' Mr Davidson asked. 'No,' replied Carol.

When she could get no reply at her front door she ran to the home of a friend, Mrs Kate Dobbin, who lived in nearby London Road. Carol continued, 'Kate opened the door and said "Oh my God." She got her son out of bed and told him to get the police and an ambulance. It was while I was waiting for the ambulance to come that I realized that I was naked from the waist down and had no shoes on. I was all cut.'

On the Saturday morning in hospital Carol recalled having a drip in her arm. 'I was feeling very, very groggy,' she said. Another thing she remembered was the police coming to see her that same day.

Mr Davidson instructed the macer to hand Carol the photographs of her injuries. As she looked through them, Carol started to shake violently, her hands barely able to hold the book. She was on the verge of collapse. It was obvious that the Dean found it distasteful to put this woman through a further ordeal by asking her what injuries she had sustained, but he had to.

Carol managed to compose herself again. She looked through the photographs and described the cuts on her fingers, hands, both her thighs and in her back passage. There had also been a bruise on the back of her head which, she claimed, had probably been caused by the blow from behind. Her hair had been shaved to expose it.

Carol's evidence came to a stop, much to her relief. It had seemed as if only minutes had elapsed since the start of her evidence but the court clock showed that an hour had flown. Lord Ross said it was time to adjourn for lunch, an extremely apt time as far as Carol was concerned. She was gently ushered out of the witness box by the macer.

Mary Stewart took her to a restaurant a few hundred yards from the court in Edinburgh's famous Royal Mile. But Carol could not eat. All she could do was nervously sip a cup of coffee. She could not see her husband and had been warned not to speak to anybody connected with the case. As she was drinking her coffee, some reporters and photographers from the press arrived at the restaurant looking for a meal. When they saw Carol they went out again. None of them dared risk being in contempt of court by speaking to her before her evidence had been completed.

Harper walked over to the restaurant for a few minutes to see how Carol was getting on. She assured him she was still fit and confident. She would survive the remainder of that afternoon.

When the jury returned after lunch, Carol was already standing in the witness box. She was reminded by Lord Ross that she was still on oath. The Dean continued, 'How did you know you had been raped?' Carol told him she only *thought* that she had been raped because, when she regained consciousness in the cabin, she discovered her legs had been lying open.

To establish the crime of rape it is vital to prove that intercourse took place forcibly and without the consent of the victim. It is not a crime of rape to have intercourse with an unconscious woman. But Carol could not remember being raped. She only *thought* she had been raped. She could remember very little of what happened that night apart from her encounter with the two boys in the road.

'Did you agree to anything after first meeting the two boys?' asked the Dean. It was a vital question. Carol replied with an emphatic 'No' and she was even more emphatic when she told him she certainly did not agree to let them have sexual intercourse with her.

Mr Davidson then turned to another chapter of events. He asked Carol to recount how she had been taken by the police to view an identification parade on 4 November after being released from hospital. 'I was feeling very tired,' she told him. 'And I was taken in by a policewoman. She had to hold me up when I went in.' The Dean asked her if she had picked anyone out. Carol agreed she had picked out five youths from the parade, but admitted, 'I was told to pick out anyone I knew from the area, anyone whose faces I had seen. I knew some of the boys from actually seeing them hanging around in the area.'

The Dean took that line no further. It was obviously not going to bear fruit. He went on to ask Carol if she could remember anything about either of the two boys who picked her up in London Road. Carol shook her head. She admitted she could not. 'Were they long, short, dark or fair?' The Dean was trying to jog her memory. Carol concentrated hard. She thought one of the boys was fair-haired and short.

The Dean asked her to look around the court. 'Do you see anyone you met that night after leaving the Mecca Bar?' The Sweeney brothers and Thomson were feet away, obviously the accused because a police officer sat on either side of them. Carol looked round, pausing briefly to glance at the three boys.

They had *dark* hair. Her eyes then started to search round the press and public benches. 'Do you recognize anyone?' the Dean repeated. Carol shook her head.

The Dean's examination was drawing to a close. Carol had not been a star witness but the private prosecution had been aware of that possibility. While she might not be able to remember everything in detail, there was more important evidence to come which could back up her story.

The Dean finally asked if Carol remembered presenting herself at the High Court in Glasgow in June the previous year. Carol remembered. She told the Dean that she had heard the case had subsequently been put off although she was never told the reason why.

In January, just four months before the present trial, she had read in the *Daily Record* that the youths were not being prosecuted. Later she read that the Lord Advocate would not stand in the way of a private prosecution. As a result, she contacted her present solicitor.

'Is that the reason you are in court today?' asked the Dean. Carol nodded. Her evidence on behalf of the private prosecution was over.

The Dean could have made his case much more emotive, with a few well-chosen dramatic questions and statements to catch the jury's attention. But he had decided before the trial began not to play it that way. The prosecution was not the forum for a big theatrical show trial. The case was too important for that. It demanded a cool, analytical review, without the jury being whipped into an outraged fervour which would only result in their emotions taking over from their common sense. The Dean agreed with Lord Ross's warning to the jury that they had to decide the case on facts and facts alone, and he was not going to sway them with theatrics.

For a moment Carol thought she had finished. The Dean thanked her and sat down. Carol looked as if she was ready to step out of the witness box but a few seconds later she found herself facing a relentless stream of questions from Mr Findlay, Joseph Sweeney's advocate.

'The only thing you were aware of was being struck in the

middle of the back of your head after you were approached by two boys?' he asked. Carol nodded.

'Between being hit on your head and waking up you could remember nothing and can give no details of what happened to you?' Again Carol answered with a simple 'Yes.' Continued Mr Findlay, 'If anyone was to try to give evidence about what may have happened to you in between being hit and waking up in the darkness, then these are details of which you have no recollection at all?' Carol again agreed, 'No recollection at all.'

As Mr Findlay questioned her he stood near the jury to encourage Carol to speak up across the court-room so everyone could hear what she had to say. He went on, 'Someone was standing over you with one foot on either side of your body. But it was just an impression. Apart from hearing words, the only physical recollection you have was seeing this shiny object.' Again Carol agreed with the young advocate but she was adamant that she had said the words, 'You don't need to use that,' when she saw what she took to be a blade.

'Might it be that you sustained the injuries you sustained, injuries of the cutting variety, *before* you were actually aware of seeing that shiny object? Is that possible?' Carol paused for a second, looking perplexed. 'I am not sure,' she admitted.

Mr Findlay was paving the way for Joseph Sweeney's defence that it was not he who slashed Carol but John Thomson. 'Do you remember hearing someone say, "I'm getting the fuck out of here," as you were lying on your back?' Carol again appeared to be in deep thought. Her head nodded once or twice, almost imperceptibly. 'Yes,' she admitted. 'I could have heard that.'

'Why did you think you were raped?' Mr Findlay asked her, his voice becoming louder and more insistent. 'Because my legs were lying open and because my hands were cut and I was all covered in blood.'

Mr Findlay then turned to Carol's drinking habits. How much had she taken that day? Had it affected her? Had her drinking caused the row between herself and her husband? Carol was forced to admit that the vodkas, Carlsbergs and wine she had consumed had affected her. It had also been the cause of the row although her husband was also angry because his tea was not ready. She also agreed that, as she left the Mecca Bar that night, she did feel under the influence of drink.

Carol insisted, however, that, as she walked home, she started to regain her senses. Mr Findlay's cross-examination was not particularly brutal. He had, however, managed to establish that Carol was drunk. That fact might have a bearing on the case to test whether she went voluntarily to the cabin, or against her will, and whether or not she could accurately remember what happened.

Gordon Sweeney's defence counsel, Mr Macaulay, however, was much more direct and ruthless in his cross-examination.

'One boy approached you, put his arm round you and took you into the yard,' he suggested. Carol stared at him and firmly denied the QC's allegation. 'If there is evidence to that effect, you completely disagree with it?' he queried. Carol raised her voice for the first time in the proceedings. 'I completely disagree,' she told him.

Mr Macaulay was not to be shaken by the forcefulness of Carol's denial. 'If there is evidence in this case to, first of all, suggest that you went to the hut with one young person and your clothes were taken off and you had intercourse with him and thereafter another young person had intercourse with you, without you showing any signs of resistance, are you in a position to say that this might have happened or didn't happen?'

Carol looked vehemently at her accuser and, in a defiant and clear voice, told him, 'That did *not* happen.'

Mr Macaulay was too skilful a cross-examiner to be put off. 'But you were unconscious and therefore you could not have resisted?' Carol admitted she had been knocked out.

For the second time Mr Macaulay put to her his allegations that she had sex willingly. For the second time Carol firmly denied it.

Mr Macaulay went on to suggest that what happened was this: one of the boys had approached her in London Road to put his arm round her. He then led her across the road saying, 'We'll go over there,' pointing in the direction of the scrap-yard in Davaar Street. London Road at that time of night was a busy road and he stopped, momentarily, in the middle to allow traffic to pass before taking her across. She had then gone willingly into the cabin to have sex, first of all with the boy who escorted her and then with the other boy who followed.

'That is a very different picture to the one you earlier alleged, being hit on the head from behind and being dragged into the cabin,' said Mr Macaulay. Carol was still adamant that her story was the true one.

Mr Macaulay continued, 'The only reason this case came to the public eye was the horrible injuries some person inflicted on you?' – 'Yes.'

'You had no idea you were raped?' – 'No.'

'It was the police who suggested to you that you had been raped?' – 'Yes.'

'And this is why this case has been given the notoriety of being "*the rape case*"?' – 'Yes.'

'You think that you must have been raped but you don't know whether you were?' – 'Yes.'

'But if there was some sexual activity between you and any young man, *you* don't know what form it took?' – 'No.'

With that last telling question and answer, Mr Macaulay sat down, leaving Carol to be questioned by Mr Morton, John Thomson's QC. He perhaps had decided that Mr Macaulay's cross-examination was sufficient to sow the seeds of doubt; consequently, he was not so hard with her. He dwelled for some time on the amount Carol had drunk. Had she consumed much more than she was prepared to admit? Had she gone voluntarily with the boys to the cabin for sex? Both these questions led to instant denials from Carol.

'Your lack of memory might have something to do with the alcohol?' suggested Mr Morton. 'No,' replied Carol.

Mr Morton did not take long and, when he sat down, it remained for the Dean to re-examine his chief witness on some of the points raised by the defence. Carol had then finished.

The day she had dreaded was over, at long last. She could have stayed in court to watch the rest of the case, but did not. Her lawyer advised her against it. Carol left the court with Mrs Stewart for a cup of coffee and was joined by her husband. Since Billy was a witness, he and Carol were advised not to discuss the case. Carol was told that, as she might be required for possible identification purposes, she would have to remain in the court precincts. She was to spend the rest of her time in the dingy, unattractive basement canteen which caters for the needs of witnesses in Scotland's High Court.

The last witness of the day was Police Casualty Surgeon, Dr Colin McKelvie, who took samples of blood and head and pubic hair from Carol and her alleged attackers. Dr McKelvie also revealed that he had examined the youths for signs of injury. He found nothing of significance on Gordon Sweeney, Thomson or Stephen Cameron, but he told the Dean that Joe Sweeney had bruises on both shoulders and the centre of his chest. He also had a weal on his lower back, two and a half to three inches long. Its edges were straight and parallel.

When cross-examined by Mr Findlay, Dr McKelvie agreed that the bruising could have been consistent with Sweeney being pulled and pushed about and the weal could have been caused by a blunt instrument, possibly a police baton. Sweeney, however, had made no direct allegation of assault by the police. Dr McKelvie's evidence only took a few minutes but what he had to say about finding injuries on Joe Sweeney was to become of crucial importance to the defence later on in the trial.

20 The Eyewitness

In raising his right hand and repeating the oath administered by Lord Ross, nineteen-year-old Stephen Cameron must have been aware of the silent enmity directed at him from the dock. Once, 'Steff' as he was known in Barrowfield, had been their friend, a member of the same gang, the Spur. He was now their enemy. To the Sweeney brothers and Thomson, Cameron was a 'grass' who had broken the criminal code of silence by speaking to the police and agreeing to give evidence. The accused youths, like many other people in Barrowfield, felt that Cameron should have been sitting in the dock too. In street confrontations groups of boys had accused him of lying to save his own skin. The three youths in the dock would do the same themselves – this time in court.

Cameron, a slightly built, dark-haired youth with a scraggy moustache, was the vital Glasgow rape case eyewitness mentioned in all the newspapers and in Parliament during the months leading up to the trial. He had originally been charged with raping and razoring Carol but he was freed in return for a promise that he would give evidence for the Crown against the remaining three.

When the new trial was set up by the private prosecution, Cameron agreed again to give evidence for Carol. She granted him immunity from prosecution and, during the preparation of the case, Harper took him before a Glasgow sheriff to give a statement under oath about the events he had witnessed. Sheriff Irvine Smith, formerly a noted defence advocate, ensured, with his customary fairness, that Cameron understood his rights. He listened as Harper questioned Cameron about the case, each question and each answer being recorded by a shorthand writer. Sheriff Smith asked the occasional question of his own.

The time had now come for Cameron to fulfil his promise. While Carol herself was being taken through her evidence, step by step, Cameron had sat outside Court No. 9 with his mother. He saw Carol come out, escorted by a policeman, and watched the next witness, a police casualty surgeon, enter. It was like sitting in a dentist's waiting room except that, for Cameron, the anxiety was worse. His turn was next.

As the minutes ticked by he retraced in his mind the arrangements made to escape from Barrowfield before the trial ended. Cameron was terrified there would be repercussions for him if he did not. It comforted him to think that, in two days, he would be taking his young and pregnant wife, the same girl he had bedded on the night of the razor assault, to a secret address in another part of Glasgow. There, he hoped, he would be safe from revenge.

Cameron also thought about his family. For months they had endured taunts from local boys, chanting 'grass' as they massed outside his mother's tenement home. There had also been threats that his house would be broken into. Worse still, his ten-year-old sister, Rose, had been approached by young thugs several times in the street and ordered to pass on a message to her brother. She would run home in tears to tell him, 'They are going to stab you.' Cameron felt that if he did not get out of Barrowfield, and get out fast, he would end up being knifed.

'Stephen Cameron' – the loud voice, plus a nudge from his mother in the ribs, jolted him out of his thoughts. Cameron stood up and followed the official into court, walking past his three former friends sitting in the dock. Their eyes were fixed on him. He looked away.

The Dean began to question him. Members of the jury shook their heads in frustration, straining their ears in an effort to understand Cameron's replies, his voice almost inaudible. At one point a juror asked if the youth could be told to speak up. When at last he could be heard, pencils furiously scribbled.

The Dean asked Cameron to start at the beginning. Had he encountered any of the accused boys on the night of the rape and assault? Cameron said he had met Joe Sweeney in the street just before 11 p.m. He told the Dean how he was invited to the Sweeney home for a couple of Carlsberg lagers.

Ten minutes later, while they were still drinking, Joe's young brother, Gordon, arrived. It was at this point in his evidence that Cameron was forced to look directly at the two brothers. 'Do you see Joe and Gordon here today?' asked the Dean. Cameron quickly pointed them out in the dock and just as swiftly turned to face the Dean again.

The Dean continued, 'What, if anything, did Gordon say when he arrived?' 'He said that he had a bird up in the scrap-yard at Davaar Street.'

'What happened next?' 'Me, Joe and Gordon went to the scrap-yard.'

The jury immediately realized that they were about to hear an eyewitness account. They listened eagerly but, first of all, the Dean asked Cameron to describe the surroundings, aided by the book of coloured photographs. Holding them up so the jury could see them, Cameron pointed out the main gates of the scrap-yard and the green container inside.

'What did you do?' asked the Dean. 'We went inside,' said Cameron.

The Dean's next question was delivered in a loud, deliberate voice. 'What did you see?' Cameron paused for a second or two. His voice faded again. 'I saw a girl with John Thomson,' he whispered. The jury just managed to make his answer out. Cameron had to point out Thomson. He did so, as he had done with the others, as quickly as he could.

The Dean asked Cameron how he had been able to see inside the darkness of the cabin. Cameron explained that a faint shaft of light from a lamp-post outside the main gate had shone through a hole in the container's side. He picked up the book of photographs to point out the hole to the jury. With the same photographs he also pointed out the position occupied by Thomson and the girl on the container floor.

'Look at what appears to be a large blood stain in the middle of the floor,' urged the Dean. 'Was that where you saw them?'

Cameron told him it was exactly the spot. 'She was lying on the floor,' he explained. 'John Thomson was on top of her.'

'What was the woman wearing?' – 'Nothing at all. She had no clothes on.'

'What was Thomson wearing?' – 'He had his trousers down at his ankles.'

'What was he doing?' – 'He was having sex.'

Cameron described how the woman lay still. Thomson was on top of her for only a couple of minutes and then he got off. Continued Cameron, 'The girl was getting up when Joe Sweeney pushed her down. He told her, "We are not finished".' Mr Davidson asked Cameron to demonstrate to the jury how Sweeney had pushed the woman back. From the dock he lifted both his arms, bending them slightly at the elbows, and suddenly thrust them out straight and downwards to show how the woman had been propelled with a push on both shoulders back to the floor. 'What happened next?' asked the Dean.

Cameron's voice lowered once more. 'Joe Sweeney had sex with her. He took his trousers down and was lying on top of the lassie and had sex. It took a couple of minutes.'

The Dean wanted to know if he had seen any sign of movement from the woman. Cameron said he had not.

'What happened after that?' – 'Joe Sweeney got up and pulled out a razor. It was in his pocket. It was one of the old barber's razors.'

Cameron, at the Dean's request, was asked to describe the weapon in more detail. It was obviously a cut-throat razor and it was open. The Dean then fired a rapid series of questions. Had he seen anything which could have justified Sweeney producing the razor? Was there any movement from the woman? Cameron answered each one with an almost silent 'No.'

He recalled, however, that the woman had said something. He had heard her words quite clearly. She told Sweeney, 'Put that away, you don't need it.'

'What was the next thing you saw?' asked the Dean. His voice was still in a monotone but the questions were becoming more and more probing. 'I saw Gordon Sweeney having sex with the woman,' said Cameron. 'She was just lying there.'

Gordon, he claimed, finished and walked out of the container. Added Cameron, 'I went with him, leaving Joe Sweeney and John Thomson inside with her.'

The Dean continued, 'Did you not have sex with the woman yourself?' Cameron looked at him quizzically, replying with a shake of his head, 'No. No, not me.'

'Why did you go out?' – 'I thought that it was finished.'

'What was finished?' – 'Having sex with the woman.'

Cameron then described how he and Gordon Sweeney walked to the main gates of the scrap-yard to stand at the corner outside. The two others had still not left the container; he asked Gordon to run back to see what was keeping them. As he went, Joe Sweeney approached them. 'He still had the razor in his hand. It was open. There was blood on his hand, a lot of blood, in fact his hands were covered in blood. He shouted out three times "I have ripped the lassie".'

The Dean asked Cameron to continue. 'What did you do next?' Cameron told him they all walked to nearby Stamford Street intending to go home, when suddenly two policemen ran after them. They appeared to go for Joe who ran through the back of a tenement. John Thomson and Gordon Sweeney continued to walk into Stamford Lane. 'I made my way home,' he said.

Cameron admitted that he went back into the street five minutes later. There was nobody about so he returned to bed. Four days later he was interviewed by police who were making investigations into the incident. He gave them a statement. Then he was charged and locked up.

The Dean, however, was not finished with Cameron's evidence. He referred to what Cameron alleged he had heard Joe Sweeney say, when he pushed the woman to the floor, '*We* are not finished yet.' Mr Davidson emphasized the word 'We'. Was he certain it was '*We* are not finished yet'? Cameron told him he was sure.

'When Joe Sweeney produced the barber's razor did you see it?' – 'Yes.'

'Did you think everyone else had been in a position to see it?' – 'Yes.'

'Were you able to see the woman's face when the razor was produced?' – 'Yes.'

'How did she appear?' – 'The lassie looked scared.'

'Were you scared?' – 'No.'

'Why did you think that it was being brought out at all?' – 'I had no idea.'

'When Joe Sweeney produced the razor, where was Gordon Sweeney?' – 'He was just inside the main door two steps away.'

'How long after Joe produced the razor did Gordon have sex with the woman?' – 'Minutes.'

'If you had wanted to have sex with the woman do you think that they would let you do it?' – 'Yes.'

'But you just didn't want to?' – 'No.'

After the barrage of questions, the Dean asked Cameron what he had expected to gain by going to the scrap-yard with the other youths. Cameron just shrugged his shoulders. He was extremely evasive. 'I said to the police that I didn't know why I went there.' The Dean chided him. 'Come on, Cameron, tell us the truth. What did you expect to happen if you went down there?' The Dean's voice, raised in earnest for the first time, jolted the youth. In just one word he gave the answer. 'Sex.'

For the second time the Dean asked him if the woman appeared to have been scared. It was a crucial point for the private prosecution. Cameron said, 'When I first saw John Thomson on top of her she was OK. She only looked scared when Joe Sweeney produced the razor.'

The Dean was angry. In his right hand he held the statement Cameron had given on oath before Sheriff Irvine Smith. All the questions to the youth had been formulated from his statement. He pressed him hard, 'Did you ever give a statement about the woman looking scared before?' Cameron just shrugged his shoulders again. 'Do you remember saying she looked scared *all* the time, but more scared when the razor came out?'

Cameron stood in the witness box as if he didn't know where to turn next. After what seemed ages he finally admitted he had said that Carol looked scared *all* the time.

It had been a long day. It was almost 4.30 p.m. Lord Ross

looked towards the Dean. 'It would be an appropriate moment to rise for the day,' he suggested. The judge got to his feet, the macer bellowed, 'Cou . . . rt', and Cameron was led away to rejoin his mother. His evidence would be continued in the morning. The first day of the trial was over.

The Sweeney brothers and John Thomson thought their bail would continue. But they found themselves being led away by the police, not to rejoin their relatives but to be taken to Saughton Prison for the night.

On the Tuesday morning at 10 a.m. Cameron returned to the witness box to face further questioning, this time cross-examination by Joseph Sweeney's defence counsel, Mr Findlay. The defence had to discredit the youth and, at one point, Lord Ross felt that the severe questioning was calculated to incriminate Cameron. He asked the Dean if it had been pointed out to Cameron that he was being granted immunity from prosecution. The Dean confirmed that he had been so informed.

Cameron told Mr Findlay that he had known John Thomson for seventeen years. They were distantly related through marriage, Cameron's brother having married John Thomson's cousin. Both families were friendly with each other.

Cameron said that, during the earlier part of the evening, he had been at a disco with Joe. 'When you were at the disco did you show Joe Sweeney anything?' asked Mr Findlay. Cameron looked taken aback. 'No,' he said.

'Didn't you have a knife with you when you were at the disco and didn't you, at one point, show it to Joe Sweeney?' Cameron's denial was more emphatic this time.

'And didn't you say to Joe Sweeney you were looking for someone in particular and that you had a knife?' Cameron replied, 'None of that happened at all.'

Mr Findlay took the youth through his earlier evidence about having been in the Sweeney house when Gordon Sweeney arrived to say that they had a 'bird' in the scrap-yard.

'Didn't he say, when he came into the house, that the two of them, him and John Thomson, had had sex with this woman?' – 'No.'

'And didn't he say that, if you and Joe Sweeney wanted to, you could go along to the scrap-yard?' – 'Yes.'

For the second time Cameron was asked why he had gone to the hut. This time the questioner was Lord Ross. 'I just went up,' he said. The judge obviously found the answer unsatisfactory and asked him again. 'I don't know,' Cameron replied, shaking his head and shrugging his shoulders. For the next few minutes he found himself on the receiving end of a stern warning from Lord Ross about the dangers of prevarication and the possibility of being locked up for it.

Mr Findlay continued as soon as Lord Ross finished. 'Come, come, Cameron, there *was* a woman in the scrap-yard and there *was* a prospect of having sex with her, wasn't there?' At last the youth admitted that that was the reason, but he insisted on having the last word. 'I went up to the cabin,' he said, 'but I didn't have sex with her.'

Mr Findlay said, 'This business about Joe Sweeney pushing this woman down and saying "*We* are not finished," is just not true, is it, Cameron? It's a lie.' – 'It is true,' said Cameron.

'You had some sexual involvement with this woman?' – 'No.'

'Didn't you take your trousers down and lie on top of her?' – 'No.'

'Why didn't you?' – 'I had sex with my own girlfriend about 9 o'clock.'

'But you went to the cabin with the prospect of having more sex.' – 'I didn't.'

'You had some sexual involvement with this woman, didn't you, Cameron?' – 'I did not.'

There was little respite for Cameron. He had lied when he claimed he saw Joe Sweeney with the razor in his blood-stained hands in the street outside the scrap-yard, alleged Mr Findlay. He had also lied when he claimed he had heard Sweeney shouting, 'I have ripped the lassie.' Cameron insisted he was telling the truth. Mr Findlay insisted that he was not.

The youth found himself questioned about the voluntary statement he had given to the police four days after the incident, in which he blamed the others. Cameron admitted that he had made the statement because he had been frightened and alarmed. 'Were you deliberately trying to shift as much blame from yourself to other people as you could?' 'I was not,' replied Cameron.

'You were playing down your own involvement and Thomson's at the expense of others, in particular at the expense of Joe Sweeney because you are, by marriage, in some way related to John Thomson?' 'No,' said Cameron.

Mr Findlay sat down, his questioning over, leaving Cameron to be cross-examined by Mr Macaulay and Mr Morton who went over the same ground. When that was completed the Dean cleared a few points in re-examination. Cameron then left the court.

It was with relief, tinged with the fear of retribution, that he travelled back to Glasgow with his mother. That night Cameron packed up his belongings, ready to move out of Barrowfield the next day.

The Dean called four witnesses in succession: Mrs Kate Dobbin and her son James, and two doctors from the Royal Infirmary, Dr Gillian Blair from the Casualty Department and Mr Robert Simpson, a Casualty surgeon. The Dobbins would describe Carol's state immediately after the attack and the doctors would reveal the extent of her injuries and how they had treated them.

It was vital evidence for the prosecution as it would prove that Carol had been attacked, the approximate time of the incident and the nature of her injuries.

Mrs Dobbin, aged sixty-six, was first to enter the witness box. She recalled that she had been watching the late-night television movie when Carol came to the door covered in blood. Mrs Dobbin told the jury she shouted for her son, who was in bed, and asked him to run to get an ambulance. She took Carol into the living room and she immediately collapsed on the floor in front of the fire, pleading with her to get help.

'I tried to give her a cup of tea,' said Mrs Dobbin. 'But she couldn't hold it. There was blood right down her – from her head to her toes. I couldn't see where it was coming from there was so much, plus dirt, all over her. Her hair was all matted. She was only wearing a wee jacket and a pair of tights.'

Mrs Dobbin was not cross-examined by the defence. Her son,

James, aged thirty-four, was next in the witness box. His evidence was as graphic as his mother's. He told the court what he had seen on his return from summoning the police and the ambulance. 'When I got back I saw Carol sitting on the floor. I thought she had a pair of black trousers on, but when I had a wee second look I saw that it was dirt and blood. She had no trousers on at all. She was shaking with shock.'

Mr Dobbin was asked if he had asked Carol about what had happened to her. He replied that it was impossible because she couldn't talk.

Dr Blair, twenty-seven, who was a senior houseman at the Royal Infirmary Casualty Department at the time of Carol's admission, was asked by the Dean if she could identify Carol from the photographs. She could not. The reason, she explained, was that, when she first saw Carol, her wounds had been gaping open. Her appearance had altered so much, after they had been stitched up and photographed, that it was impossible to recognize her. Surprisingly, Dr Blair had very little recollection of Carol the person, rather than Carol the patient, doubtless because she was just one of dozens of people treated every week in the hospital for serious injuries. She had to refer to the bulky medical records on Carol's case history to enable her to give evidence at all.

The case history had been handed to Dr Blair by the Dean and, looking at it, she was reminded that, when Carol arrived at the Royal Infirmary, she had multiple lacerations on her face and thighs. She was very pale and distressed and her blood pressure was significantly low. The doctor said it was obvious, because of low blood pressure and her colour, that she had lost a considerable amount of blood though she was not bleeding to death. Nevertheless, Carol was given a transfusion.

The Dean asked Dr Blair if she had been able to find out from Carol what had happened. Again she referred to the case notes. She told him, 'It was rather difficult to get a history from the patient because of her distressed mental state. Apparently the patient had said, in the presence of the nursing staff, that she had been raped, but it was not said to me.'

Dr Blair said that, because of Carol's extensive injuries, a general anaesthetic had to be used while they were stitching her up. Before that, Carol was taken to have her skull X-rayed to see if there were any fractures. There was none. One of the wounds, she explained, was on the scalp across her forehead. It had gone right down to the bone but not into it. The injury gaped so much that the doctor was able to examine the skull for a possible fracture by running her fingers through the wound along the bone. All the other wounds were gaping too.

During his cross-examination Mr Macaulay won a vital point for the defence. He told the doctor that, in her evidence, Carol claimed to have an injury at the back of her head where she said she had been struck from behind. Had Dr Blair detected such an injury? The doctor asked if she might go through the medical records; after a few minutes she stated that they disclosed no injuries of that nature. Later on, however, when re-examined by the Dean, Dr Blair agreed that, while the records did not note the alleged injury, Carol might still have sustained it.

Mr Simpson, the Casualty surgeon who stitched up Carol's wounds, followed Dr Blair into the witness box. He was asked by the Dean to itemize Carol's injuries one by one. He described four cuts, each four inches long, on her face, forehead, eyebrows and cheeks, and one across the tip of her nose. In addition there was a two-inch cut on her neck. On the side of her right thigh there were three cuts, each again four inches long, with a fourth cut intersecting them. The left thigh had three four-inch slash wounds on it.

Mr Simpson was asked to describe the severity of the injuries. Some, he revealed, had gone right down to the thigh bone. The wounds were also full of dirt and blood. Under a general anaesthetic he inserted fifty very fine stitches in Carol's face, a further thirty-six in her left thigh and sixty-six in her right thigh, making a total of 152. She also had other cuts which did not require stitching.

Mr Simpson revealed that Carol was in so much pain and distress that she had to be given powerful pain-killing injections. The Dean asked if there had been any danger to her life. One of the wounds, explained Mr Simpson, had gone close to her eyes; another had travelled inbetween her eyes. The wound in her neck was dangerously close to the jugular vein.

'What would have been the likely result if action had not been taken in hospital?' asked the Dean. The surgeon replied, 'It is likely that severe scarring of the face would have resulted, difficult to set right by any operation at a later date. It is also possible that severe infection, perhaps even death, might have resulted from the wounds on her thighs.'

Part Four

21 Confessions

The jury had now heard Carol's story, the allegations by the eyewitness and the medical evidence. Gradually, the private prosecution case was building up. Now it was time for the voluntary statements, the publicity surrounding which had almost prevented the court action. The voluntary statements by all three accused were the cornerstone of the entire prosecution.

Starting late on the Tuesday afternoon the police officers involved in collecting statements for the case began to appear, grouped in pairs so that they could corroborate each other's evidence.

The first two officers to go into the witness box were Detective Constables Adam Drummond and Arthur Chatfield, who had been in on the investigation from the moment Carol was wheeled into the Royal Infirmary until they formally charged the youths with rape and razor assault.

Drummond gave evidence first, followed by his colleague. Both detectives told how they had gone to the Sweeney home at 185 Barrowfield Street to bring the brothers in for questioning.

The door had been opened by their father, Mr Gordon Sweeney, senior, who told them the boys were in, but sleeping. The jury heard how the detectives went into their rooms and immediately advised them they were making enquiries into a serious incident which had taken place the previous Friday. Both boys agreed to go back to the police station. They were put in separate cars and, when they got to Tobago Street, placed in separate rooms.

The two detectives also revealed that, when they formally cautioned young Gordon that he need not say anything but that 'anything he did say would be noted and could be used in evidence', he stared at the floor in total silence for fifteen seconds. Then, they alleged, he looked up and told them, 'All right, I knew it would happen. The whole scheme [area] is talking about it.' The two detectives asked him what he meant by that and Gordon, the jury heard, replied, 'I was into it, but she wasn't cut up when I left.'

It was at this point, both detectives claimed, that they realized Gordon was a juvenile and, as such, could only be questioned in the presence of a parent. They sent for his father while Gordon remained in the police station's general office.

In the meantime, Drummond and Chatfield told the court, they interviewed Stephen Cameron who had also been taken by them from his home at 61 Fraser Street to the police station. Cameron was also cautioned and the jury heard that he replied, 'I saw them all getting into her, but not me. I thought Joe was kidding when he said he had ripped her.'

Detective Constable Drummond told the jury that he later charged Joseph Sweeney and Cameron with the crimes. Sweeney, he alleged, replied, 'I didn't think she was that bad. I will tell you what I did.' Cameron, he claimed, said, 'Look, I will make a statement. I never did her.'

Detective Constable Drummond told the court that, when Mr Sweeney arrived at the police station, his son, Gordon, agreed to give a voluntary statement. Drummond wrote it down in his official police notebook in the presence of Mr Sweeney and his colleague, Chatfield. When the statement was completed he asked Mr Sweeney, his son and Chatfield to sign the book; he then signed it himself.

Mr Cameron now handed him the small black book with pages numbered and lined. 'Will you please read it out to the ladies and gentlemen of the jury?' he asked. Detective Constable Drummond duly obliged. But before he began Lord Ross asked him to read the statement slowly so that he and the jury could make notes.

The youngster had begun his statement by accounting for his movements earlier that night. He had gone to the disco in Queen Mary Street School and had left about 10.30 p.m. along with some other boys whom he named. He also described how he got a taxi for an older boy. He had been with John Thomson at the time.

Detective Constable Drummond continued to read from the statement.

When we got to London Road we saw a lassie. John ran after her and I ran behind him. He grabbed the lassie and he dragged her into Wilson's Yard at Davaar Street. After he got her into the yard he said to me, 'Close the gate over.' I closed the gate and then I went into the hut and he was taking her clothes off. He said to me, 'You stay outside just now.' I went out and waited a while and then I went back into the hut.

He said 'Shut the door.' I then had sex with the woman. She was naked. After that I went out of the hut again and went down to my house and got Joe and Steff, this is Joseph, my brother, and Steff is Stephen Cameron. The three of us went to the hut. She was still lying on the floor with no clothes on, and then Joe had sex with her. Me and Steff came out, and Joe and John came out behind us.

Both Joe and John had blood all over their hands. We went down the road and the police chased us. They told us to leave, and they started running after Joe. Joe, and the police who chased him, ran through the first close in Stamford Street.

When I got to my close I saw the police run up the stairs after Joe. Joe ran into the house and changed his shirt and trousers and jumped out of the verandah and away. That's all that happened, and I went to my bed.

Detective Constable Drummond told the court that, soon after, along with Detective Constable Chatfield, he formally charged the Sweeney brothers and Cameron at the police station. Cameron, he alleged, replied: 'No,' when asked if he had anything to say. The Sweeney brothers made no reply at all.

Later on, the next afternoon, John Thomson was brought by other officers to the police station. Detective Constable Drummond said he was informed that Thomson, too, had made a statement under caution as he travelled in the car en route to Tobago Street. When he arrived he cautioned Thomson who replied, 'I didn't know Joe had a razor at first. I just screwed her.'

Thomson had indicated that he wished to make a written voluntary statement and Detective Constable Drummond went to his home to get a parent. Both parents refused to come but an older sister agreed to go with him. Drummond was not present when Thomson made his voluntary statement but afterwards he formally cautioned and charged him at the police station. Like the Sweeney brothers he made no reply.

After Drummond and Chatfield's evidence the court adjourned for the day. When it resumed on Wednesday morning two more detectives, Constables Thomas Moulds and Leslie Darling, went into the witness box to describe what Joseph Sweeney had said to them in the police station.

Constable Moulds, who was first to give evidence, told how he cautioned Sweeney in the presence of Darling. The youth said nothing. They left him for a while in the room where he was being detained and returned soon after. They cautioned him for a second time and questioned him about his movements on the night Carol was attacked and raped. Sweeney told them he had been at a disco and had left at 10.30 p.m.

They left him again and went out to make more enquiries. When they returned they told Sweeney they were not satisfied. 'Did he say anything else?' Mr Cameron asked. 'He did My Lord,' said Moulds, asking the judge for permission to read out the statement from his notebook. 'You know I fucking done it, but that cunt Thomson held her down. I'm not taking all the fucking blame.'

Moulds told the jury that, in the afternoon, he brought Thomson back to the police station for questioning and cautioned him in the car en route. Thomson, he claimed, said, 'The four of us screwed her, but Joe just went too far with the razor.'

During his cross-examination Moulds faced a serious allegation put to him by Joe Sweeney's defence counsel, Mr Findlay.

Mr Findlay asked, 'Was it not the case that, during the course of the morning, you and other police officers subjected this youth to intensive interrogation and told him he had better speak up and, by your manner and demeanour, tried to frighten him into making a statement.' Moulds emphatically denied the allegation.

'Did you at any time take a hold of his clothing and push and pull him about the room where he was being kept?' – 'No.'

'Did you strike him with a police baton or any other similar object?' – 'No.'

'If he had on his body the type of bruising which might be consistent with pulling him about by his clothes, and weals which could have been caused by a police baton, did you see anything in Tobago Street which caused either or both of these injuries?' – 'No.'

'If it happened in Tobago Street, do you have any idea how it happened?' – 'No.'

Mr Findlay then went on to accuse the detective of fabricating Sweeney's statement. 'It is true,' he protested.

Mr Macaulay pressed him about the propriety of taking a juvenile to the police station without his parents. 'Did you not realize when you went to the Sweeney house you were dealing with Gordon, a very young boy – a schoolboy?' Moulds told him he hadn't.

'Is it not a serious matter to arrest a young boy and take him to the police station without his parents?' – 'He didn't seem that young.'

'He was fourteen.' – 'He didn't look that age. He looked older. He could have been eighteen.'

Mr Macaulay continued to press him but Detective Constable Moulds insisted, 'I had no thought about the age of this boy.'

'Did you hear the father ask if he could go with his son to the police station when you took him away?' – 'I have no recollection of that.'

Detective Constable Darling followed Moulds into the witness box to go over the same ground as his colleague. Mr Cameron prepared him for the allegations which would be put to him later by Mr Findlay and Mr Macaulay.

He asked him if, as he made his statement, Joe Sweeney had shown any signs of distress. 'I would say he was distressed,' Darling told him. 'He was dejected.'

'Did you see any signs of his having been assaulted?' – 'No.'
'Did he make any allegation of having been assaulted?' – 'No.'

'Did he make any allegation of having pressure put on him by police officers in one form or another?' – 'No.'

'It may be suggested to you that the statement he gave is pure fabrication. What would be your reaction to that?' – 'He gave that statement.'

The two formal police witnesses who gave evidence about the voluntary statement given in the police station by John Thomson in front of his sister, were to go into the witness box next. Detective Sergeant William Mackie and Detective Constable George Cowie, both officers in the Strathclyde Serious Crime Squad, told the jury that they had been asked by telephone to go to the Eastern Division to take the statements.

Before Thomson began his statement, Detective Sergeant Mackie asked him if he wished to write the words of the caution himself. Thomson declined. The detective told Mr Cameron that he wrote it down himself and asked Thomson and his sister, Helen, to sign it afterwards. He read out the text of the caution to the court:

I have been cautioned by Detective Sergeant William Mackie that I am not obliged to make any statement, and that any statement I care to make will be taken down in writing and can be given in evidence in any proceedings which may be taken against me. I have also been advised that I can have a solicitor present (and/or parent where appropriate). I do not wish a solicitor to be present.

Asked Mr Cameron, 'Did John Thomson then go on to make a statement?' – 'Yes,' said the detective.

'Was it a voluntary one or did you prompt him in any way?' – 'It was a voluntary one.'

'Will you please read it out aloud to the ladies and gentlemen of the jury?'

As they had done with Gordon Sweeney's alleged statement the jury scribbled down what they had to hear, in their notebooks.

Thomson's statement, like Sweeney's, also began with a description of what he had been doing earlier that night.

We went to a disco on Friday night. Came out of the disco at 10 p.m. and went up to Barrowfield Street. We bought some wine out of the licensed grocers, me and Joe Sweeney. We sat up a close in Stamford Street. Then we came out of the close and walked about for a wee while. Then we went to the top of the lane in Barrowfield Street. We met wee Gordon and we saw the big boys coming off the bus. We walked down towards them and one of the boys asked us to put another guy in a taxi.

We saw this lassie across the road walking up towards Parkhead, and me and wee Gordon Sweeney walked up beside her. Then we took an arm each and took her across the road into the scrap-yard. We took her into this big container and we took the bottom half of her clothes off. Then wee Gordon Sweeney went on top of her. Then I went on top of her.

The statement added that Gordon left to get his brother and Stephen Cameron, and continued:

The woman didn't fight or resist. She was drunk. The other three boys came back just as I was going to get out. The three of them ran into the container. Stephen Cameron got on top of her. One of the boys had pulled the bottom half of her clothing right off. Then Stephen Cameron got off and Joe Sweeney got on.

At this point in his statement Thomson made an allegation that Joe Sweeney had razored the woman.

Joe Sweeney got up and started hitting her with a razor on the back of the legs. Then Stephen Cameron and Gordon Sweeney ran past me as I was standing at the door. I went in and pulled Joseph Sweeney by the back of the collar and pulled him out of the container. Then I started to run out of the front gate. I stopped to wait for Joe Sweeney. He came out and we ran to the corner of Davaar Street leading into Barrowfield Street. Joe Sweeney came out behind us shouting, 'Spur Rule', and he said to me he had chibbed her.

Thomson's statement also revealed how they were approached by the police. He described Joe Sweeney running away, chased by one of them.

The other policeman said to me and Gordon Sweeney, 'Where were you going?' Gordon Sweeney stays down the road. So he told us to get to fuck down the road. We went down to Gordon Sweeney's house and when we got into his house Joe Sweeney crept out of the verandah. One of the policemen followed us. Then he came upstairs and chapped the door. Gordon Sweeney opened the door and the police asked him where his brother was. Gordon said he didn't know where he was. Then his mother got up. She asked what was happening. Gordon told her the police were looking for Joe. Then Gordon's mother went to the door and let them in. They started searching the house looking for Joe Sweeney. Then me and Gordon went out.
We walked up to the corner of Barrowfield Street. Joe Sweeney ran right passed us. He didn't say anything to us, he just kept running. Then I said to Gordon, 'I'm going up the stair.' That's it, but I never raped the lassie or chibbed her. She wasn't struggling when me and Gordon Sweeney were there.

Detective Sergeant Mackie told Mr Cameron that, when Thomson finished his statement, he read it over to both him and his sister. He wrote at the bottom: 'This statement has been read over to me and it is true. I do not wish to make any changes or say anything more.' Thomson and his sister signed it and Mackie said it was countersigned by himself and Detective Chief Inspector Cowie.
The jury had now heard two voluntary statements. It would be up to them to decide if the statements had been taken fairly and accurately and, if they had, whether they added up to admissions from Gordon Sweeney and John Thomson that they had raped the woman or simply had sex with her consent. There was clear evidence from both statements that neither of the two boys had taken part in the razor assault. Gordon Sweeney had been outside the hut, in the street, and John Thomson had alleged that Joe Sweeney had slashed the woman but that he had tried to prevent further injury by dragging him off.
'I call Detective Chief Inspector Alex Cowie,' announced Mr Cameron. Mr Cowie was the detective in charge of the Eastern

Division CID, the man responsible for the day-to-day running of his detectives and answerable for the actions they took.

In the witness box he looked more like a sharp businessman than a senior policeman. Dressed in a natty tan suit and wearing tinted glasses, there were times during his evidence when the shorthand writer found he could not cope with the detective's rapid speech.

Within seconds of beginning his evidence Mr Cowie told how, after Joe Sweeney had been cautioned and charged, he asked him if he wished to make a voluntary statement. Sweeney agreed. Mr Cowie asked him if he wanted a solicitor to be present and Sweeney declined.

'Did you write down his statement?' asked Mr Cameron. 'Yes. But I asked him if he wanted to write it himself. He asked me if I would write it because he couldn't read or write very well.'

Cowie then described how Sweeney dictated the statement to him slowly, pausing frequently. In the room with them was uniformed Constable Robert Carrigan, whom he had asked to be present as a witness. Neither he nor Carrigan put any questions to the youth. The jury went on to hear the detailed confession to the crime which, when its existence was revealed in the *Daily Record* earlier in January, had led to the angry Parliamentary debate on the case, the dismissal of the Solicitor General (indirectly) and now the private prosecution trial itself.

'Will you please read out Joseph Sweeney's statement?' asked Mr Cameron. Before he could begin, Lord Ross asked Cowie if he could read slowly because he and the members of the jury had to note it.

Detective Chief Inspector Cowie adjusted his spectacles and, holding the three-page document in his right hand, began:

On Friday I left the house at 7.30, me and Stephen Cameron's big brother. I met him down the street. We went to the disco in Queen Mary Street School. I had a bottle of wine. I met a lot of my pals at the disco, big Lockie, Andy Wynn, Bill Hailey, and some others. I came out of the disco at 10 with James Cameron. I stood at the corner of Barrowfield Street and Stamford Street, and about a quarter to

eleven I met Stephen Cameron. We went up to my house for a drink.
We were drinking Carlsbergs – the wine was finished.

My wee brother, Gordon, came along into the house. He told us
that they – him and wee John Thomson – had a lassie in Wilson's
Yard. 'We got her at the London Road,' he told me, and said, 'Come
on down, we're having a line up.'

Me, Stephen and Gordon went to the yard and went into the big
thing. We shut the door. I saw a lassie lying on her back. She was
naked and wee John told me that he had done it to her. He said to
me, 'It's your turn to do it,' but I couldn't do it because I was that
drunk. Steff never touched her but Gordon had a go at her. I had
another go and managed to do it to her.

She started screaming again, and I had a razor, so I gave it to her
and then I came out. We left her there and the four of us walked
down the road. We walked back to Barrowfield at the corner again.
There was a lot of people standing there from my gang, the Spur. I
saw the police coming and I ran like fuck because my hands were all
covered in blood. The police never caught me. I ran through a close
and then up to the house. I went out onto the verandah, waited for
the police, but they never came. I jumped the verandah and went
back out onto the street again.

There was hardly one member of the jury who did not write
down the key points of Sweeney's alleged voluntary statement.
Some of the men and women looked astounded. One man shook
his head.

Cowie said that, afterwards, Sweeney signed the statement
confirming it had been read over to him and that it was true.
Before he started he had also signed an eight-line confirmation
that he had been properly cautioned and offered the services
of a solicitor if he wished. Mr Cowie said the youth had turned
down the offer.

Mr Cameron asked Cowie to recollect the events of Thursday, 1 April when the three High Court judges granted Carol's
application for the private prosecution. Detective Chief Inspector Cowie said that he instructed one of his officers, Detective Inspector Phil Smythe, to attend the High Court in
Edinburgh that day. He had been ordered to contact him with
the news of the judgment immediately it became known.

At noon the inspector phoned to tell him the Bill for Crimi-

nal Letters had been granted. Within it there was a warrant
to arrest the three boys and he issued instructions for Thomson
to be detained while he personally went with other officers to
apprehend the Sweeney brothers. He took them back to the
new police station in London Road – Tobago Street had been
closed down months before – and all three were given the
news. By this time, Cowie revealed, he had the original Criminal Letters with him and he read the document out to the boys
and gave them copies. Then they were charged but they made
no reply.

Cowie then faced cross-examination by Mr Findlay and an
onslaught of allegations which included one that he had manu-
factured Joseph Sweeney's statement. Mr Findlay seized on
what he obviously considered was a major flaw in police procedures. Detective Chief Inspector Cowie was the officer in
charge of the division, yet he had personally taken a voluntary
statement from Sweeney.

'When you take voluntary statements from people it is not
unknown to get officers from outside divisions to take them,
is it not?' he asked. Cowie told him that was sometimes necessary, agreeing it was done so that the officers brought in could
not possibly know anything about the case. It ensured they
could not prompt the accused or add any details to the statement because, of course, they had no knowledge of the finer
points of the investigation.

Mr Findlay hammered this line of questioning for several
minutes. Cowie was the officer in charge of the CID; he su-
pervised those who were investigating the case; therefore he
must have known details about it.

Cowie, however, insisted he knew nothing whatsoever about
the investigation. It had been an extremely busy weekend
when the incident occurred and he had been in other parts of
his division investigating a whole string of crimes varying
from attempted murder to assault and robbery. Things had
been so hectic that he left the officers under his own command
to get on with it.

The young advocate then changed course and began to
attack the policeman from a different line. 'At no time did you
or Constable Carrigan ask Joe Sweeney if he wanted a solici-

tor?' The reaction to that from Mr Cowie was swift. 'We did,' he said. 'He signed a confirmation to that effect.'

Mr Findlay continued, 'You had this man who is obviously very distressed. . . .' Cowie jumped in quickly at the end of his sentence. 'He didn't appear to be distressed to me at that time,' he claimed.

'You took him into this room and you wrote out the caution and the reference to the solicitor and you told him to sign it and he signed it simply because you had told him to, is that not right?' – 'No.'

'And while Constable Carrigan engaged Joe Sweeney in conversation you wrote down the replies but not at dictation speed?' 'That,' said Cowie, 'is a lie.'

For the next few minutes Mr Findlay questioned the detective about the young constable's nickname. Mr Findlay told him Carrigan's nickname was 'Ginger' and said Sweeney had heard him call Carrigan that as they conducted their alleged interrogations. Again he received an instant rebuff from Mr Cowie. 'I didn't know his nickname was Ginger,' he said. 'And even if I did, it would have been highly improper for a senior officer to call a constable by his nickname. I might call somebody by his nickname off-duty, but certainly not on official business.'

'Did you not hear Carrigan speaking to Joe Sweeney about his brother, not his brother Gordon, but another brother?' – 'PC Carrigan did not utter one word during the taking of that statement. He just sat in the room.'

'Isn't it true you wrote the statement out yourself, put it to him and said "Right, sign it"?' – 'No.'

'But you could have. You knew what the investigation was all about?' – 'I didn't have any facts with which to write down this statement.'

'The statement was *not* made by Joe Sweeney?' – 'The statement *was* made by Joe Sweeney and anything else you say is not true.'

'It was pure fabrication wasn't it?' – 'I deny that emphatically, very emphatically indeed.'

'Joe Sweeney is a very dim individual?' – 'I can't say that. I had only met him once.'

Mr Findlay finished with a summary of all the allegations that he had been asked by Sweeney to put to the detective. Cowie's last word on the subject was yet another denial, this time a most strenuous one. 'Complete and utter lies,' he said, shaking his head. 'It happened as I said it happened!'

The jury had to hear one more important chapter in the private prosecution evidence. It was to be the last chapter because, midway through the afternoon, the Dean would close the case.

When Inspector George Cuthbertson, of the Scottish Criminal Records Office in Glasgow, took the stand, the jury was reminded of the fingerprint said to have been taken from a disused gas fire outside the cabin where Carol alleged she had been attacked.

Inspector Cuthbertson, a noted expert in fingerprints, told the jury he had examined the print. He came to the conclusion that it was identical with Gordon Sweeney's right fingerprint. It was not a damning piece of evidence taken in isolation because the container had been daubed with gang slogans and the print could have been left by young Gordon at any time before Carol was assaulted. But when this was taken with the report of the two forensic scientists who were next in the box, it became another important link in the chain of circumstantial evidence.

Keith Eynon and Ian Hamilton told how they had examined blood samples on clothes and shoes from the accused and Carol. Her blood group was present in only 4 per cent of the population. The three accused boys and Stephen Cameron had a different blood group and theirs was all the same. It occurred in only 14 per cent of the population.

Various items of clothing taken from Joseph Sweeney by the police were handed to Mr Eynon in the witness box: a pair of trousers, polo-neck sweater, two pullovers, underpants, socks and shoes. Eynon identified each item and went on to reveal that, when he examined them, he found faint blood staining on the front of Sweeney's underpants, more on the left side of his right shoe and some further staining in the middle of the sole of his left shoe.

Both he and Hamilton told the court that the stains were

subjected to tests and the blood was identified as being in the same group as Carol's. It could therefore have come from her but *not* from any of the four boys.

Thomson's clothes, a leather bomber jacket, trousers, jersey, socks and shoes, also yielded blood clues. Stains were found in the lower lacing area of his left shoe and the right cuff of the jacket. This blood, too, was of the same group as Carol's and could therefore have come from her but not from the four boys.

The two forensic experts told how they also found blood on one of Gordon Sweeney's shoes but it was too faint to make a positive identification. Nothing of note was found on the belongings of Stephen Cameron.

An examination of Carol's pants and a swab said to have been taken from her after the attack, proved the presence of human sperm. This, of course, proved not that she had been raped but merely that she had had recent sexual intercourse.

The last witness that Thursday afternoon was Carol's husband of only a few weeks, Billy. He recalled the argument which led to Carol walking out on him that evening and of his shock at seeing her in hospital the next day. He had been forced to leave his job as a shipyard painter to look after her because she couldn't do anything and could hardly walk.

The Dean asked him about Carol's injuries and the scars. 'I would like to think that the scarring is fading,' he said. 'The surgeon made a good job of her face. I *know* it is still there but I try to convince her it is fading. But I *know* it is still there.'

Cross-examined by Mr Morton about Carol's drinking habits, Billy admitted that, at weekends and usually only at weekends, she had a 'few'.

'Did she drink much?' – 'I wouldn't say that.'

Billy took his seat at the back of the court. The Dean stood up and, as quietly and undramatically as he had announced the start of the trial, closed the evidence for the private prosecution.

Before leading any evidence on behalf of their three clients each defence counsel rose in turn to announce that they would like to put forward legal submissions. Such legal debates are always held without the jury's presence; the jury suddenly found itself being sent home for the rest of the day by Lord

Ross. As they made their way out of the High Court building the defence was already arguing that there was insufficient evidence to convict the three boys on any of the charges; the private prosecution was claiming the opposite. At the end of the two-hour debate Lord Ross came to a decision on the submissions and announced his findings to all parties in private. The few reporters who were in court could not publish the details. The judge would reveal his decision to the jury in the morning.

22 The Accused

Thursday morning, the fourth day of the trial, provided a major shock for the jury. They knew something important had been going on because they had not been allowed to hear the previous day's legal submissions. Lord Ross told them the result as soon as he sat on the bench that morning.

'There is insufficient evidence in law to convict Gordon Sweeney and John Thomson of the most serious of the two charges, that is, the charge involving the assault with the razor,' he announced. Some members of the jury looked astonished. But the judge told them there was no evidence to suggest the boys had assaulted the woman with the razor, or were even parties to such an assault. Lest they forget, however, he reminded the jury that Joseph Sweeney still faced trial on that charge and all three were still accused of raping Carol.

Seconds later, the Dean formally closed the prosecution case.

Mr Findlay rose. 'Are you calling any witnesses for the defence?' asked the judge. 'Yes. I call Joseph Sweeney,' was the reply. A hush went round the court, reporters already turning new pages in their notebooks to write down Sweeney's name and address as he walked to the stand, still dressed in the same dark-blue suit, light-blue cut-away-collar shirt and maroon tie that he had been wearing since the trial began.

Without wasting any time Sweeney alleged that, at the disco before the assault, John Thomson had produced a knife with a nine-inch blade, saying he was going to 'get a guy' with it. Sweeney was at pains to tell the court that the knife was 'shiny'.

Asked why he went to the cabin with Stephen Cameron
after his young brother had arrived to tell them they had a
woman there, Sweeney admitted that he assumed they were
going for sex. He also admitted trying to have sex with the
woman but told the court he was too drunk. He was not to
admit much more during the rest of his evidence.

Sweeney's first denial was that he pushed Carol down on
the ground and held her there so he could have sex with her.
'She just lay there,' he told the jury. Cameron, he alleged, had
lied in the witness box when he claimed he had refused to
have sex with the woman. 'He took his turn after I tried,' he
said.

Sweeney told Mr Findlay that it was so dark in the cabin he
could not see the woman's face clearly and that he did not
know whether she was conscious, although she had made no
response as he tried to have intercourse with her.

His brother and Cameron went outside and, as soon as they
disappeared, Thomson, he alleged, called the woman a cow.
Sweeney went on, 'He pulled something shiny out of his pocket.
The blade was shiny. He started to hit her with it on the body.
He hit her three times and was still hitting her when I left
the hut.'

Questioned more closely about the part he was said to have
played in the incident that night and what he was alleged to
have done afterwards, Sweeney again denied that he had
harmed the woman or cut her up. The others who had said
they heard him shouting outside that he had 'ripped her' were
all lying.

Mr Findlay then turned to the confession that Sweeney was
said to have made to Detective Chief Inspector Alex Cowie.
Mr Cowie, Sweeney alleged, had made it all up. Mr Findlay,
'Why then did you sign it?' Sweeney claimed, 'I signed it because I was told to by Mr Cowie.'

'Why should he do that?' – 'I was frightened. Officers had
been pushing me about by the clothes. I was hit by a trun-
cheon. They slapped me and pushed me. When I went to see
Mr Cowie I was shaking. I felt terrible.'

Mr Findlay reminded Sweeney of the evidence of another
two statements he was alleged to have made. The first one: 'I

didn't think she was that bad. I'll tell you what I did,' and the second: 'You know I fucking done it, but that cunt Thomson held her down. I'm not taking all the fucking blame.'

'Did you make these statements?' asked Mr Findlay. 'No,' replied Sweeney.

'As far as you are concerned you admit you attempted to have intercourse with the woman. Is that right?' – 'Yes.'

'According to the police you have admitted using a weapon to injure this woman. Is that right?' – 'No.'

'There was evidence you had blood on your hands. Is that right?' – 'No.'

'Then you came out of the cabin with the razor covered in blood, shouting, "I have ripped her." Is that true?' – 'No.'

'Do you know who cut that woman to inflict these injuries?' – 'Yes.'

'Who was it?' – 'John Thomson.'

Thomson shook his head as Sweeney made the allegation and in so doing completed his defence. It was now the turn of Mr Macaulay, Mr Morton and the Dean to cross-examine Sweeney. Mr Morton energetically countered the allegations against his client, John Thomson, despite the fact that Thomson had already been found not guilty of the razor charge by direction of Lord Ross. Sweeney, nevertheless, had to be attacked and attacked ruthlessly; that is what Mr Morton did.

Why, he asked him, when he had been taken into custody, did he not tell the police, 'OK, I know all about it. It was John Thomson. I'll tell you what I have got to say'? Sweeney claimed he did not because the police kept hitting him with batons.

Mr Morton then took him, line by line, through the confession. Sweeney stuck to his claim that the police had made it all up and that nearly all of it was not true. Mr Morton, 'According to you, everyone who is giving evidence in this case is telling lies, is that right?'

Mr Findlay jumped up to object to the question, but Sweeney had already answered, 'Yes.' In any event Lord Ross refused the objection. 'Let him give his answer without any assistance,' he insisted.

Mr Morton continued, 'The woman victim was lying.' 'Yes,' replied Sweeney.

'Were all the policemen telling lies in saying they did not assault you in the police station and that they took a statement from you?' – 'Yes.'

'That is a total concoction, isn't it?'

Surprisingly, Sweeney answered that question with a 'Yes,' and, quick as a flash, Mr Morton was on to him. 'So the whole group got together to say, "We are going to get Joe Sweeney," is that the case?'

Before Sweeney could answer, Lord Ross interrupted to ask the youth if he knew what the word 'concoction' meant. Sweeney did not. But there was no respite from Mr Morton. 'They got together and formed a plan in which they were going to hit you and take a false statement from you. Is that the position?' Sweeney nodded.

'They were going to do that, according to you, so that the person who did the slashing could get off. Why should they make up this story which would have the result of the person you say is guilty, John Thomson, getting off?'

This time Sweeney shrugged his shoulders. 'I don't know,' he answered.

With a fleeting smile, Mr Morton asked, 'Is John Thomson related to the whole of the Glasgow police force?'

It was a very sheepish youth who answered that he didn't know.

Mr Morton rounded on him again. 'Why should they do this?' But he answered the question himself, a split-second later. 'The answer is they did *not* and the statement you gave to the police is basically true.' 'No, sir,' replied Sweeney.

'You at some stage lost your temper with this woman and started slashing her.' – 'No.'

'And you came out glorying in what you had done, announcing it to the others in the street,' – 'No.'

'And you ran away from the police because you had the razor.' – 'No.'

The next series of rapid questions had Sweeney in a tight corner. It started when Mr Morton asked him about being assaulted in the police station.

'You must have been sore by that time after having been hit by batons,' he stated. 'Why did you not tell that to Dr

McKelvie who examined you afterwards?' Sweeney told Mr Morton that he had.

'You never told your solicitors or those acting for you.' – 'Yes I did.'

Lord Ross intervened again. 'Did you tell your solicitor that you told the doctor the police had hit you?' he asked. 'No,' replied the youth.

'Why not?' inquired Mr Morton. 'I don't know,' replied Sweeney.

Mr Morton suggested it was 'rather odd' that, if he had been assaulted, he never mentioned it to his defence counsel, Mr Findlay, so that he could ask Dr McKelvie, during the trial, to confirm the allegation.

'I never told Mr Findlay,' said Sweeney.

'Did you write to the Chief Constable telling him police officers had assaulted you?' – 'No.'

'Before you went to the identification parade on the Tuesday did you see your solicitor?' – 'Yes.'

'Did you make any complaint to him that you had been hit by policemen?' – 'No.'

'Why not?' There was total silence from the bemused youth.

'It is against the law,' continued Mr Morton, 'for people to assault other people, especially for policemen to assault other people. Why did you not tell your lawyer then?' Sweeney prevaricated. 'I don't know if I told him. I might have.'

'The reason you don't, Sweeney, is that you are inventing it as you go along.' – 'No.'

Mr Morton's cross-examination had been devastating and not once had he raised his voice during it.

Before sitting down he switched back to the razor assault in the cabin. 'When you went there you were fairly drunk,' he suggested. 'Yes,' replied Sweeney.

'And you tried to have intercourse and failed.' – 'Yes.'

'And before that you pushed this woman down.' – 'I didn't. She was just lying there.'

'You started hitting her and John Thomson came in from outside the door and pulled you off.' – 'No.'

'That in fact is the truth of what happened.' – 'No.'

'Your whole story is untrue.' – 'No.'

Mr Morton sat down and the Dean stood up to confront Sweeney; he was immediately on the attack, his emotionless, clinical voice rarely changing tone. Within a few minutes he, too, had tied Sweeney up in a knot.

'Is your position, Sweeney, that, after you were taken into custody by the police, you told them nothing about what you had been doing on the Friday night apart from being at a disco?' asked the Dean.

That was the opening move. Not seeing any trap before him, Sweeney answered, 'Yes.'

'You were not cautioned and the statement was written out while you were sitting there?' – 'Yes.'

'And while all this was being done you said not a word?' – 'Yes.'

The Dean then reeled off the names of the various boys who Sweeney said, in his statement, had been with him earlier that night: Bill Hailey, Andy Wynn, big Lockie. 'Had you seen them at the disco?' asked the Dean. 'Yes,' the youth replied.

'Did you tell the police that?' – 'No. I didn't tell the police anything.'

'Who else,' asked the Dean, 'who else could have told them that but you?' Sweeney paused for a few seconds and then looked over at John Thomson. 'Who else?' asked the Dean for a second time. 'John Thomson,' he replied.

The Dean continued to read Sweeney's statement, line for line, and eventually succeeded in forcing a confession from the youth that some of the things it contained were true. For instance, he intended to have sex when they left for the cabin. 'That's what happened,' said Sweeney.

'She was naked and wee John had done it to her.' 'Yes,' said Sweeney. 'That's what I saw.' The Dean continued with yet another line from the statement. 'I tried to do it to her but I couldn't because I was that drunk.'

'Is that true or false?' he asked. 'Correct,' replied Sweeney with a cockiness creeping into his voice. 'Who else could have told the police but you?' asked the Dean. For the second time Sweeney pointed the finger at John Thomson.

But the Dean told him that John Thomson had not been taken into custody by the time Sweeney gave his statement.

So was he still insisting that he had never said these things
to the police?

'I didn't tell them that,' said Sweeney. 'Who did?' asked the
Dean. This time Sweeney switched the blame to Stephen
Cameron.

Mr Davidson took Sweeney through each line of his statement. He asked him about the allegation that he had seen
Thomson slashing the woman. Sweeney told him he was on
the other side of the cabin when it happened and added that
he immediately said, 'Get to fuck out of it.'

The Dean then handed him the book of colour photographs
showing the injuries he was alleged to have inflicted on Carol.
He asked him to look through them. 'If what you say is correct,
having seen these blows struck, you left the cabin and didn't
go back. So whose blood was found on your shoes?' Sweeney
admitted, 'It may have been the woman's.'

During the rest of his evidence Sweeney continued to deny
almost everything put to him by the Dean. At the end of it he
returned to his seat in the dock looking decidedly pale.

Then came his brother Gordon's turn. He was taken through
his story by the quiet-voiced Mr Macaulay. Gordon told the
court he was only fourteen at the time of his arrest and was
still at school. On the night of the incident he had been walking home with John Thomson from the disco when they saw
a woman in London Road.

John Thomson, he claimed, went over to her, put his arm
round her and took her across the road towards the scrap-yard.
Gordon said he did not hear the woman object at any time. As
she went with Thomson across the road they stopped in the
middle to let traffic pass. The woman did not shout for help
and there were no signs of a struggle.

Gordon went on to claim that he walked twenty-five to thirty
yards behind them and, consequently, couldn't hear what the
two were talking about. When they all got to the entrance of
the scrap-yard – by this time they were together – they found
a gap in the gate and he helped Thomson to take her through.

'John got hold of one of her arms and I held the other so she
could go through the gate,' he said.

Mr Macaulay asked him if he was certain he was assisting

her and not forcing her and that she had wanted to go with them. 'Yes,' he replied. 'She never said she didn't want to go.'

Gordon described how Thomson went into the cabin while he remained at the front gate. 'I pulled the gate over a wee bit,' he added. 'It was sticking out and people walking past could have banged their head off it.'

Eventually he went to the cabin and, when he looked in, he saw Thomson and the woman lying on the floor having sex. The woman was half-dressed. Thomson, he claimed, told him to shut the door and wait outside. When he opened it for a second time a few minutes later, Thomson was pulling up his trousers.

'What happened next?' asked Mr Macaulay. Young Gordon replied, quite matter-of-factly, 'I went in and had sex with her too.' He told his QC that the woman was not unconscious. Her eyes were open and she gave no indication she was unwilling. There had been no struggle.

'In your statement you told the police you had sex with her,' said Mr Macaulay. 'Is that correct?' 'Yes,' said Gordon, 'but after John Thomson.'

'Had you ever had sexual intercourse before?' – 'No.'

'Was this the first time you had tried it?' – 'Yes.'

'Whose idea to have sex with her was it?' – 'Mine.'

'Was this woman unwilling to have sex?' – 'No.'

'What did she do?' – 'She opened her legs up.'

'Did you have any reason to believe she was unwilling?' – 'No.'

After that Gordon said he went home to tell his brother and, when he arrived back at the cabin with Joe and Stephen Cameron, the woman was still with John Thomson. He couldn't see whether he was having sex with her. Joe, he said, then tried to have sex. She was still conscious because he could see her legs moving. He added, 'I saw Joe getting up and I went away to go home.'

Gordon then described the details of his arrest at 7 a.m. a few days later. The police arrived at his house, went into his bedroom, told him to get his clothes on and then took him by car to the police station.

Mr Macaulay asked if he knew by that time that the woman

had been slashed. He claimed he did not know. Gordon admitted, however, that he had given the police a statement. When asked why, he said, 'My dad told me to. He told me to tell the police the truth.'

'And did you tell the police the truth to the best of your ability?' – 'Yes.'

'You heard the statement read out. Did you tell the truth?' – 'Yes.'

Mr Macaulay reminded the boy that there was a passage in his statement which said that he and John Thomson had dragged the woman to the cabin. 'Was that true?' he asked. 'No,' Gordon told him.

Like his brother before him, Gordon embarked on a series of allegations against the police. They continually accused him of ripping the woman, he claimed, and, at one stage, a detective picked up a wine bottle and struck him on the back of the head with it. 'They frightened me,' he said.

Gordon ended his evidence with a claim that, when Thomson took the woman to the cabin, he had got the impression that Thomson knew her. 'She had also been drinking,' he added.

The Dean, in cross-examination, immediately challenged Gordon's evidence that he had told the police the truth. Mr Davidson selected a number of sample passages from the voluntary statement and asked whether they were true.

' "John grabbed the lassie and *we* dragged her into the yard." Was that true? "Both Joe and John had blood all over their hands." Was that true?' Gordon denied making both statements. He had never spoken these words to the police, he claimed. 'I might have said they had something *like* blood on their hands.'

The Dean launched into a blistering attack. 'Isn't it the truth that it was perfectly obvious Joe's hands were covered in blood?' Gordon insisted, 'I am not saying that they were covered in blood.'

'Didn't you hear your brother shout "I ripped her" more than once?' – 'No.'

'Is the truth of the matter not this: she was dragged into the yard by you and Thomson?' – 'No.'

'And before that happened she was struck on the back of the

head.' – 'No. I never saw John do that, and I never did it myself.'

'Did you have sex with her once, or more than once?' – 'Just once.'

'After Joe arrived, did the woman not try to get up and Joe pushed her back and said "*We* are not finished"?' – 'She never tried to get up. She never moved.'

'If Cameron said that, it's a lie?' – 'Yes.'

'As far as you can say, did the woman know what was going on?' – 'Yes.'

'So if she said she couldn't, that would be quite wrong?' – 'Yes.'

'You have heard Mrs X. say that she did not consent to anything that happened after she met you and Thomson in London Road.' – 'It is a lie.'

'Isn't the truth of the matter that you were one of the two boys who dragged her into the yard and then forced her into sexual intercourse?' – 'No.'

With this final denial, Gordon's cross-examination ended. It only remained now for the last of the three to give evidence. 'I call John Thomson,' announced Mr Morton.

It came as no surprise that, for the first few minutes, Thomson trotted out almost the same story as Gordon Sweeney.

Describing the encounter with Carol in the street, he said, 'She was a wee bit drunk. I walked up beside her, by myself at first, and put my arm round her and asked her where she was going. She said she was going home. I said, "Come on, we'll go over there for a wee while." She made no reply.'

Mr Morton asked him if the woman had gone quite willingly. 'Yes,' he confirmed. Thomson also claimed that, after he crossed the road, Gordon caught up with them and took the woman's other arm before she went into the scrap-yard. Again she didn't object.

Thomson's story then diverged from Gordon Sweeney's. He described how they both undressed the woman. 'I took the top half of her clothing off and Gordon took the rest of her clothing down to her knees. I lifted her blouse above her chest. She bent down and lay on the ground.'

'Did you ask her to do that?' asked Mr Morton. 'No,' replied

Thomson. 'Did Gordon Sweeney?' – 'No.' 'She just did it herself, then?' – 'Yes.'

'What happened next?' – 'She said she would have to go away after this.'

Thomson then turned the tables on Gordon Sweeney. Gordon, not he, had sex with the woman first, he claimed. 'He got on top of her and asked me to go outside. He got off and then I got on top of her.'

Asked by Mr Morton what happened to Gordon at this point, Thomson told the jury his friend just disappeared.

'I got up and pulled my trousers up and, just as I got outside, Gordon Sweeney, Stephen Cameron and Joe Sweeney came running in.'

When asked what had happened after that, Thomson claimed that he saw Joe Sweeney immediately get on top of the woman. He alleged that Stephen Cameron took his turn, too.

'When he got off and Gordon ran past me, I looked back inside and I saw Joe. I think he was punching the lassie. He was standing at the side of her, his arm moving back and forward. I went back in and tried to pull him off. I managed to get him out.'

Mr Morton then asked him what, if anything, he had seen next? 'There was a bit of light,' said Thomson. 'As I got him out I saw a razor in his hand.' Joe Sweeney, he said, left the cabin shouting the war-cry of his local gang. 'He was shouting "Spur Rule" and "I chibbed her." The razor was still in his hand.'

The QC then dealt with Thomson's voluntary statement. The youth confirmed he had given it to the police in the presence of his sister.

'Is what you told the police in that statement true?' asked Mr Morton. 'Yes,' replied Thomson.

Mr Morton handed him the original. 'Can you read?' he asked. Eyebrows were raised throughout the court when the youth replied, 'No. I can hardly read.'

Mr Morton helped him. For the next few minutes he read out the entire statement asking Thomson to listen carefully.

At the conclusion the youth agreed it was all true. He was not contesting any of it.

'Did you rape this woman?' asked Mr Morton. 'No,' replied Thomson. 'She agreed to have sex.'

'Did you chib her with a razor?' There was an even more emphatic 'No.'

Thomson's main adversary now was Mr Findlay, in view of Joe Sweeney's special defence that Thomson, not he, had committed the razor assault.

Mr Findlay suggested to Thomson that he was lying when he claimed that he had left the cabin while Joe remained inside. This was met with an instant denial. 'I was outside until I went back to pull Joe off the woman,' Thomson protested. He told Mr Findlay that Sweeney had even tried to resist his efforts to pull him off.

'Have you tried to suggest to anyone before, that the reason you had blood on your jacket was for the reason that Joe Sweeney struggled with you?' – 'No.'

'Do you not find you need an explanation because it was you who assaulted that woman with a knife?' – 'No.'

'It was *you* who got stuck into her with a knife, wasn't it?' – 'No.'

'And ever since you have been at pains to heap blame on everyone but yourself?' – 'No.'

'And at no time did Joe Sweeney ever have any weapon in his possession that night, did he?' – 'Yes.'

It was now the Dean's turn to cross-examine. Thomson vehemently denied that he had stopped Carol in the street to ask her for a light and that, while she was reaching into her bag, he had struck her from behind. He also denied that, helped by Gordon Sweeney, he had dragged her into the yard.

Thomson abandoned his usual monosyllabic replies. 'These are the two biggest lies I have heard of in this case ... her being hit over the head and dragged into the yard.'

Undaunted, the Dean continued, 'Are you asking the jury to accept your account that, at the age of fourteen, a woman twice your age and without any word being spoken between you, went into the yard with you?' Thomson replied with an almost defiant, 'Yes.'

'Isn't the truth of the matter that you, Thomson, struck her over the head, dragged her with Gordon Sweeney to the cabin, placed her on the floor and then removed her clothing, held her down and had sexual intercourse against her will?'

Thomson's last word on the subject was again a flat denial. The evidence for the defence was finished.

23 The Closing Submissions

Late that afternoon, after a day of conflicting and confusing stories from the three boys, the Dean rose to address the jury as undramatically as he had begun the private prosecution case four days before, reading from a carefully prepared speech.

He told the jury there were two questions they had to ask themselves: what was the evidence that Carol could rely upon as proving her case and how much of it, if any, did they accept?

Dealing first of all with Joseph Sweeney and the razor assault charge the Dean submitted that the first part of the case against him was the evidence of the voluntary statement, the most critical part of which was his admission of having had intercourse and razoring Carol after she started screaming. The second part of the case was the evidence of Stephen Cameron who claimed he saw Sweeney produce something which looked like a razor in the cabin and, later on, saw him emerge, his hands covered in blood and shouting that he had ripped her. The third element was Sweeney's suspicious behaviour in running away from two patrolling police officers. 'You may think that he had a very good reason not to be seen by them,' he said. The Dean also referred to the evidence of the blood found on Sweeney's clothing which could have come from Carol.

'In my submission, if you take all that evidence at face value, then I suggest you would be entitled to hold the charge proved and that Joseph Sweeney is guilty of it.'

The Dean submitted there was no good cause to reject, even

to doubt, the essential truth of the police evidence, particularly
that of Detective Chief Inspector Cowie who took Sweeney's
voluntary confession. He also reminded the jury of Sweeney's
claim that the police had made it all up. 'You might like to
look at it from the other side of the fence. If Joseph Sweeney
is right, then you may think that there is a quite remarkable
and rather ingenious conspiracy on the part of several police
because, if the statement was in fact taken from him or written
down, it is quite extraordinary that, by that time, the police
seemed to be so well into the case that they could reproduce
not merely generalities, but so much detail from the background of what was said. And you may think that there are
some quite notable sentences in that statement which could
have come from no one but Joseph Sweeney.'

The Dean conceded that Dr McKelvie had noted certain
injuries on Sweeney which were consistent with a variety of
causes. The Dean claimed that it was very significant that
Sweeney made no complaint to the doctor and more significant
that, on the same day, he had access to a solicitor and made
no allegation to him.

The Dean continued, 'It is really for you to come to a concluded opinion in these matters. Did, for example, Joseph
Sweeney volunteer the statement that he made to Chief Inspector Cowie? I suggest that the weight of the evidence is
that he did. And if that is so then you have a foundation for
the case set out on the razor assault charge against Joseph
Sweeney. On top of that, I suggest you have strong supporting
evidence, if you accept him as being essentially credible, from
Stephen Cameron.

'In my submission, on that evidence you are entitled to hold
Joseph Sweeney did attack the complainer repeatedly, strike
her upon the head and body with a razor or similar instrument,
all to her severe injury, permanent disfigurement and to the
danger of her life, and I therefore ask you to bring in a verdict
of guilty against him on that charge.'

The Dean then turned to the rape charge against Sweeney
and suggested to the jury that it approach this by asking, first
of all, was it proved that Sweeney had sexual intercourse with

Carol and, secondly, if it was, then in doing so did he overcome her will by force or by threat of force?

'So far as the first question is concerned I suggest that the evidence which you have heard is quite clear. There is evidence in the statement which he gave to that effect. He said, "I tried to do it to her, but I couldn't do it because I was drunk. Stephen never touched her, but Gordon had a go at her. I had another go and managed to do it to her." So again, if you take the statement as being correct, you have a basis for concluding that, and you have had evidence also from Stephen Cameron to that effect.

'Was her will overcome by force or by the threat of it? For this part of the case you will recall some of the events earlier that evening. You may think, and the evidence does suggest, that in the course of the day and evening, in the afternoon and evening of 31st of October, the complainer had a fair amount to drink.

'Her ability to resist an approach such as she experienced may have been reduced, it may have been impaired, and it is really for you to judge that. But on the evidence given by her, and to some extent on the evidence given by even Gordon Sweeney, there is no question of her being unable to give or refuse consent to sexual intercourse.'

The Dean submitted that Stephen Cameron's evidence in relation to this was of considerable importance. According to him, when he and Joseph Sweeney arrived at the cabin Thomson was having intercourse with the woman. After Thomson got up she tried to get up. At that point, Cameron had claimed, Sweeney said, 'We are not finished yet,' pushed her back and then had intercourse with her.

Continued the Dean, 'Now, if that is the position I submit that you are entitled to hold that he had intercourse with her against her will. It is not so much the question of pushing her down it is the fact that, having done that, he then lay on top of her and had intercourse with her. You may well think that, if he had not done what he did, she would have got up and would have gone away. He prevented her from doing that. Therefore, I submit that, if you accept the evidence of Stephen

Cameron about that episode, you are entitled to conclude that her will to resist was overcome by what he did.'

The Dean asked the jurors to recall the part of Sweeney's statement in which he was alleged to have said that the woman started screaming again. That suggested there had been a clear indication, before Sweeney had intercourse, that Carol was not consenting.

The Dean also reminded the jury that, when he was cautioned by Detective Constables Moulds and Darling, Sweeney was alleged to have said, 'You know I fucking done it, but that cunt Thomson held her down.' The Dean pointed out that that caution related to the charges of both rape and razor assault, adding, 'I suggest that the answer fits more easily into the rape charge because there is no indication, so far as I can recall, of it being alleged that Thomson held her down for the purpose of the assault with the razor. I suggest that it fits much better with the suggestion that it was in relation to the rape.

'When you consider all that evidence, I submit that you are entitled to conclude – and I submit that it is plain that the first charge against Joseph Sweeney has been proved beyond reasonable doubt and I ask you to bring back a verdict of guilty against him.'

Mr Davidson then moved to the case against Gordon Sweeney and John Thomson and asked the jury to accept the story given by Carol that she was hit on the back of the head when approached by two boys asking for a light. He admitted that there was no mention of the head injuries in the hospital records, but suggested that this was because the razor injuries might have absorbed the major part of the attention of the doctors. There was, however, evidence from Carol's husband of a bald patch on the back of her head and of scars or sores. The condition of the heels of her new shoes also gave strong support to the allegation that she had been dragged to the cabin.

The Dean said, 'What you are asked to accept is that she willingly allowed two unknown boys to guide her from London Road to a filthy cabin in a scrap-yard for the purposes of having sexual intercourse, instead of carrying on home. That raises very sharp issues of credibility and I suggest that you are entitled to take that factor into account in weighing up the credibility of the two main stories, given by the accused in their evidence today.

'So, in relation to Gordon Sweeney and John Thomson, my submission is that you are entitled to hold that the charge of rape is made out. You are entitled to hold on the evidence which has been led that both of them were involved in the events which comprised the striking her on the head with an unknown instrument whereby she became unconscious, dragging her into the cabin, placing her on the floor, forcibly removing her clothes, holding her down, lying on top of her and repeatedly raping her.

'I agree that it may also be open, subject to My Lord's correction, to take a less serious view of the charge of rape but, on the basis of the confessions and the other facts, you might be persuaded to find a lesser charge proved. In my submissions, however, that decision would not reflect accurately the whole evidence or the gravity of the events which you have heard described. And so in that state of affairs I regard it as my duty to invite you to bring verdicts of guilty upon charge one in relation to all three accused, and of guilty in relation to the second charge against Joseph Sweeney.'

With these words the Dean closed his closing submission and the court adjourned for the evening. Before leaving, the jury was warned by Lord Ross that, as it had only heard one side of the story, it should keep an open mind until the morning when the three defence speeches would be heard.

On Friday, the last day of the trial, Mr Findlay, Joe Sweeney's defence counsel, launched his closing submission with attacks on the press and the police.

He told the jury there was a section of the press which, when dealing with the case, seemed to be not so much concerned with justice as with some form of hysterical cry for vengeance or revenge. The advocate added, 'The tenor of some of the reporting was not that justice should be done, but that these three young men should be convicted. Well, ladies and gentlemen, if you were in any doubt before you came to the court, I

am sure that you are in no doubt now – vengeance or revenge
play no part at all in our judicial system.'

Mr Findlay reminded the jury of Sweeney's special defence,
blaming Thomson for the razor assault. 'If you are of the
opinion that the private prosecution have not proved it was
Joe Sweeney, as I submit most earnestly they have not, you
do not then require to go on to say, "Well, if it wasn't him,
who was it?" Nor do you take into account that, if you acquit
Joseph Sweeney, then no one will be convicted of that charge.
Gordon Sweeney and John Thomson have been acquitted. They
have been acquitted because, at a particular point in this trial,
there was not sufficient evidence to allow the matter to proceed
any further. That does not mean to say that John Thomson
did not do it, or could not have done it. It doesn't really matter
whether he did it or not. The question is, has it been proved
that Joseph Sweeney committed this assault? If you are of the
opinion that Joseph Sweeney should be acquitted, even
although that makes you realize that no one will be convicted
of that assault, then that is the verdict you must bring in.'

Mr Findlay admitted there was an overwhelming body of
evidence against Sweeney. People were almost running around
in circles trying to point the finger at him. He continued, 'So
what? That doesn't matter, because if it is not evidence of a
quality that you are prepared to accept, then you cannot con-
demn Joseph Sweeney.'

Mr Findlay submitted that the manner in which Carol
arrived at the scrap-yard cabin had nothing whatsoever to do
with Joseph Sweeney. He had only been told by his brother
that there was a bird there, and it was plain that he went for
one reason and one reason only – that he thought she was
'providing it for the boys'. It was a nasty mean thing to do,
but condemnation was not sufficient for a charge of rape.

He continued, 'He may have taken advantage of her, but
where is the evidence that he used force? He is not connected
with any bash that she received on the head, if she received
a bash on the head. There is no indication that he knew she
had been forced there, if she was forced there. There is one
reply to the police to suggest that she may have been held

down. Well, I will have something to say about the police shortly.'

But before turning to the police, Mr Findlay attacked the evidence of Stephen Cameron, and asked the jury to reject it because Cameron had been at pains to shift blame onto the others. Cameron had maintained that he took no part in the incident because he had already had sex with his girlfriend that night. Commented Mr Findlay, 'Well, if he had already had sex with his girlfriend, why did he go along? It is obvious. There is evidence to the effect that Cameron did have intercourse with that lady that night and, if that is so, then he is a liar on that point. He is also a liar when he says that Joe Sweeney held her down. I would suggest that if you have two lies on two important points then you must be very wary about treating his evidence as in any way reliable.'

Mr Findlay then launched his promised attack on the police. It was a scathing one. He said that, in his experience, the police often made mistakes, bent the rules and even broke the rules. Mr Findlay gave this advice to the jury, 'You do not believe the evidence of a policeman simply because he is a policeman. You must test his evidence in the same careful way as you would test all the evidence at face value. Bear this in mind: police officers are professional witnesses, trained and experienced in giving evidence and expert in dealing with cross-examination.'

Sweeney, he said, was no more than a boy when he was taken to the police station, and what was he to do when he maintained that officers had assaulted him when it was only his word, and his word alone, against them? There was nobody to back up his story. Mr Findlay also asked the jury if it was purely coincidence that Sweeney had injuries consistent with him being pulled about by his clothing and being hit by a police baton. He added, 'Even if a baton was used, and even if he was pushed and pulled about, that does not mean to say he didn't make the statement. But it does, does it not, make you wonder about what acceptance you can put on the evidence of the police?

'They deny emphatically that any form of violence was used towards Joseph Sweeney. Members of the jury, the weight of evidence is, I submit, that violence was used against Joseph Sweeney, and almost certainly was used against him in that police station.'

Mr Findlay suggested the possibility that various police officers were lying. 'They are as capable or as incapable of committing perjury as anyone else,' he alleged. 'I invite you without any hesitation to reject the statement, to reject the evidence of the police and to allow it to play no further part in your consideration. It is a very serious thing to ask you to do, but all I have are tiny, little details. But those tiny, little details scream at you some very big questions.

'Bear in mind that this young man was alone in a police station. How would you feel if any son of yours on his way home from a school disco was grabbed and taken away to a police station to spend two or three hours in police custody, the police turning round later, saying, "Oh, he has said various things"? Would you be happy? Would you be content? Would you not be demanding that you should have been there and that he should have had a solicitor? Would you not be asking, "How can this be? A sixteen-year-old son of mine kept by the police and now he is supposed to have said these things? This cannot be right."

'Ladies and gentlemen, it is not right, not right at all, and I ask you to reject that police evidence. It will be difficult I know, but I ask you without hesitation and with every ounce of urgency I have.'

No sooner had Mr Findlay finished his powerful attack on the police than Mr Macaulay was standing up to address the jury on behalf of Gordon Sweeney. He stressed that Gordon had walked free from the shadow of the claim that he had razored Carol, and emphasized that the jurors had now to consider whether what happened was rape or some stupid sexual frolic between a woman who had drunk too much and two boys seeking sexual adventure. He added, 'There is a world of difference between a silly woman going with two young boys to a hut while she is half-drunk and the boys taking advantage of her condition, and what is required to prove rape.'

Mr Macaulay said one of the main problems was that there was no real account from the woman about what had happened

– which could be tested. She had said in evidence she didn't consent to anything, but perhaps the proper way to have put it was that she didn't *remember* consenting to anything that happened.

He went on, 'If the prosecution can speculate can I just for a moment? Is it a picture like this: a drunken and depressed woman has just fallen out with her boyfriend, walked out of the house and indulged in further drink? She is wandering home and is picked up by Thomson and Sweeney, taken into the yard, helped through the gate and there, having gone, perhaps stupidly – a lot of funny things happen in life – she succumbs or grants them their sexual wishes?

'She thinks it is all over and is getting ready to go when, lo and behold, what I might call the second wave suddenly appears and she says, "No, no, it is not on. I am not having any more." Does that fit in with the picture, if you believe Cameron, that Joe Sweeney arrived on the scene as the woman was getting up from voluntary sex? When she saw him he pushed her back and said, "We're not finished yet," and then had sex.

'That particular episode, if you find it proved, might constitute rape as far as Joe Sweeney was concerned. If that picture is even a possibility in this case, then it casts a complete shadow on the prosecution case against the others and I would ask you to accept that view of it.'

Mr Macaulay submitted that, even if Carol protested minimally and Gordon Sweeney genuinely, but mistakenly, had reason to believe she was willing to have sex with him, he could not be guilty of the crime of rape. He continued, 'People who are not sober do stupid things, and when they sober up and someone tells them what they did, they regret what they may have done under the influence of drink. You may wonder whether the cloak of unconsciousness put before you in the witness box by Mrs X is, in fact, a cloak for her own drunken condition.

'Having sex with a woman is not a crime. Even taking advantage of a woman is not necessarily rape. It all depends on the circumstances, the state of the woman and the degree of violence used and all the rest of it. I ask you to remember

this is a fourteen-year-old boy living in the age of curiosity.
You remember when you were that age – fourteen, fifteen and
sixteen. Perhaps in days gone past we never heard of it but,
nowadays, people of that age are curious about sex. It is a fact
of life. Sex, just like eating, sleeping and drinking, is just
another activity.

'Having seen Gordon Sweeney in the witness box you could
hardly say he was the brightest individual, his own best friend,
from the way he gave his evidence. Is he not just the type of
boy, at the age of fourteen, who would tag along with Thomson
to see what all this was about, have a bit of sex and go back
home? It was just a sexual adventure on the part of this boy
with this woman under the influence of alcohol.'

His jury speech over Mr Macaulay sat down, the well of the
court to be taken by Mr Morton on behalf of Thomson. He
began by commenting about Joseph Sweeney's allegation that
John Thomson had used the razor. He asked the jury, 'Who
ran away at 12.30 a.m. on November 1st, 1980 when the police
arrived? It wasn't John Thomson – it was Joseph Sweeney. It
is crucially important what happened initially.

'Who made a statement that he didn't do it, but another
person did, and has stuck to that statement without qualification, has made no allegation that the police have invented
it, or have hit him, and have done this, that or the other to
him? It is John Thomson.

'You have heard me go through his statement word for word
because he can't read. He is not like a CIA or KGB agent who
can adapt to another character. He is not perhaps the brightest
character in Glasgow but, if he tells the same consistent story
all along, isn't it likely to be true?'

Mr Morton said that what was clear in the evidence was
that, when Joseph Sweeney, his brother Gordon and Stephen
Cameron arrived at the cabin, John Thomson took no further
part in anything except to pull Joseph Sweeney off the woman
as Sweeney was using the razor. He stressed to the jury, 'Your
concern in deciding whether John Thomson is guilty of rape
comes down to the first stage – how did Mrs X get to the cabin,
and what happened before Cameron and the two Sweeneys
arrived?

'Was she struck on the head as she claimed? She said she was hit on the head while she was reaching into her handbag to get a lighter, because she had been asked by these two boys for a light. She said she had two lacerations, her hair was shaved and she wasn't drunk at that time. She had recovered from the effects of the drink. She says she was knocked out, but she remembers being dragged before she lost consciousness. Now that is vital evidence because, of course, if that is established that is force and that is very obvious. You have got to find corroboration of that somewhere.

'But where is there support for the idea that she was hit on the back of the head? First of all, she said she was going, for a cigarette lighter, into her shoulder bag. Every article of her clothing has been found but there is no shoulder bag. She said she ran out of the house because she thought her boyfriend was going to attack her or hit her. Could she possibly have gone out without her shoulder bag at all?'

Mr Morton also referred to the evidence of the doctors who had no record of any injury to the back of her head. The only evidence to support Carol had been very vague and inconclusive – from her husband. Mr Morton commented on the other evidence relied upon by the private prosecution, that of her damaged shoes. 'The shoes she was wearing are over *there*,' he continued, pointing towards the bench where all the Crown productions were lying. 'They are a very light sandal type of thing. It is astonishing, if she was dragged backwards, that there is not much damage on the back of the heels to the leather.'

Mr Morton submitted that the 'terrible assault' on Carol by Joseph Sweeney might have affected the accuracy of her recollection of previous events. She had also been questioned time and time again by lawyers, police and the press. 'After you have been through all that do you imagine it is easy to remember exactly what did happen and what somebody else has suggested to you may have happened? Is she reliable? In my submission, when you come to consider that evidence, you can't really say either that you can accept her account as being accurate and reliable, taking all the circumstances, or, secondly, you can't find the corroboration of the strength, quality and character that you would need to be able to say beyond reasonable doubt this is what happened.'

So how did Carol get into the cabin? Mr Morton said the only answer was that she went willingly but unwisely because she had had too much to drink. Cameron's evidence that, when he arrived, she was all right, conscious, trying to get up, but scared, was not evidence to corroborate rape. She became scared afterwards, but that was only after Thomson had left. He took no further part in the sexual attack if there was one. Mr Morton said the Dean had posed the question: what woman would voluntarily go to such a hut? The QC continued, 'With all respect to the Dean, that seems to me to put the cart before the horse because, if you accept John Thomson, that he put his arm round the lady and said "Come along here," then the lady couldn't have known she was going to that particular hut at that point. She was just going along with him. She may have been going to a house. She may have been going anywhere. Is it not an obvious place, if the gate was open, for a boy to take a girl if you live in a slum in Glasgow? Where else?'

Mr Morton said that, during the closing submissions, the possibility of the jury bringing in a verdict of guilty to the lesser charge of indecent assault had been mentioned. He added he was 'a bit puzzled' as to exactly where a charge like that could arise. 'But, if it is open to you, naturally it would be better than a conviction for rape. But please do not say, "Oh well, this is a halfway house, we will go there." This isn't a form of option. You have sworn an oath to tell the truth. You have got to make up your minds on the evidence you have heard and nothing else. In my submission the proper verdict for Thomson on the rape charge is a verdict of not guilty or of not proven.'

24 The Summing-Up

The trial was now reaching its conclusion. All that remained for the jury, before it retired, was to hear Lord Ross's summing up of the complicated and sometimes contradictory evidence.

Lord Ross told the jury men and women that they had to decide the case on facts and facts alone, subject to his directions in law.

'It is for you to decide what facts are proved and what facts are not proved. It is for you to decide what evidence is acceptable; which witnesses you believe and which you reject; which you regard as reliable and which as unreliable; whether you accept the whole or only part of a witness's evidence; what weight you attach to a witness's evidence; and what inferences fall to be drawn from any facts. All are matters for you to determine and have nothing to do with me.'

He also stressed the necessity to put out of mind anything seen in the newspapers or on the television regarding the case or rape generally, and the need to remain free from all prejudice and preconceived ideas in order to arrive at a verdict solely on the basis of the evidence. 'At the outset you will recall that you took an oath that you would well and truly try the accused and give a true verdict. So you have sworn to return a true verdict which you can only do if you obey these directions which I am giving you. That is a very important direction as I am sure you will appreciate.'

Outlining the law on evidence Lord Ross said that, in any criminal trial, the burden of proving guilt rested firmly on the prosecution. Under the law a man was presumed to be innocent until he had been proved guilty. The law also provided that no person could be convicted of any offence upon the evidence of one witness alone, however credible or reliable that witness was.

He added, 'Before any accused person may be convicted, there must be evidence to establish his guilt coming from more than one source. The evidence may be the evidence of more than one eyewitness, or it may be evidence of one eyewitness and other witnesses speaking to facts and circumstances, but the important thing is that you must find evidence from more than one source, each tending to fit in with each other, and so satisfying you that an essential matter has been proved before you can hold that essential matter to be proved.'

Different considerations, however, applied for defence evidence. 'It is never necessary for an accused person to prove anything, or indeed to give evidence at all, because the onus or burden of proof is upon the prosecution. If an accused gives evidence which tends to exculpate him, then, if you believe him you must acquit him even if his evidence stands alone. He does not require to be corroborated. Moreover, even if you don't altogether believe an accused person, if what he says raises a reasonable doubt in your minds as to whether the prosecution has proved its case beyond reasonable doubt, then it would be your duty to acquit. And I must stress, too, that even if you reject an accused's evidence, that does not mean that the contrary case is necessarily established.'

Lord Ross then turned to the vital evidence of Stephen Cameron, the eyewitness. He told the jury Cameron was in a somewhat special position because he appeared to have been involved, at least to some extent, in what was alleged to have happened. 'At one stage he appears to have been a suspect and, indeed, to have been charged with the offences which are the subject of the present proceedings. Depending on what you make of that evidence, you may feel that he might have been in the dock with the other accused. But in this connection I should explain to you that it is perfectly competent for the prosecution to lead evidence from a person whom they believe has been involved to some extent in the commission of the offences charged.

'I have to tell you that you must regard his evidence with great care: there may be a tendency, a desire on his part, to fix the blame firmly on the accused in order to distract attention from anything which he may have done himself. Of course, ladies and gentlemen, you are quite entitled to accept what he says but you should apply to his evidence a special scrutiny, over and above the general examination which you apply to all the material evidence in this case.'

One of Lord Ross's most vital directions was to spell out the law relating to the evidence of voluntary statements. He told the jury that, if they were satisfied that the three statements by the accused boys were freely made and that they were accurately recorded by the police, then they could accept them in so far as they related to the person who actually made them. If they took the view that they were not accurately recorded, that someone did not accurately write down what was said, then, of course, they should not accept the statements. He continued, 'It is important that, in so far as anything is said in such a statement which implicates a co-accused, it must, of course, be ignored because, if made without the presence of the co-accused, it cannot be evidence against the co-accused. If Joseph Sweeney, in his statement, makes some remark which would tend to implicate one of his co-accused, then what Joseph Sweeney says in his statement may be used in evidence against him, if you find it acceptable, but it can't, under any circumstances, be evidence against the co-accused, and I am sure that is obvious. At the same time I must point out to you, of course, that it is quite different when the accused gives evidence because, if an accused person gives evidence which is then, as you can see for yourselves, subject to cross-examination on behalf of the other accused, it is then part of the evidence in the case like any other evidence that has been put before you. But a statement is in a different position and the rule which I have explained to you applies so far as a statement is concerned.

'The sort of question that you should ask yourselves in relation to any statement which has been challenged is this: was the statement unfairly obtained? Was there any question of bullying, of pressure, or inducement, or third-degree methods?

Was there anything in the nature of cross-examination when the statement was being taken? And if any of these questions fall to be answered "yes," then you should disregard the statement and exclude it from your deliberations as being unfairly obtained and not a true and voluntary statement. On the other hand, if you hold that there is no unfairness, no bullying, no pressure, no inducement, no third-degree methods and no cross-examination, then you may accept the statement as a voluntary and spontaneous statement of the accused who is said to have made it and then attach to it such weight and value as you feel it deserves.'

'The law of rape is the carnal knowledge of a woman forcibly and against her will. It has to be done by force and the woman has to withhold her consent. Penetration also has to be proved, although the extent of the penetration is not material to guilt.'

The judge went on to define the law on rape: 'It is of the essence of the crime of rape that there must be force by which the physical resistance of the victim has been overcome. That may be effected by direct violence, as, for example, taking hold of someone in such a way that she cannot prevent intercourse. It may also be done by threats of the kind of violence which put a woman in fear of her life or serious injury. If the will to resist is overcome in this way, the crime is rape, even although no actual physical violence is committed. But, of course, you must not judge too harshly or allow yourselves to be too wise after the event as to what the victim might or might not have done.

'You have got to look at all the circumstances properly disclosed by the evidence and, if the threats were serious enough to induce her to believe that they might be carried out unless she yielded, then the man who has threatened her and induced her to yield in this way commits the crime of rape.'

At this point Lord Ross sounded a warning. One of the issues in the case was drink and he told the jury that, if a woman voluntarily consumed alcohol to such an extent as to be virtually insensible, it was *not* rape to have intercourse with her, just as it was not rape to have intercourse with a sleeping woman. 'It might be indecent assault,' he said, 'but it would *not* be rape.

'Where a woman is not insensible but is drunk, that is to
say under the influence of alcohol, the matter, of course, is
different, and in such a situation what you must determine is
whether intercourse took place forcibly and against her will.
The fact a woman is drunk may mean that a lesser degree of
violence is necessary to overcome her resistance than in the
case of a sober woman. On the other hand, if a woman is drunk
it may mean that she is less inclined to withhold consent and,
of course, if she was capable of withholding consent and did
not, in fact, withhold consent, there is no rape.

'The next question you may ask when you are considering
rape is: what of a woman who has become unconscious? Under
our law it is not rape to take advantage of a woman who is in
an unconscious state and is thus incapable of exercising will
power so as to give or refuse consent, because it is only rape
if intercourse takes place forcibly and against the woman's
will. But, of course, it would be rape for a man to have intercourse with a woman whom he had rendered unconscious by
violence because, in that situation, he has used violence to
overcome her resistance.'

There were alternatives, however, and Lord Ross painstak-
ingly outlined them to the men and women of the jury. If they
were not satisfied that the facts amounted to rape but were
satisfied that the accused assaulted their victim and attempted
to ravish her, then they could convict of attempted rape. Again,
if the jury was not satisfied that there was an attempt, in the
sense of taking some positive steps towards effecting a rape,
but that there was an assault with the intention of ravishing
the woman, it could convict of assault with intent to ravish.
There was another alternative – indecent assault. This was an
attack upon a woman accompanied by circumstances of inde-
cency. Lord Ross referred to Carol's evidence about being
assaulted in London Road. He told the jury there was no
suggestion that Joseph Sweeney was there or was responsible
for what took place in London Road. 'The prosecution merely
say, in relation to the charge against Joseph Sweeney, that
you should consider this because it explains how she got to be
in the cabin, but I do stress there is no question of Joseph
Sweeney being responsible for her getting into the cabin.'

Dealing with what was alleged to have happened to Carol in the cabin, Lord Ross said it was important for the jury to determine whether it thought she was conscious or not at the relevant time.

'As I told you, under our law it isn't rape to take advantage of a woman who is in an unconscious condition and is thus incapable of exercising will power so as to give or refuse consent, and it is not suggested that Joseph Sweeney took part in any alleged assault in London Road which she says rendered her unconscious.

'On the other hand, there was some evidence that she was not unconscious the whole time, and that you may think is important. In fairness she wasn't really able to say very much but she did indicate, as I understood her evidence, that for part of the time in the cabin she was conscious, to some extent at least.

'Joseph Sweeney, as I recall his evidence, said something to the effect – and you may or may not think this is important – that the woman never knew what was going on, which might suggest that she was not conscious. On the other hand the evidence of his younger brother Gordon, as I recall it, was that she did know what was going on and, indeed, that was really the evidence of Thomson as well.

'So there is a conflict here because both Gordon Sweeney and John Thomson maintained that the woman agreed and that there was no question of her being unconscious. On the other hand the complainer said that she was unconscious at least part of the time and, I think on her evidence, for most of the time, and Joseph Sweeney, too, said that she didn't know what was going on. Well it is up to you, ladies and gentlemen, to determine that, because this obviously raises an issue of fact.

'If she was unconscious when Joseph Sweeney either had, or tried to have, sexual relations with her, then that would not be rape or attempted rape. On the other hand, if she was conscious then you must decide, firstly, whether Joseph Sweeney had intercourse and, secondly, whether the woman's resistance was overcome by force. Joseph Sweeney denied having sexual intercourse and therefore you have got to consider whether it has been established beyond reasonable doubt that he did.

'There certainly is evidence, if you accept it, which would justify you in holding that he did have sexual intercourse but it is entirely a matter for you on the evidence. If he did not have intercourse the question then is, did he overcome her resistance by fear or, more correctly, has it been established beyond reasonable doubt that he overcame her resistance by force?'

Lord Ross referred to a passage from Joseph Sweeney's alleged voluntary statement in which he was quoted as saying, 'She started screaming again.' The prosecution suggested that meant, firstly, that Carol must have screamed before and, secondly, it indicated she was not willing. 'But it is for you to consider what you may of the evidence,' he told the jury.

The judge also referred to Cameron's evidence of the production of the razor in the cabin. If the jury accepted that, it might be relevant to the assault, but it wasn't relevant to the rape because there was no suggestion in the charge that a razor had been used to overcome the woman's resistance.

Dealing with the razor assault, Lord Ross told the jury they might think that there was quite a body of evidence in support of the prosecution case that it was Joe Sweeney who carried out the assault. 'I can certainly say that there is sufficient evidence, if you accept it, to justify you in bringing in a verdict of guilty against Joseph Sweeney on this charge. But it is entirely a matter for you as to whether you accept that evidence and are satisfied beyond reasonable doubt.'

Lord Ross then went on to sum up the case in respect of Gordon Sweeney and John Thomson. He said the jury first of all had to decide whether it believed Mrs X's account of what happened in London Road, a very critical point in relation to the two boys.

Lord Ross referred to what Carol had drunk that afternoon and evening, but told the jury to bear in mind that she was a person who had suffered very serious injuries in the assault and to consider whether the injuries might have affected her recollection of events. Nobody, in evidence, had suggested that she was really drunk or incapable.

The judge continued, 'She said that two boys asked her for a light somewhere near the railway bridge; and she was struck on the head from behind. She remembers being dragged, she became unconscious, and she came to. Well now, do you believe her? And this is really crucial because, unless she was rendered unconscious and dazed, you might want to ask yourselves why she didn't resist and why she didn't struggle if two young boys were trying to have intercourse with her. So, do you believe her?

'Well now, you have been reminded of the fact that the hospital surgeon said that there was nothing in the hospital records to show any injury to the back of the head, which is something you might have expected if she had been struck from behind, but it is your recollection of his evidence that matters. If he had found cuts on the back of the head then he would have noted them and that is perhaps what you would have expected. He also said, I think, that her head had not been shaved, and you would really have to ask yourselves whether you think that the surgeon could, in some way, have missed this cut, injury, on the back of her head, or could have forgotten about it, being too concerned with the more obvious and major injuries apparently caused by the razor.

'Could they be mistaken, could they be wrong about this? Because certainly she said, as I recall her evidence, that the back of her head had been shaved and that there were some kind of cuts there. If there was no mark on the back of her head you might think that that would be surprising if her story was true that she had been struck a blow on the back of her head, but it is up to you.

'The other thing on which the prosecution rely, as in some way supporting her story, is the state of her shoes. You may remember her shoes were produced in court. She gave an account of being dragged along to this cabin and drew attention to the fact that the heels of her shoes, which I think she said had, in fact, been in fairly good condition beforehand, were damaged.

'Well, it is for you to determine whether you think that supports her story or not. And the prosecution also says that, in her evidence, she indicated she had never agreed to anything that took place after events in London Road.

'Of course, as regards that early period in London Road, evidence has been given by both Gordon Sweeney and John Thomson – and they deny any assault – that she went voluntarily with them. So you really have to choose between these versions and ask yourself whether the prosecution has established beyond reasonable doubt that she was assaulted in London Road and struck on the head, whereby she became unconscious.

'The prosecution point out that the defence really means that this woman, in her late twenties who is living with a man, voluntarily went off in order to have sexual relations with two boys aged fourteen and fifteen, and they say, "Is that likely?" But, of course, on the other hand the defence point out that, on the evidence, this woman had had a fair amount of drink and she might therefore have been doing something which she wouldn't normally do and which, indeed, she might well regret in her sober moments.'

Lord Ross said that Gordon Sweeney had given evidence that he believed he had the consent of the woman. The judge, however, stressed that a man must have reasonable ground for thinking, for honestly believing, that a woman had consented. The issue depended on what the jury made of the evidence relating to London Road. If Carol had gone along quite quietly and entered the cabin without force or protest and lay down as was suggested, the jury might well conclude that, whether or not she was willing, the boy had good reason to think that he was dealing with a woman who was consenting, even though she didn't consent. That would mean he would be entitled to be acquitted.

'Because Gordon Sweeney admits having intercourse, therefore there could be no question of attempted rape or assault with intent to ravish, but there might be the other alternative of indecent assault. If you took the view that the prosecution had not proved rape, that is, that it had not been proved that sexual intercourse took place forcibly and against the woman's will, but that she was assaulted and that the assault was accompanied by conduct of an indecent nature – that is, forcibly removing her clothing – then you could bring in a verdict of guilty of indecent assault. But I have to remind you, and this is important, that for assault there must be an intention to do harm, and before you could bring in a verdict of indecent assault you would have to be satisfied that she was assaulted by the accused intending to do her harm and you would have to ask, "Was there any intention to do her harm?"

'If she was consenting to the removal of her clothing or if Gordon, genuinely and reasonably, believed that she was so consenting, then that would not be an assault and, on that view, there would not be room for a finding of indecent assault.'

Lord Ross then dealt with the case for and against John Thomson, the evidence being very similar to Gordon Sweeney's. Thomson had claimed that sex was with the woman's consent. Stephen Cameron had given evidence that he could see the woman's face when Thomson was on her, that she had looked all right, that he had seen no sign of movement from her and that there had been nothing to suggest force.

Lord Ross added, 'That evidence you may think, if anything, would tend to negate any question of intercourse taking place forcibly and against the woman's will but, of course, it is entirely for you to determine whether you accept that evidence and what you make of it.'

Lord Ross said that the prosecution relied on one particular passage in the statement made by Thomson to the police: 'We saw this lassie across the road walking up towards Parkhead and me and wee Gordon Sweeney walked up beside her. Then we took an arm each and took her across the road into the scrap-yard. And took her into this big container and we took the bottom of her clothes off.'

The jury had to decide whether there was any significance in the continued use of the word 'took' and whether it indicated that some degree of force had been used: 'On the other hand, I think he goes on later to say, "The woman didn't fight or resist. She was drunk." '

There was also evidence from Thomson to the effect that he believed the woman to be willing. 'You will remember what I said a moment ago about the position of a man who has intercourse with a woman without her consent but, in the circum-

stances where there are good grounds for genuinely believing
that he does have her consent, such a person is not guilty of
rape. And then again, you will remember what I said about
the possible alternative of indecent assault. If you weren't
satisfied that he had sexual intercourse with her forcibly and
against her will, you could still bring in a verdict of indecent
assault if you thought that he had assaulted her in an indecent
manner, and that would be in the terms of the indictment by
forcibly removing her clothing.

'But you could only do that if you thought that he had acted
with an intention to injure her and that he was doing so when
she either didn't consent or, at least, that he had no reason to
think that she did consent.'

Lord Ross was almost finished. 'I don't want to trespass into
your field of fact,' he told the jury. 'And I hope you will believe
that I am not in any way attempting to usurp your function.
But I am bound to say, I think that the evidence which does
exist in the rape charge against Gordon Sweeney and John
Thomson is slender. I have concluded that there is sufficient
evidence, if you accept it, to entitle you to convict, but I make
no secret of the fact that I reach that conclusion with some
hesitation.

'Fortunately, if there is a conviction and I am wrong in that,
there is a court of appeal that can put that right, but what I
have to say to you at this stage is this: that where evidence is
slender against the second and third accused I have really to
give you this direction.

'I have reminded you of what the evidence is upon which the
prosecution relies, and what I would say to you is this: if you
are unable to accept any of the evidence upon which the prosecution rely, or are not satisfied by any material part of the
evidence, then the result would inevitably be that there would
not be sufficient evidence in which to convict the second and
third accused of rape.'

After being instructed on the three possible verdicts they
could bring in, not guilty, not proven or guilty, the jury retired
to consider one of the most important verdicts in Scottish legal
history.

25 The Verdicts

At 5.25 p.m., two hours and sixteen minutes after it had retired, the jury returned to announce its verdict.

QCs and advocates had spent much of the time, while the jury was out, pacing up and down Parliament Hall under its ornate ceiling beams and supports.

At one point, while considering the evidence, the jury had rung the bell in its private room to ask the clerk of court if it could examine the sandals Carol had been wearing. Members had been unable to see them properly during the course of the trial.

There was a hurried debate in Lord Ross's chambers, the defence objecting to the jury's request. Lord Ross ruled it could see documentary productions – but not the shoes.

But that was all water under the bridge now. The moment of truth had arrived after four days of evidence. With, or without, the sandals, the jury had arrived at its decision on charge one, the razor assault which only Joe Sweeney faced, and on charge two, the rape which concerned all three. Journalists were trying to guess who they had selected from their number as a foreman to speak for them. There was one obvious candidate, a man sitting in the front row, nervously clenching a slip of paper in his right hand.

As soon as Lord Ross took his place on the bench the clerk rose, faced the jury and asked, 'Ladies and Gentlemen, who speaks for you?' The man in the front row stood up. 'What is your verdict in respect of the first named, Joseph Sweeney, on charge number one?' asked the clerk. The foreman said, 'Guilty as libelled.' 'Is that unanimous or by a majority?' 'Majority,' replied the foreman. Other members of the jury started shaking their heads. The foreman began to stutter. 'Sorry, unanimous.' 'Is it unanimous?' asked the clerk for the second time. 'Yes. Sorry about that, I apologize.'

'And on charge number two, in respect of Joseph Sweeney, what is your verdict?' 'Guilty as libelled.' 'And again, is that unanimous or by a majority?' 'Unanimous.'

'What is your verdict in respect of the second named, Gordon Sweeney, on charge number one?' 'Guilty of indecent assault.' 'Is that unanimous or by a majority?' 'Unanimous.'

'What is your verdict in respect of the third named, John Thomson, on charge number one?' 'Guilty of indecent assault.' 'And again, is that unanimous or by a majority.' 'Unanimous.'

The clerk then returned to his desk, to record the verdicts in the official court ledger.

The three boys sat impassively during the whole proceedings. QCs, advocates and lawyers, however, were looking quizzically at each other. It was a bizarre verdict. Sweeney, for instance, had been convicted of something which the prosecution and the judge accepted he did not do, namely, ambushing Carol in the street, striking her on the back of the head with an unknown instrument and dragging her by force to the container in Davaar Street. While all this was allegedly being done by him, Joe had been at home with Stephen Cameron, drinking cans of lager.

The verdicts were even more odd in respect of Gordon Sweeney and John Thomson. For a start, the jury did not specify the nature of the indecent assault of which it had found them guilty. The verdict was open to two constructions.

Firstly, did the jury believe that Carol had gone willingly, though under the influence of alcohol, to the cabin, had perhaps been assaulted by the removal of her clothing but, thereafter, had agreed to sexual intercourse? Or, secondly, had the jury decided there was insufficient evidence to prove that Carol had been dragged to the cabin but enough to prove that she was unconscious when sex took place? That being the case it had perhaps taken Lord Ross's advice that it was not rape to have sex with an unconscious woman unless she had been rendered unconscious for that purpose. Which view the jury took no one would ever know except the jury itself.

The Dean rose to his feet. 'My Lord, on behalf of the complainer, I move for sentence.'

Lord Ross motioned Mr Findlay to address him. The young advocate pointed out that the judge had already received a Social Enquiry Report on Joseph Sweeney. He referred to a line in it which disclosed that, when Sweeney had been interviewed by a social worker, he had 'impressed as a normal eighteen-year-old youth, with nothing in his past to indicate a predisposition towards violent acts or behaviour of any kind'.

Mr Findlay added, 'I think all I can say, My Lord, is that I have been involved in this case from an early stage. I have seen Joseph Sweeney on a number of occasions, as indeed has my instructing solicitor, and neither he nor I can see anything in this young man which would in any way explain, in particular, the violence of which he has been convicted of using against this unfortunate lady.

'Indeed, it is in my own experience a unique degree of violence of a particularly cruel kind and one has to face up to that. It is very hard to conceive of any basis upon which anyone could, coldly and deliberately, use such violence in the circumstances in which it was used. It would seem that, whatever made that young man lose his temper, he must have lost control of himself to such a degree that, on a commonsense view, one might describe it as a moment of madness. Beyond that I really find it impossible to say anything to explain his behaviour.

'In the whole circumstances I can really only ask Your Lordship to bear two things in mind: in particular, that he is only eighteen years of age and, whilst this had undoubtedly been an ordeal for the complainer, it has also been an ordeal for Sweeney himself because, on two occasions, he has been brought to the High Court, with the Bill itself and then this trial. I would ask your Lordship to bear that plea in mind when considering sentence. But really, in the light of the verdict of the jury, I regret that there is nothing I can really say on behalf of my client.'

Lord Ross nodded. 'I understand, Mr Findlay,' he said. He then asked Mr Macaulay to address him.

Mr Macaulay said that Gordon Sweeney was now sixteen years old. He told the judge that his family had had to live under the constant blaze of publicity focused on their sons. They had received abusive letters and their boys had become the 'subject of attention' in the area. Mr Macaulay also referred to the Social Enquiry Report on Gordon. It described him as a boy of 'considerable potential'. He went on, 'Of course, it is rather difficult to see what his potentiality is until it has been tested, but the conclusion reached is that his involvement in the offence would appear to be completely out of character in that he has no past history of any predisposition to this type of behaviour.

'I find myself in some difficulty addressing Your Lordship in the light of the nature of the jury's verdict, because Your Lordship has only obtained from the jury the name of an offence without the specification, and therefore I do not know any more than does Your Lordship what the nature of the indecent assault is.' Lord Ross told him that, in any view, it was certainly a very much less serious charge than the crime of which his brother had been convicted.

Continued Mr Macaulay, 'I can only surmise that the jury has taken the view that the initial stages in this episode with Mrs X, involving Gordon Sweeney and Thomson, in fact arose out of her own doing to a large extent, in getting herself into a drunken condition, and the boys taking advantage of her in that condition. That is the only broad and reasonable view I can take as an interpretation of the jury's verdict in the absence of any specification.

'This case has been going on for a considerable length of time, as Your Lordship will appreciate, through no fault of Gordon Sweeney who has lived through a considerable period of strain for a young man.'

Mr Morton then addressed the judge on behalf of John Thomson. He said he was also puzzled about the nature of the offence of which the jury had found Thomson guilty. He went on, 'Your Lordship has the benefit of a Social Enquiry Report which shows that to say he was disadvantaged is an understatement

as regards his educational attainments and capabilities. He
was in a situation where it would be very difficult to see that
he had any hope. I think all I can suggest to Your Lordship is
that the period of eighteen months this has been hanging over
his head must have added considerably to the difficulties that
he has had to face, and ask you to be as lenient as possible.'
Mr Morton said that, if the boys had been charged with indecent assault, they would never have appeared in the High
Court.

Lord Ross then began to sentence the three boys. He turned
to Joseph Sweeney first. 'Rape is an appalling crime and this
court always takes a very serious view of it. The rape here was
a particularly cowardly one and this court must do what it can
to protect women, including those under the influence of drink.
The fact that a woman has been drinking is no excuse for
taking advantage of her.

'Not content with raping this woman, you thereafter
assaulted her in a horrific way. It was a brutal and senseless
attack with a razor which inflicted some of the worst injuries
to a victim of slashing that I have ever come across. It has
been repeatedly said in this court that a serious view will be
taken of assaults involving weapons, and those who commit
such an offence can expect no mercy. That is particularly so
when the victim is a woman.

'The sentence I am about to impose will mark the fact that
this case, in my view, is a very bad one and that you are a
very dangerous young man. I have listened to what your counsel has said. I accept that this matter has been hanging over
you and I accept that, for some time now, you can't have found
life very easy. The sentence will recognize that. But it must
be a substantial one and, in respect of the two charges of which
you have been convicted, I sentence you to be detained in a
young offenders' institution for twelve years.'

Sweeney showed no emotion whatsoever. The judge then
turned to Gordon Sweeney and John Thomson and, addressing
them jointly, said the offence of which they had been convicted
was very much less serious than rape and, in normal circumstances, would not have come before the High Court. Lord
Ross continued, 'Taking into account all the circumstances,

including your ages and the period that this has been hanging over you, I think that justice would be served if I deferred sentence upon each of you for a period of one year. That means that I will not impose any sentence today. If you behave yourselves throughout the forthcoming year you will be brought before me in one year's time and you may take it that you will then be dealt with very leniently. On the other hand, if, during that year, you do not behave yourselves you will be brought back before me and will be punished.'

The proceedings were almost over. The Dean rose for the last time and asked the judge if he could make a few observations. He wanted to express his thanks to Strathclyde Police for their behaviour in a very delicate situation and for the thoroughness of their investigations. The Dean's last few words gratefully summed up the debt owed by Carol to reporters from all over the country, in particular the *Daily Record* which had spotlighted her case and her long struggle for justice. 'I would like to express appreciation of the fact that it was because of publicity in newspapers earlier this year that these proceedings came under way. The publicity, admittedly, caused some difficulty at an early stage but, nevertheless, I think it right to emphasize that, without it, this prosecution probably would not have gone ahead.'

Lord Ross gathered up his notebook and pencils, shifted his chair to face the jury and addressed it for the last time. 'Ladies and gentlemen of the jury, it only remains for me to thank you now. You will appreciate this case as being almost a unique one. It is, I think, the first private prosecution to take place in Scotland for over seventy years and one would like to think, at the end of the day, that justice has been done and been seen to be done. If that is so, then you have certainly played a very important part in it.'

The macer shouted, 'Cou . . . rt,' for the last time and Lord Ross walked out. The spectre of the Glasgow rape case which had haunted Carol, the three boys, the eyewitness, the Crown Office, Parliament, the ex-Solicitor General and justice itself, had been laid to rest at long last. Or had it?

As Gordon Sweeney and John Thomson headed out of court

with their relatives to return to Barrowfield and Joseph Sweeney began his first night in detention as a convicted rapist and
razor slasher, the three defence teams were already announcing that the question of an appeal was under consideration.

26 Back to Normal

Carol was not in court or anywhere near it when the sentence was passed. She had been taken by a reporter to the BBC, Edinburgh television studios to await the verdicts and to be interviewed for her reaction afterwards. Carol learned the results from a telephone call and, within a few minutes, the champagne corks were popping in an unofficial celebration.

She was delighted that the youths had been convicted, but the main emotion which swept over her was relief that her anguish had ended. There were no triumphant feelings of revenge because Carol was just glad. It was all finished.

There was another reason for celebrating – Carol thought she was pregnant and was awaiting the results of tests to confirm it. Her joy, however, was later to turn to tears when the tests revealed her pregnancy was a false alarm, almost certainly brought about by strain.

As the lawyers and counsel representing the three boys began to study the possibility of an appeal that evening, Carol and Billy, after appearing nationally on television, were driven to the quiet village of Drymen, not far from the shores of Loch Lomond, for the weekend. It was a relaxing two days, courtesy of the *Scottish Daily Express*. Carol, however, had agreed to meet representatives of all the press, anonymously but forthrightly. She recognized that her case was one of national interest and she was anxious to show a corresponding responsibility.

Later, Carol and Billy returned to their flat in the East End of Glasgow hoping that, at long last, they would get back to normal. Billy started work again and, as the weeks passed, the young couple's thoughts turned towards a summer holiday. Glasgow's traditional annual holiday, the Glasgow Fair, takes place in the second half of July and, as it loomed, the young couple made plans to join the exodus.

At the last minute they were able to secure a cut-price holiday in the Greek island of Rhodes. Carol had never been abroad before and, in the days leading up to their well-deserved break, she began excitedly to pack her suitcases and buy in suntan lotions.

The thought of lying on a beach in her swimming costume, her thighs horribly scarred for all to see, worried Carol. But she put her fears to the back of her mind by recalling how Billy had taken her to the swimming baths in Glasgow just a few weeks before the trial. She had not wanted to go, believing everyone would be staring at her injuries, but Billy had persuaded her. As she stood at the poolside that afternoon, Carol received a pleasant surprise – no one looked at her twice. She was not the object of the perverse curiosity she expected.

The fortnight in Rhodes flew past and, before they knew it, Carol and Billy were on the plane heading back to Glasgow, ready to take up the threads of life together. But, as the weeks turned into months, they were both to discover how slender and delicate were the strands of their marriage. When Billy was working they got on well, as happy as any young married couple. It was when Billy was not working that their relationship began to sour. Billy would go out to the pub, a pleasure so often denied him when he was looking after Carol during the height of her torment – and when he returned Carol would be watching television. 'You don't seem to want to talk to me,' he would complain. 'What have we got to talk about?' Carol would ask. 'We've been talking all day, every day, for a whole week. The conversation has been exhausted.'

The result was a series of rows and, eventually, an unhappy Carol walked out on her husband after a particularly serious one. She went to stay with an aunt and, a few days later, turned up at Harper's office asking him to raise a divorce. Harper, however, persuaded Carol not to take any hasty action and, a few weeks later, she returned home.

But it was not long before another rift appeared in Carol's marriage and she left Billy again to return to her aunt's. Carol made weekly visits to Harper's office to discuss her criminal injuries compensation case and various other matters, including the possibility of an appeal, and her marital unhappiness. The compensation claim, however, would not be disposed of until the appeals had been heard. The appeals could not take place until the official court shorthand writer had transcribed and typed the notes of Lord Ross's summing up to the private prosecution trial jury.

In the meantime, Carol was living with her father, having left her aunt. She heard that her first husband and two children had returned to Glasgow, staying in a flat he had bought not far from the East End. Carol wanted to see the children and her ex-husband persuaded her to spend a few days with them. He talked once more about the possibility of them getting together again, but Carol knew it would never work out, said farewell to her husband and returned to her aunt's home.

Her life by now was a topsy-turvy mess with no really permanent home, save Billy's, and she did not want to go back to him. Her health, both mentally and physically, was beginning to deteriorate, almost to the same level as at the time soon after her assault.

Harper tried to get her spirit back but his efforts were to no avail. Carol was going downhill and visiting pubs in an effort to rid herself of her unhappiness. Eventually, the lawyer decided that something had to be done. He phoned the lady psychiatrist – who had declared that Carol was fit to give evidence during her private prosecution – and asked for her help. The psychiatrist agreed, Harper made a tentative appointment for Carol and persuaded her to go during her next visit to his office. Even the psychiatrist was shocked when she saw Carol. Carol began to have weekly sessions with the doctor.

In the meantime, the lawyers representing the Sweeney brothers and John Thomson, having analysed all the points for an appeal, were advising their clients to go ahead with one. Joe decided to appeal and so did John Thomson. Gordon Sweeney decided that he did not want to see the inside of a court again in connection with the Glasgow rape case.

27 The Appeal

The 21 October 1982, two years after the start of Carol's ordeal, saw the commencement of the final chapter of the case.

The scene was the court-room in Edinburgh where Carol had been granted leave to conduct the private prosecution. Two of the original judges, Lord Emslie and Lord Cameron, were joined by a third judge, Lord Wylie, who, as a former Lord Advocate, was a modest but brilliant politician and was now a respected member of the judiciary.

The occasion was the appeal by Joseph Sweeney and John Thomson against their conviction; Sweeney against the rape charge alone and Thomson against the indecent assault. In addition, Sweeney was asking the court to reduce his twelve-year sentence which he claimed to be excessive.

Joe had been brought to court from the Young Offenders' Institution at Glenochil, Clackmannanshire, where he had been given a rough time by other inmates because he was a convicted sexual offender. An outcast, he had been knocked about and threatened to the extent that he had asked the prison authorities for a move to a Young Offenders' Institution at Dumfries where he thought he would be safe.

He was glad of the day out in Edinburgh, his first visit to the outside world since his conviction. He knew, too, that it would be one of the last for many years to come. He did not have the expectation felt by many prisoners who sit at the High Court of Criminal Appeal hoping that, perhaps, a legal technicality will get them off altogether, because he was not appealing against the razor-assault charge. The question for

him was – could he get a few years of his sentence reduced
and escape the stigma of a rapist?

Joe sat in the dock alone, wearing the same suit he had
worn during the trial; alone, except, that is, for two prison
officers. John Thomson was not required to appear personally,
for his appeal.

The main thrust of Joe's appeal was the jury's odd decision
to find him guilty of assaulting Carol in London Road by
knocking her unconscious and dragging her to the scrap-yard
– despite being expressly told by both Lord Ross and the Dean
of the Faculty that these acts took place long before he arrived
on the scene.

His counsel, Mr Findlay, argued that the verdict contained
a fatal flaw and, therefore, should not be allowed to stand. He
also argued that, in any event, there was insufficient evidence.

Mr Morton, presenting the appeal for Thomson, argued that
there was no room for any other verdict save either guilty or
not guilty of rape. Since the jury did not find him guilty of
rape Mr Morton argued that the verdict of indecent assault
was ambiguous, lacking in specification, and, on the evidence,
could not be allowed to stand.

Answering the arguments put forward for both youths the
Dean, first of all, submitted that the jury verdict in relation to
Joe was a 'mere mistake', but it was obvious they still held
him guilty of rape. In relation to Thomson he submitted that,
while the jury might not have been prepared to convict him of
rape, they might have thought that, if Carol was unconscious
in the cabin for whatever reason when her clothing was removed and intercourse took place, there was room for a verdict
of indecent assault.

The legal arguments spanned two days, at the end of which
Lord Emslie announced that the court would issue a written
judgment. The three judges were extremely attentive towards
the arguments put forward against the convictions. Many ob-
servers, who had listened to the proceedings, left with the
impression that the case might never again be called the Glasgow rape case.

On Wednesday, 3 November, Lord Emslie announced the

clear opinions of the court. Dealing first of all with John Thomson he revealed, to the relief of the private prosecution team, that Thomson's conviction must stand.

Lord Emslie said that the clear inference from the jury's verdict was that it either disbelieved Carol's evidence about being knocked unconscious in London Road or was not satisfied that her account of it was established by corroborative evidence.

Lord Emslie said, 'Upon the evidence before them it was open to the jury to accept that the complainer was drunk – perhaps very drunk – and that, because of her condition, the two boys took her to the filthy conditions of the cabin, with the physical assistance which was required, for the purpose of taking advantage of her condition.

'The complainer's evidence was that she knew nothing of what was done to her in the cabin and gave no consent to anything. In our opinion, the jury was entitled to accept this, even though it rejected her explanation for her state, namely, unconsciousness produced by a blow on the head.

'There was ample evidence that she was drunk. If the jury was entitled to approach a verdict upon the view of the complainer's condition which we have just described, then the admitted acts of Gordon Sweeney and John Thomson, namely, removing her clothing and having sexual intercourse with her, constituted the act of indecent assault. There is no doubt that, in the law of Scotland, to take advantage in this way of a drunken woman, whose intoxication is solely due to her own voluntary actions, and who is, as a consequence, in no condition to refuse or resist, constitutes the crime of indecent assault.'

Lord Emslie then turned to Sweeney's appeal and announced that this had failed also. He said that, as the evidence came out, the jury was left in no doubt that a guilty verdict depended upon the jury holding that the events in the cabin – and only the cabin – were proved, and that Sweeney held Carol down, lay on top of her, and repeatedly raped her.

He continued, 'The reality of the trial was, accordingly, that the jury knew perfectly well that the only part of the libel [the charge] which remained relevant in relation to Joseph Sweeney was represented by the words: "Hold her down, lie on top of her, and repeatedly rape her."

'Now it is to be observed that the jury's verdict was returned in answer to this question: "What is your verdict in respect of the first named, Joseph Sweeney, on charge one?" In answering the questions in the words, "Guilty as libelled" it is, we think, obvious that the verdict meant "Guilty as libelled" in so far as the libel was relevant against Joseph Sweeney.

'In the context of this trial it would be quite absurd to construe it otherwise and it is not, in any way, inconsistent with the verdicts returned against Gordon Sweeney and John Thomson in relation to the quite separate chapter of events in which they alone were concerned.

'The remaining question is whether there was sufficient evidence to support that verdict as it falls properly to be understood. In our opinion there was.'

In the last few sentences the judge referred to Sweeney's reply to the police under caution and subsequent confession, the details of which were revealed by the *Daily Record*. 'You know I fucking done it, but that cunt Thomson held her down.' And, 'I had another go and managed to do it to her. She started screaming again.'

Lord Emslie emphasized the word 'again' in the confession and added, 'The jury was well entitled to interpret the reply and the statement as confessions of intercourse with the complainer against her will and by force.'

Sweeney had condemned himself by his own words. The Glasgow rape case was finally over.

28 The Aftermath

As Carol's story draws to a conclusion, she is already just another statistic buried away in a mass of crime figures for criminologists and civil servants to study.

In 1981 in Britain there were 1238 cases of rape reported to the police; England and Wales shared 1068 of the total, Scotland 170. But those organizations who deal with and care for women who have been sexually abused believe that these figures are just the tip of the iceberg. For instance, Rape Crisis reckon that 25 per cent of all women raped are either too humiliated and terrified by the crime, or too fearful of a court trial, to go to the police.

Carol hopes that, as a result of her case and the publicity given to it, including this book, some lessons can be learned for the future and some comfort given to others who have the tragic misfortune to be victims of the same crime that so shattered her life.

Many people have asked her why she went through it all. In Carol's words the answer is simple, 'I wanted justice done and seen to be done, not only for me but for other women whose cases may be treated in the same way. Even if, at the end of the day, these boys had got off scot-free, I would have been upset and annoyed but not defeated. At least, I would have been able to say to myself later, "Well I tried." There's no more I could have done than that. I managed to come through it all, and I feel very relieved that it all really did come my way at the end. If the decision not to prosecute had still been a secret buried away in the Crown Office, then I dare say I might have cracked up completely by now, not knowing what was happening. Perhaps I would not be here today to talk about it.

'If the boys hadn't been prosecuted then, in the eyes of the people round here, they would reckon there must have been a reason for it, namely, that I was the guilty party and that I was to blame for perhaps encouraging them. I couldn't have lived in the area again if that was the way people were thinking. So having the case brought to a trial allowed the public to make up their own minds with the benefit of the facts that were aired in court. People still point their finger, "That's her, that's the lassie it all happened to. What a terrible shame," instead of "Look at her, she encouraged those boys".'

These genuine fears displayed by Carol pinpoint one of the many wide-ranging issues thrown up in the Glasgow rape case. The decision to drop the charges was not made known to the victim herself. The Lord Advocate admitted, during the four-day hearing which sanctioned Carol's private prosecution, that this was 'regrettable'.

While the Crown Office possesses the right to proceed with, or drop, a case, the victim must surely have the right to be informed of a decision not to prosecute?

Carol's ordeal had two positive and beneficial effects.

Firstly, as the Lord Advocate said, during the initial debate in the House of Lords about her case, no murder or rape case would, in the future, be dropped without a specific reference to the Lord Advocate himself. The Lord Advocate thus took away the power and discretion from his Advocate Deputes in connection with two categories of crime and so classified these two categories as being the most serious in the calendar of justice.

A further positive and beneficial result was disclosed when the new Solicitor General, Mr Peter Fraser, QC, replied to a question by Mr Donald Dewar, MP for Garscadden, during a previously unreported exchange held in the House of Commons on 17 November 1982. Mr Fraser said that 'Procurators Fiscal had been instructed that they should, in general, inform persons who had alleged that they had been the victim of crimes and who had given statements to the authorities, if it was eventually decided not to proceed with the charge.'

The effect of the Lord Advocate's direction means that, for the first time, the law recognizes, officially, that the interests of justice demand that the victim has a right to know. Up until that time it could properly have been argued that the machinery of the law proceeded without reference to an interested partner, the victim. Perhaps in future this direction may well be extended so that the victim's right to know will include the right to be notified of the results of the prosecution as well as the absence of a prosecution.

During the public debate on Carol's case it was frequently suggested that a rape victim be spared the ordeal of giving evidence. Such a suggestion ignores the reality of life. Justice for the victim cannot be obtained at the expense of justice for the accused. Ever since Biblical times, when Jacob was falsely accused of rape by Potiphar's wife, history has been redolent with dramatic incidents of men being falsely accused by women of one of the worst crimes. We live in an imperfect society and require to determine guilt by using human, and not divine resources.

When there is an available arbiter, judge or jury, evidence has to be given; that evidence has got to be the subject of question and cross-examination to determine the truth.

Nevertheless, for women who have been the victims of rape, the prospect of giving evidence and reliving the degradations they have suffered in the full glare of publicity, can be just as humiliating as the actual experience itself. So is there a need for change in the way the authorities deal with rape victims? This book is about Carol and her experience, so again, who better than she to answer such a controversial question?

'It wasn't the physical, but the mental, pain which hurt me so much. The police were sympathetic but, nevertheless, they harassed me even in hospital, to the point where they would come in and ask visitors to leave the bedside so they could question me. I realize now why this had to be so, but no one told me at the time. When their investigations ended I was just told that I would be getting a citation to appear at the High Court in the future. During all those months waiting to appear I was tensed up . . . uncertain . . . facing an unknown situation . . . terrified to see the boys again and terrified to relive it all in what I thought would be a public ordeal. Perhaps if, at an early stage, a policewoman had been detailed to explain the procedure to me – the fact that courts are always cleared of the public – it would have put my mind at rest. It was left to a young man in the Procurator Fiscal's office, shortly before the trial, and I wasn't mentally prepared for the harsh way he explained it all to me. It was too much and it triggered me off.

'Looking back on it all, there is no doubt that there should be more support for women who have been raped. I was taken, eventually, to see a psychiatrist but it was too late. Every woman who has had to go through what I suffered, even to a lesser degree where there has been no violent assault, should automatically be referred to a psychiatrist; should have the facts of rape and court procedure explained to them by the police and the prosecuting authorities at regular intervals, and should even be handed over to organizations like Rape Crisis for further guidance and support.'

The Glasgow rape case is now over – recorded as a 'questionable decision' in a Crown prosecution . . . questioned by some that the case did not proceed . . . questioned by some that the victim was not re-examined by a psychiatrist . . . questioned by others that the case was dropped without the victim being informed.

The vigour, the flair and the adaptability of Scots law were, however, beyond question. The law responded to the needs of one individual in a way which she could not have anticipated.

When Charles Kemp Davidson, QC, Dean of the Faculty, said simply and directly to Carol's solicitor, 'I shall act without any stipulation whatsoever about fees,' he was following the finest and most hallowed traditions of Scottish law. When a person's need is greatest and the cry is loudest, lawyers must surely strive with all the power at their command to establish a right. Whether their cause is to prosecute or defend, a right is as inalienable as the sanctity of the law itself.

As it was, the Government, having recognized the change

in Carol's condition and having so properly raised the question of private prosecution in parliamentary debates, decided that the state would meet the whole expense of the private prosecution. This involved the payment of all legal expenses and the witnesses' costs, not only for the prosecution but also for the defence.

Meanwhile, Carol is anxious to help others. She attends weekly art classes and, as a result of recent psychiatric counselling, has taken what she hopes will be a final decision: she is now back with Billy, endeavouring to lead a normal and happy life. Her struggle is over and yet it has just begun.

The memories of what happened that night, Halloween 1980, have, to some extent, evaporated with the passage of time. But when the winds of winter blow, the scars turn purple and ache. When she journeys alone across a darkened street, the fears return. It will be a long time before these fears go away.